CLIVE BARKER'S
HELLRAISER

REQUIEM

ROSS RICHIE Chief Executive Officer • MATT GAGNON Editor-in-Chief • WES HARRIS VP-Publishing • LANCE KREITER VP-Licensing & Merchandising • PHIL BARBARO Director of Finance
BRYCE CARLSON Managing Editor • DAFNA PLEBAN Editor • SHANNON WATTERS Editor • ERIC HARBURN Assistant Editor • ADAM STAFFARONI Assistant Editor • CHRIS ROSA Assistant Editor
BRIAN LATIMER Lead Graphic Designer • STEPHANIE GONZAGA Graphic Designer • DEVIN FUNCHES Marketing & Sales Assistant • JASMINE AMIRI Operations Assistant

For information regarding the CPSIA on this printed material, call: (203) 595-3636 and provide reference #EAST – 418790. A catalog record of this book is available from OCLC and from the BOOM! Studios website, www.boom-studios.com, on the Librarians Page.

BOOM! Studios, 6310 San Vicente Boulevard, Suite 107, Los Angeles, CA 90048-5457. Printed in USA. First Printing.
ISBN: 978-1-60886-087-6

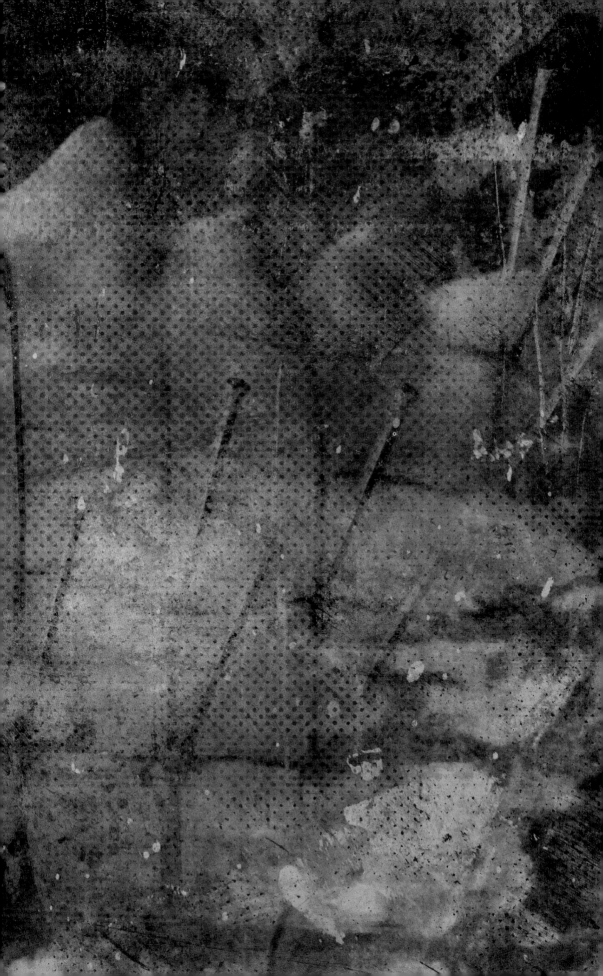

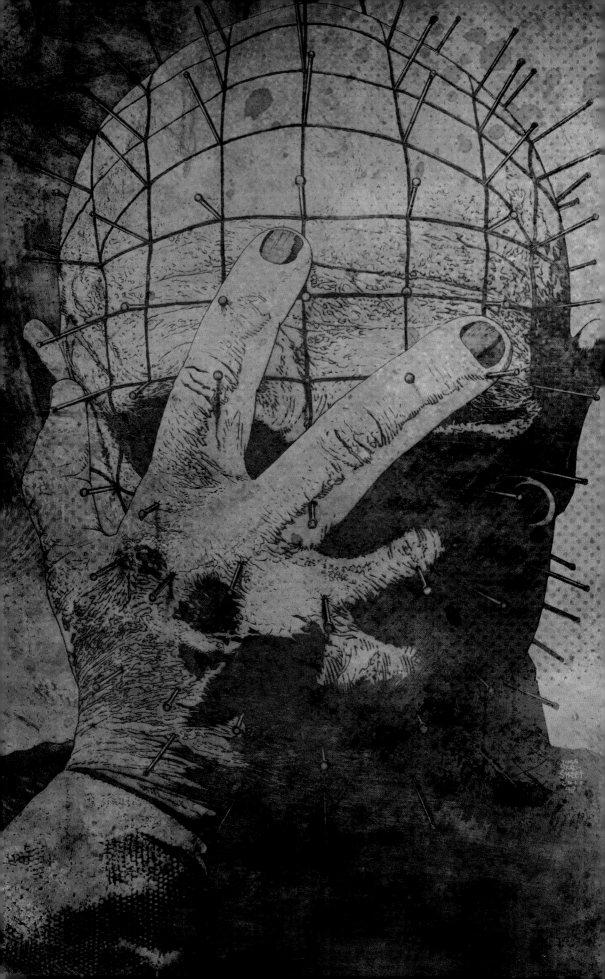

WRITTEN BY

CLIVE BARKER

AND **CHRISTOPHER MONFETTE**

ART BY

STEPHEN THOMPSON
CHAPTERS 6, 7 & 8

JANUSZ ORDON
CHAPTERS 7 & 8

JESÚS HERVÁS
CHAPTER 5

COLORS BY

JORDIE BELLAIRE
CHAPTERS 6, 7 & 8

DARRIN MOORE
CHAPTER 5

LETTERING BY

TRAVIS LANHAM

EDITED BY
MATT GAGNON

ASSISTANT EDITOR
CHRIS ROSA

TRADE DESIGN
BRIAN LATIMER

COVER BY
NICK PERCIVAL

Seraphim Films Creative Consultant Robb Humphreys
Special Thanks To Mark Miller And Ian Brill

CHAPTER FIVE

REQUIEM

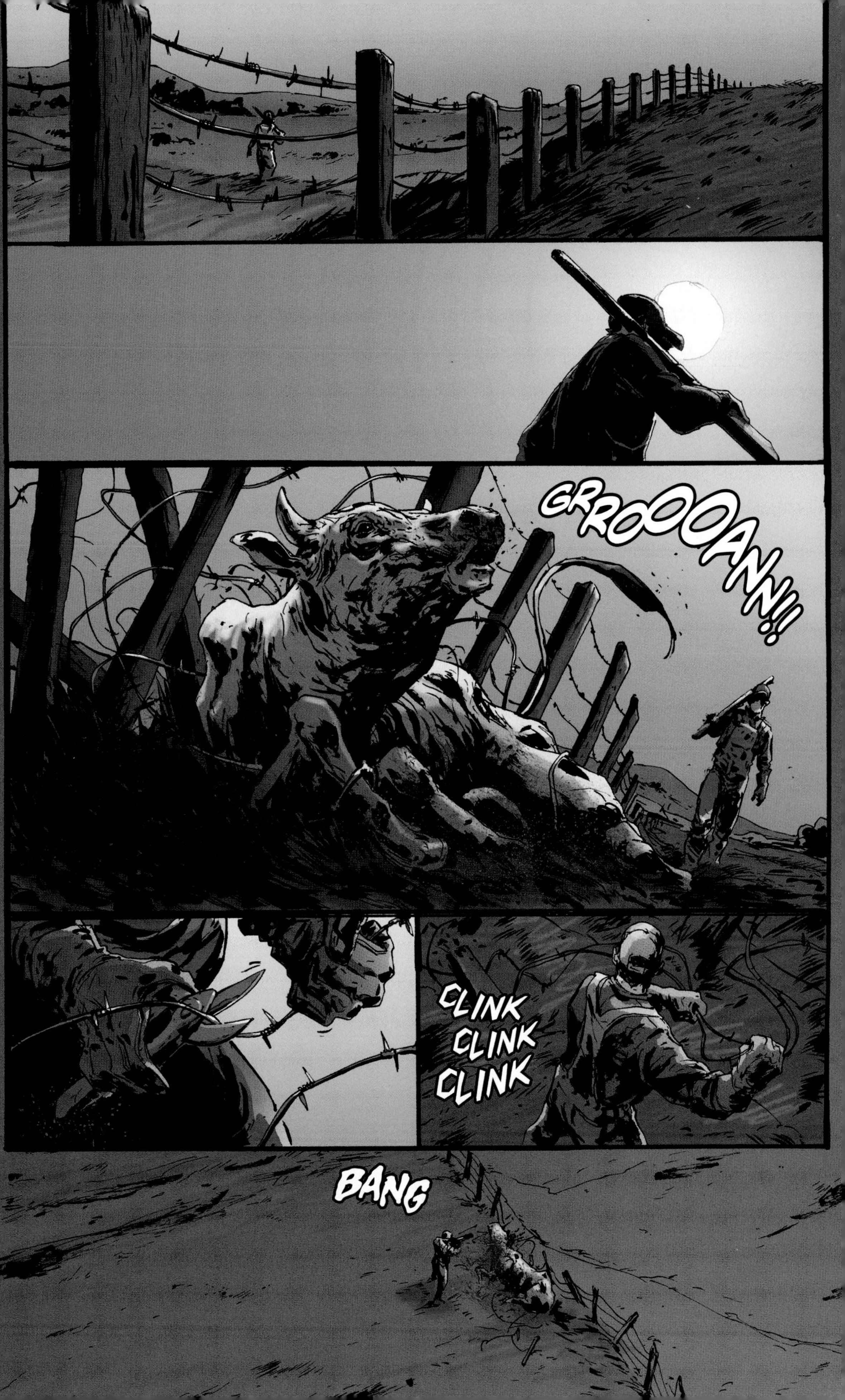
GRROOOANN!!
CLINK
CLINK
CLINK
BANG

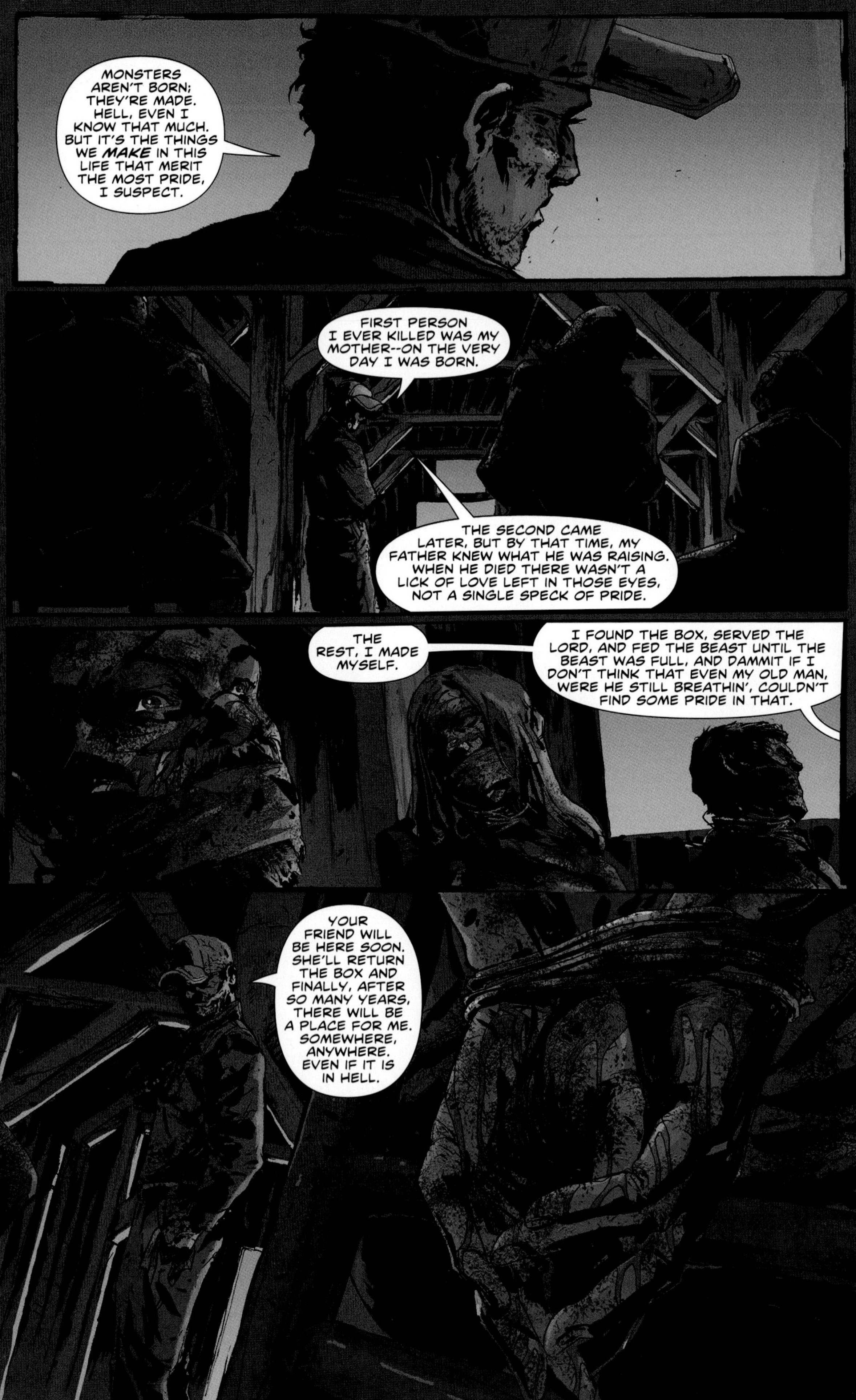

MONSTERS AREN'T BORN; THEY'RE MADE. HELL, EVEN I KNOW THAT MUCH. BUT IT'S THE THINGS WE *MAKE* IN THIS LIFE THAT MERIT THE MOST PRIDE, I SUSPECT.
FIRST PERSON I EVER KILLED WAS MY MOTHER--ON THE VERY DAY I WAS BORN.
THE SECOND CAME LATER, BUT BY THAT TIME, MY FATHER KNEW WHAT HE WAS RAISING. WHEN HE DIED THERE WASN'T A LICK OF LOVE LEFT IN THOSE EYES, NOT A SINGLE SPECK OF PRIDE.
THE REST, I MADE MYSELF.
I FOUND THE BOX, SERVED THE LORD, AND FED THE BEAST UNTIL THE BEAST WAS FULL, AND DAMMIT IF I DON'T THINK THAT EVEN MY OLD MAN, WERE HE STILL BREATHIN', COULDN'T FIND SOME PRIDE IN THAT.
YOUR FRIEND WILL BE HERE SOON. SHE'LL RETURN THE BOX AND FINALLY, AFTER SO MANY YEARS, THERE WILL BE A PLACE FOR ME. SOMEWHERE, ANYWHERE. EVEN IF IT IS IN HELL.

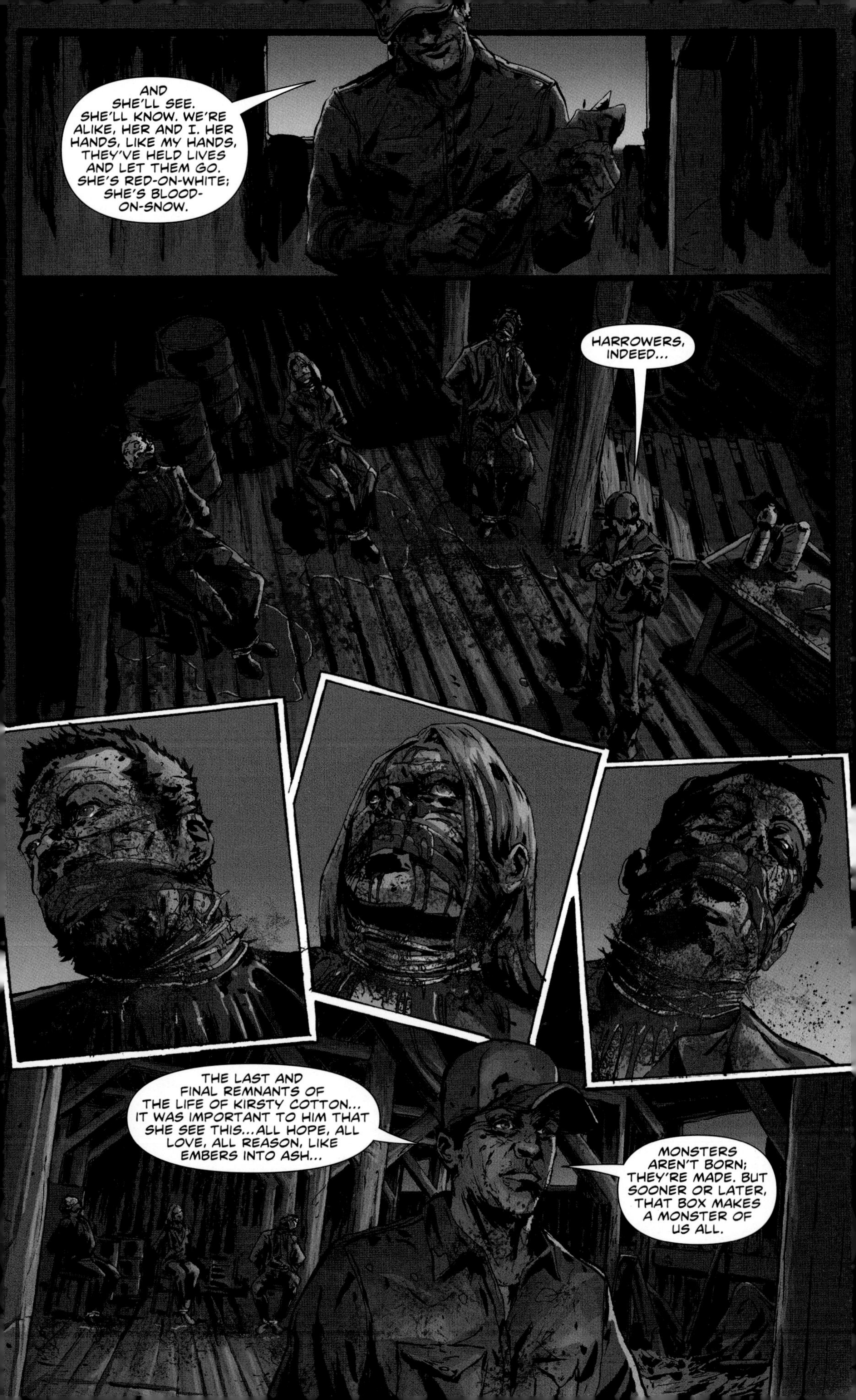
AND SHE'LL SEE. SHE'LL KNOW. WE'RE ALIKE, HER AND I. HER HANDS, LIKE MY HANDS, THEY'VE HELD LIVES AND LET THEM GO. SHE'S RED-ON-WHITE; SHE'S BLOOD-ON-SNOW.
HARROWERS, INDEED...
THE LAST AND FINAL REMNANTS OF THE LIFE OF KIRSTY COTTON... IT WAS IMPORTANT TO HIM THAT SHE SEE THIS...ALL HOPE, ALL LOVE, ALL REASON, LIKE EMBERS INTO ASH...
MONSTERS AREN'T BORN; THEY'RE MADE. BUT SOONER OR LATER, THAT BOX MAKES A MONSTER OF US ALL.

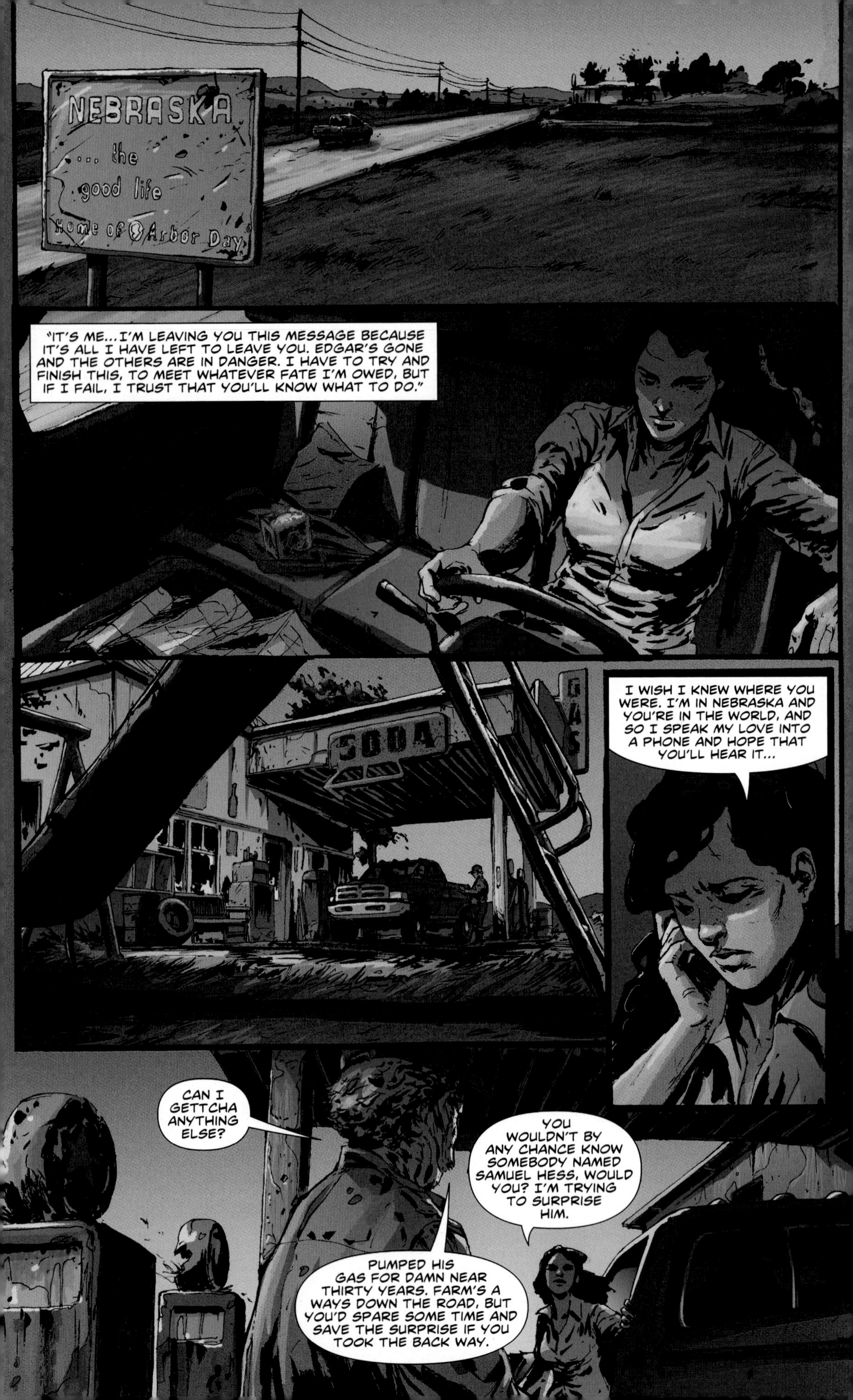
NEBRASKA
... the
good life
Home of Arbor Day
"IT'S ME... I'M LEAVING YOU THIS MESSAGE BECAUSE IT'S ALL I HAVE LEFT TO LEAVE YOU. EDGAR'S GONE AND THE OTHERS ARE IN DANGER. I HAVE TO TRY AND FINISH THIS, TO MEET WHATEVER FATE I'M OWED, BUT IF I FAIL, I TRUST THAT YOU'LL KNOW WHAT TO DO."
SODA
GAS
I WISH I KNEW WHERE YOU WERE. I'M IN NEBRASKA AND YOU'RE IN THE WORLD, AND SO I SPEAK MY LOVE INTO A PHONE AND HOPE THAT YOU'LL HEAR IT...
CAN I GETTCHA ANYTHING ELSE?
YOU WOULDN'T BY ANY CHANCE KNOW SOMEBODY NAMED SAMUEL HESS, WOULD YOU? I'M TRYING TO SURPRISE HIM.
PUMPED HIS GAS FOR DAMN NEAR THIRTY YEARS. FARM'S A WAYS DOWN THE ROAD, BUT YOU'D SPARE SOME TIME AND SAVE THE SURPRISE IF YOU TOOK THE BACK WAY.

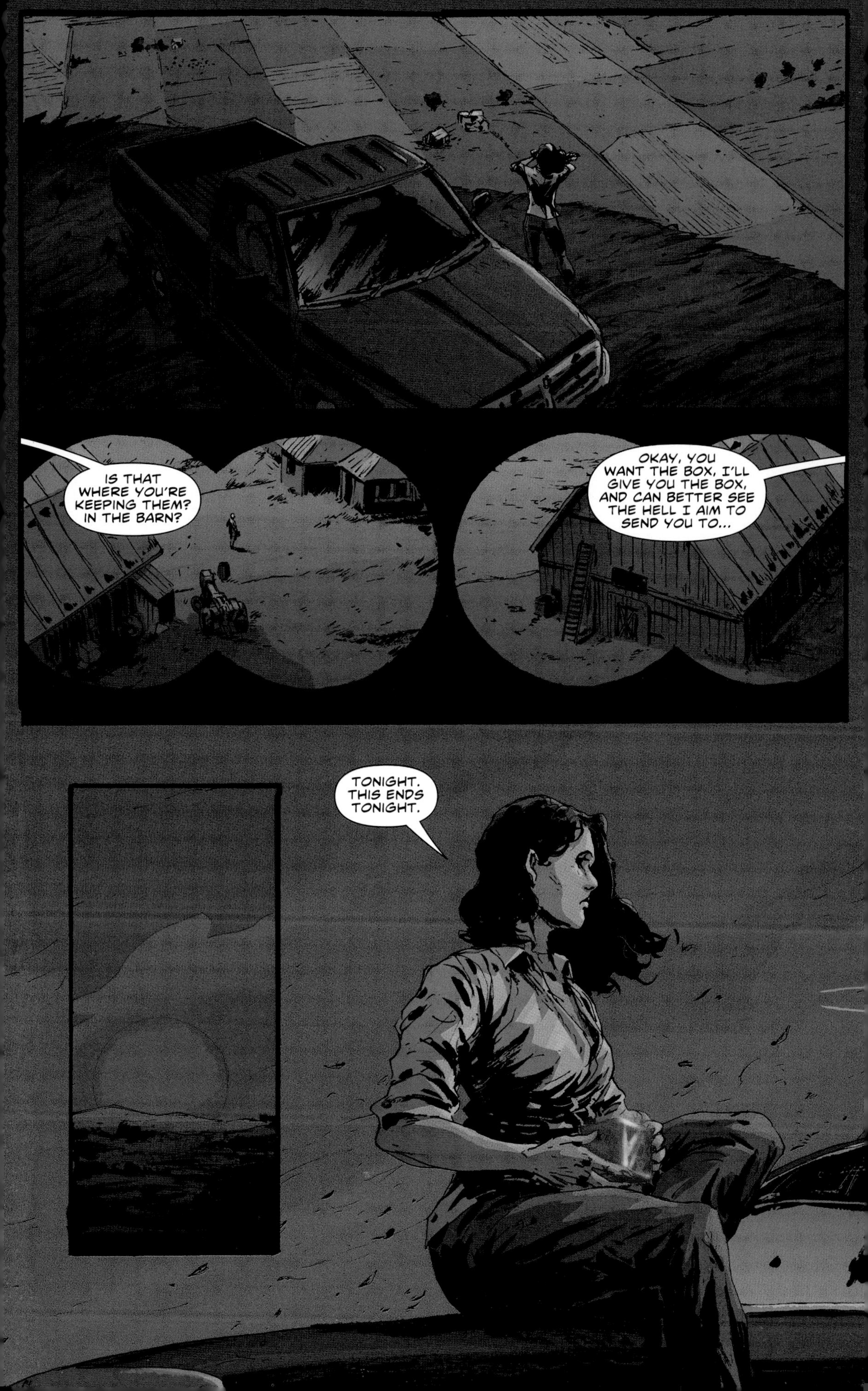
IS THAT WHERE YOU'RE KEEPING THEM? IN THE BARN?
OKAY, YOU WANT THE BOX, I'LL GIVE YOU THE BOX, AND CAN BETTER SEE THE HELL I AIM TO SEND YOU TO...
TONIGHT. THIS ENDS TONIGHT.

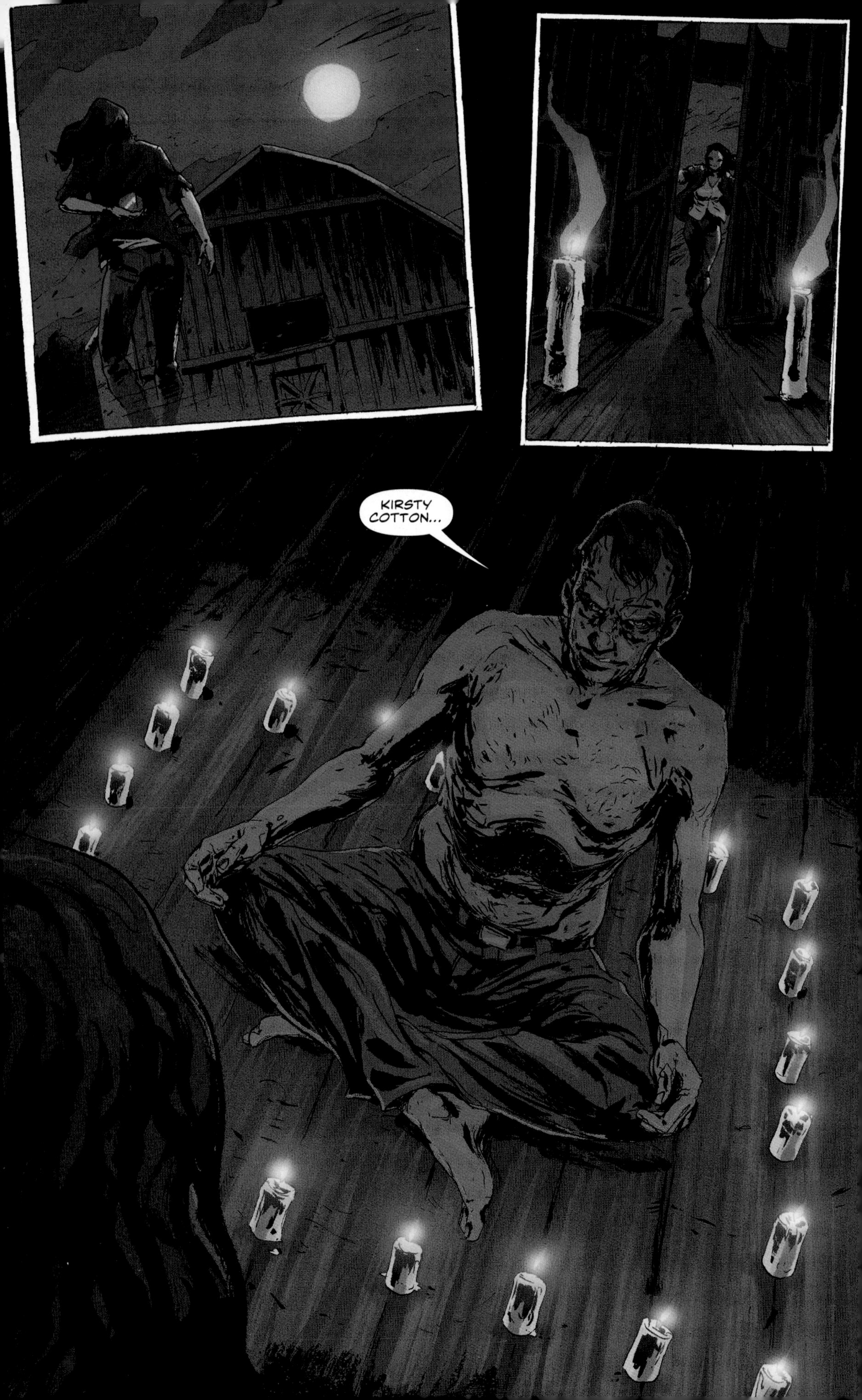
KIRSTY
COTTON...

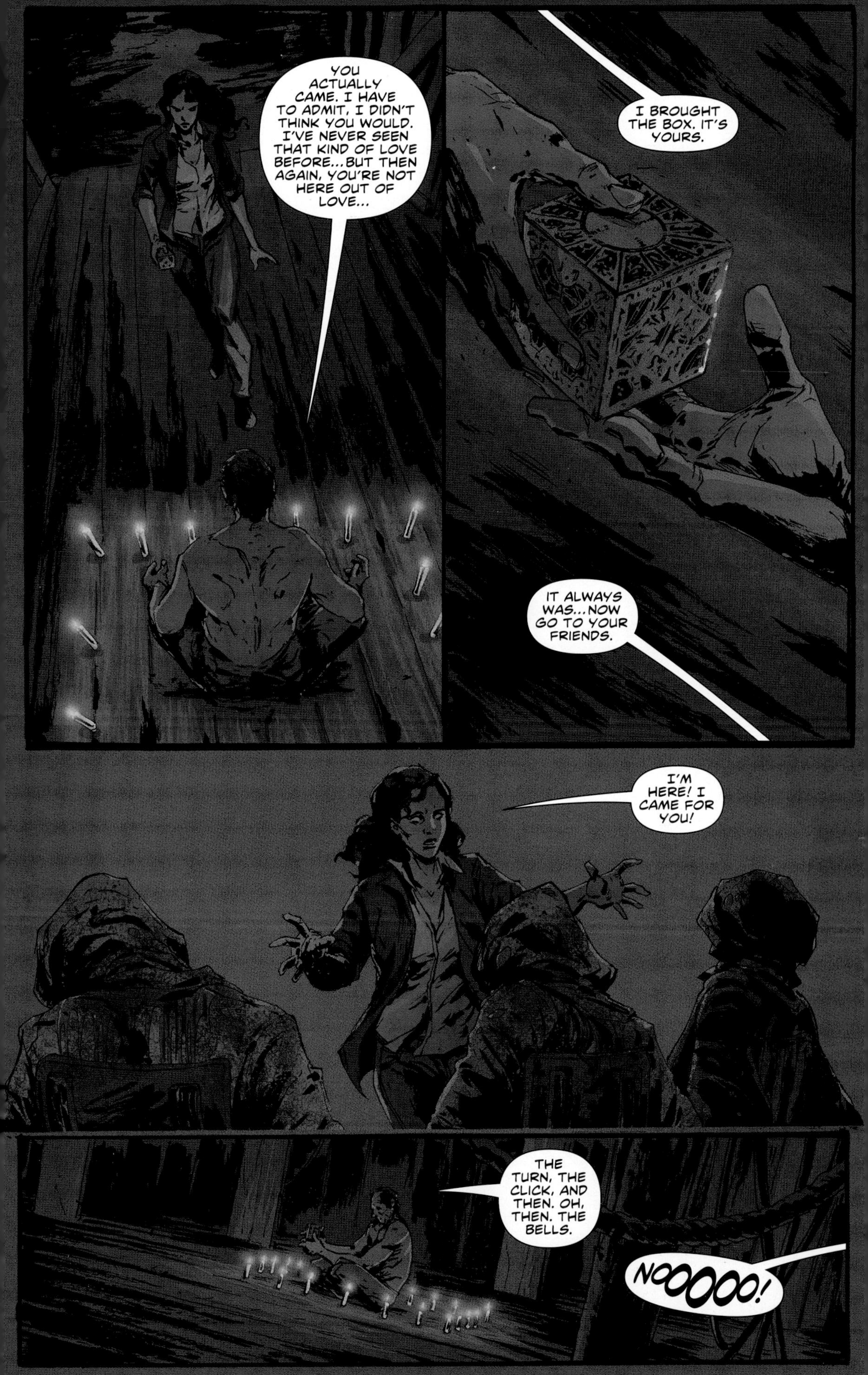
YOU ACTUALLY CAME. I HAVE TO ADMIT, I DIDN'T THINK YOU WOULD. I'VE NEVER SEEN THAT KIND OF LOVE BEFORE...BUT THEN AGAIN, YOU'RE NOT HERE OUT OF LOVE...
I BROUGHT THE BOX. IT'S YOURS.
IT ALWAYS WAS...NOW GO TO YOUR FRIENDS.
I'M HERE! I CAME FOR YOU!
THE TURN, THE CLICK, AND THEN. OH, THEN. THE BELLS.
NOOOOO!

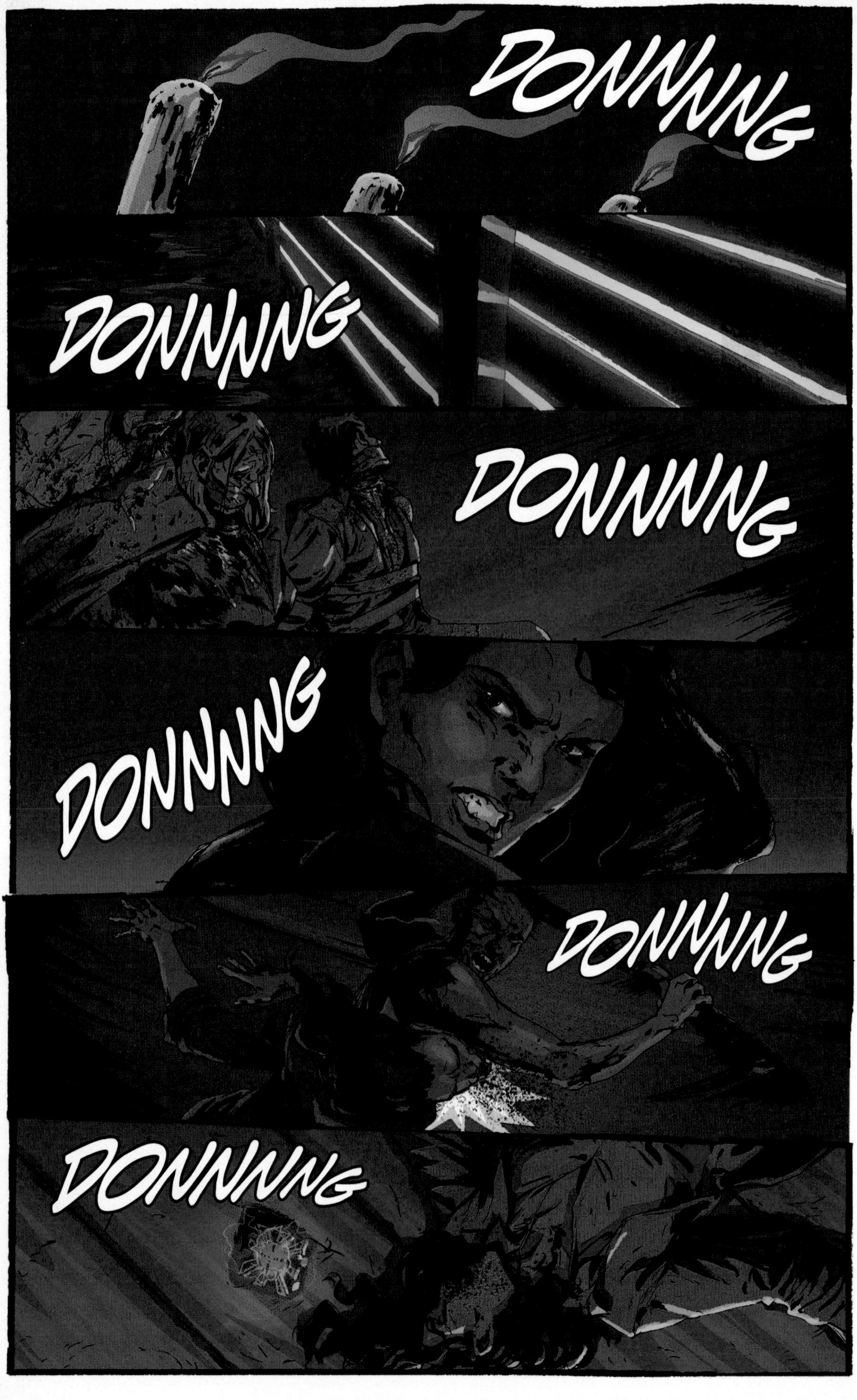
DONNNNG
DONNNNG
DONNNNG
DONNNNG
DONNNNG
DONNNNG

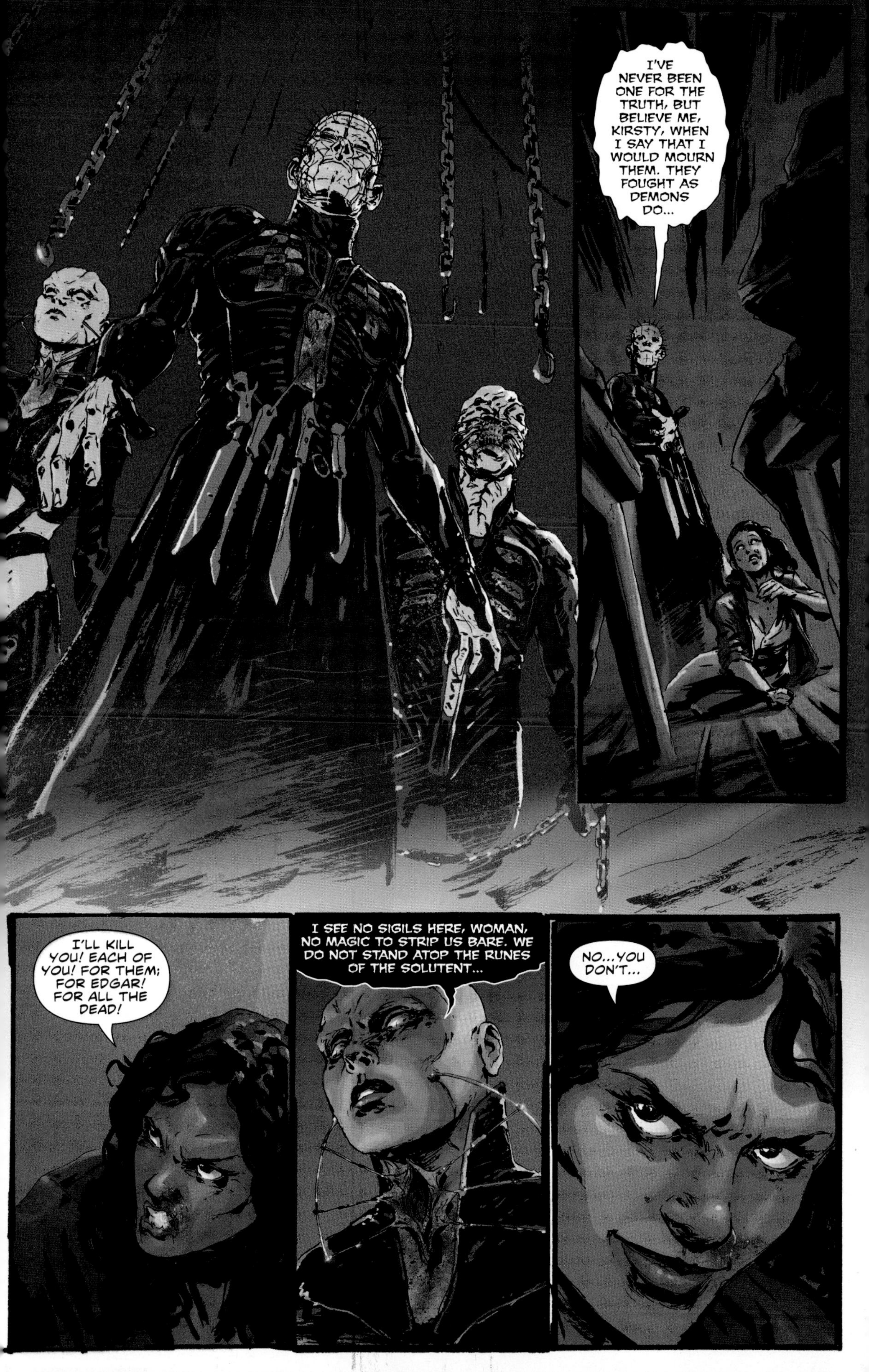
I'VE NEVER BEEN ONE FOR THE TRUTH, BUT BELIEVE ME, KIRSTY, WHEN I SAY THAT I WOULD MOURN THEM. THEY FOUGHT AS DEMONS DO...
I'LL KILL YOU! EACH OF YOU! FOR THEM; FOR EDGAR! FOR ALL THE DEAD!
I SEE NO SIGILS HERE, WOMAN, NO MAGIC TO STRIP US BARE. WE DO NOT STAND ATOP THE RUNES OF THE SOLUTENT...
NO...YOU DON'T...

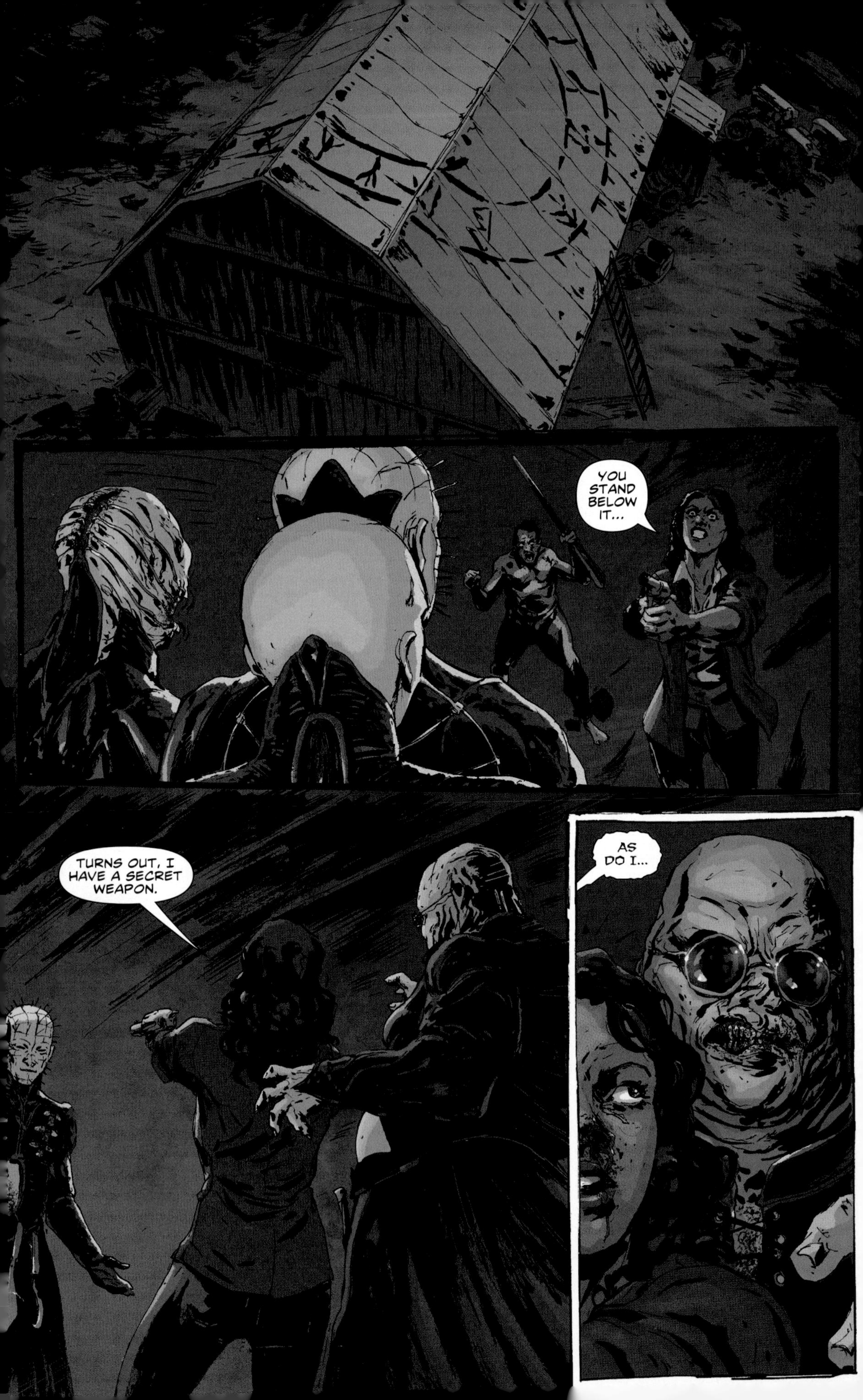
YOU STAND BELOW IT...
TURNS OUT, I HAVE A SECRET WEAPON.
AS DO I...

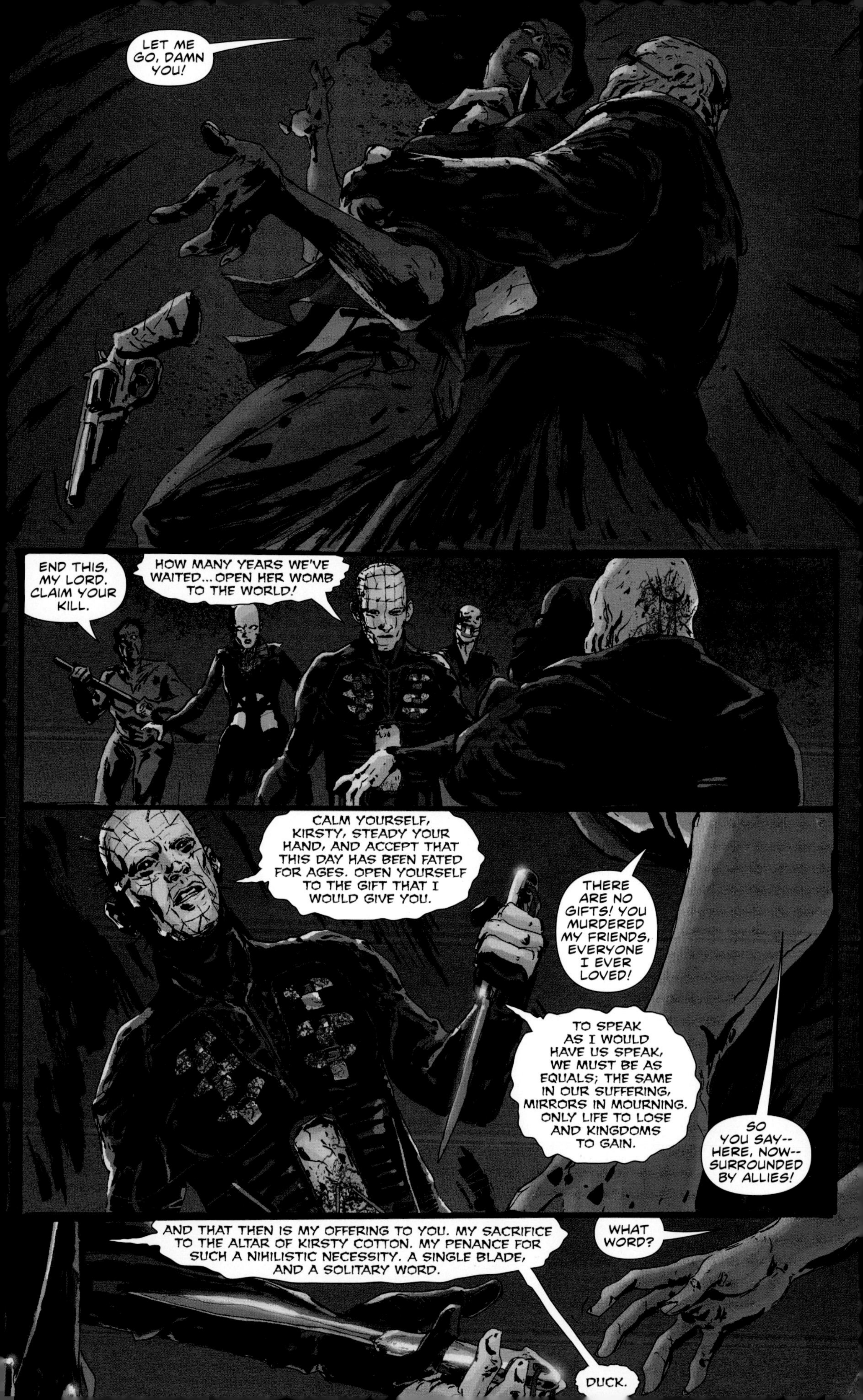
LET ME GO, DAMN YOU!
END THIS, MY LORD. CLAIM YOUR KILL.
HOW MANY YEARS WE'VE WAITED... OPEN HER WOMB TO THE WORLD!
CALM YOURSELF, KIRSTY, STEADY YOUR HAND, AND ACCEPT THAT THIS DAY HAS BEEN FATED FOR AGES. OPEN YOURSELF TO THE GIFT THAT I WOULD GIVE YOU.
THERE ARE NO GIFTS! YOU MURDERED MY FRIENDS, EVERYONE I EVER LOVED!
TO SPEAK AS I WOULD HAVE US SPEAK, WE MUST BE AS EQUALS; THE SAME IN OUR SUFFERING, MIRRORS IN MOURNING. ONLY LIFE TO LOSE AND KINGDOMS TO GAIN.
SO YOU SAY-- HERE, NOW-- SURROUNDED BY ALLIES!
AND THAT THEN IS MY OFFERING TO YOU. MY SACRIFICE TO THE ALTAR OF KIRSTY COTTON. MY PENANCE FOR SUCH A NIHILISTIC NECESSITY. A SINGLE BLADE, AND A SOLITARY WORD.
WHAT WORD?
DUCK.

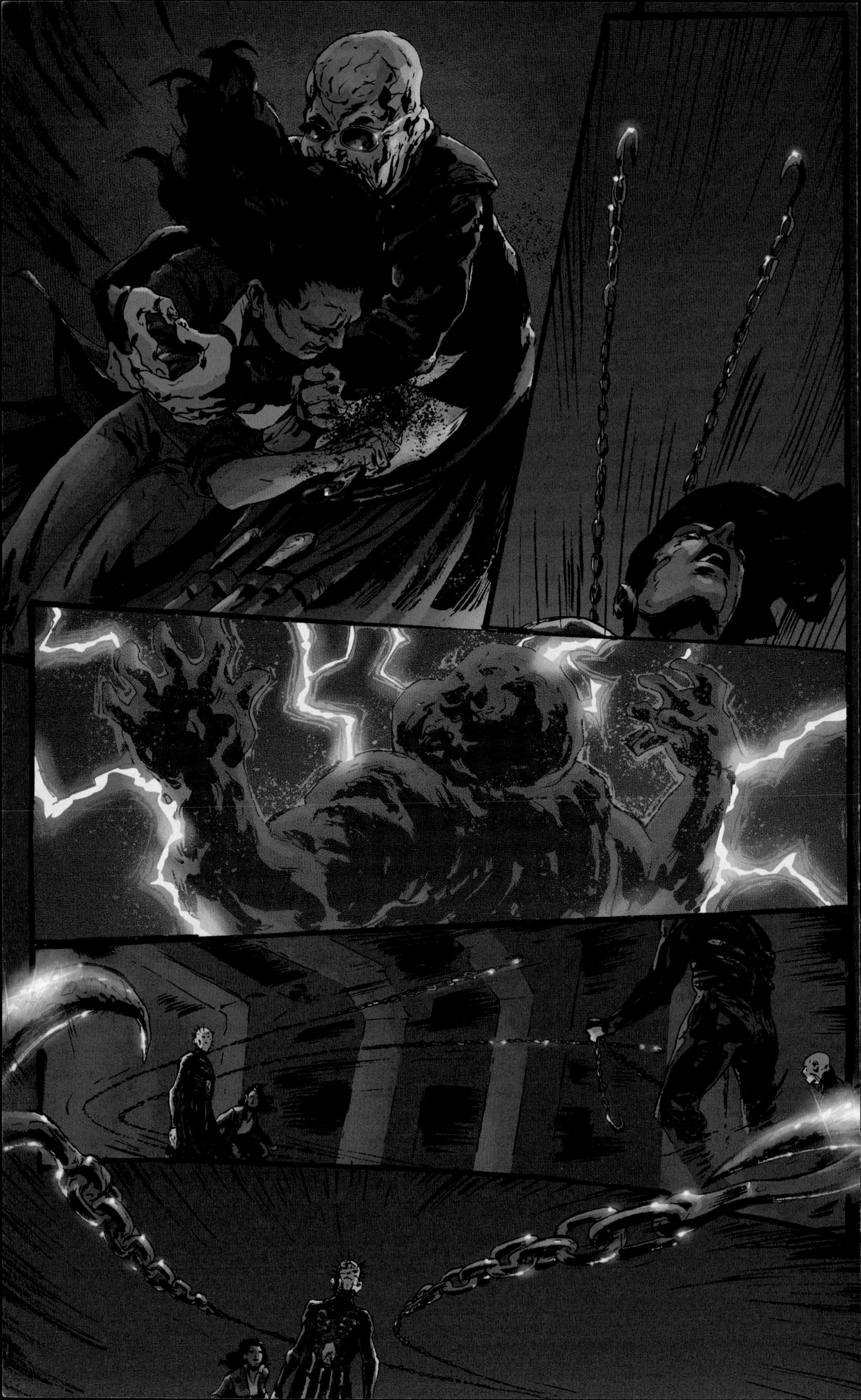

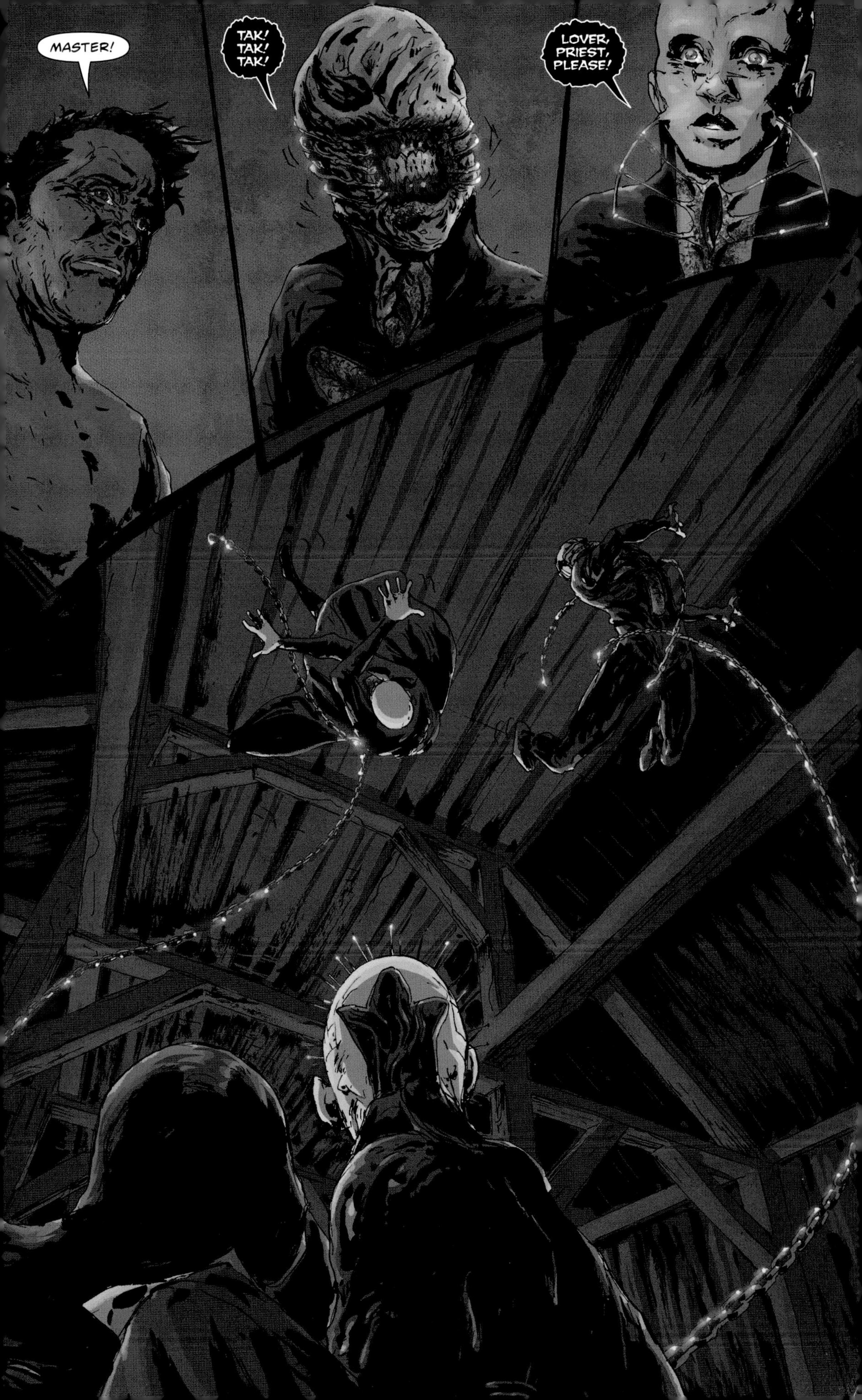
MASTER!
TAK! TAK! TAK!
LOVER, PRIEST, PLEASE!

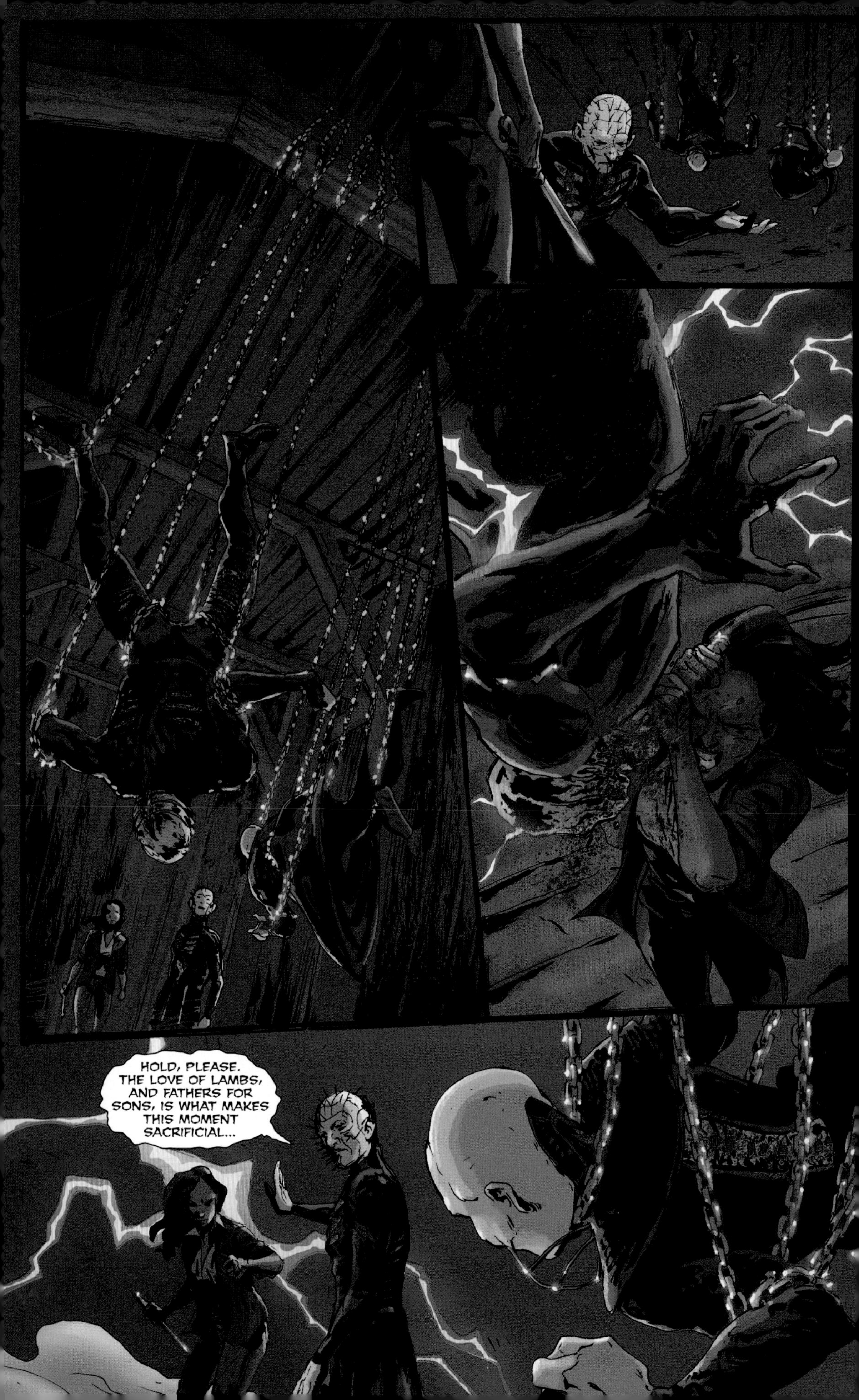
HOLD, PLEASE. THE LOVE OF LAMBS, AND FATHERS FOR SONS, IS WHAT MAKES THIS MOMENT SACRIFICIAL...

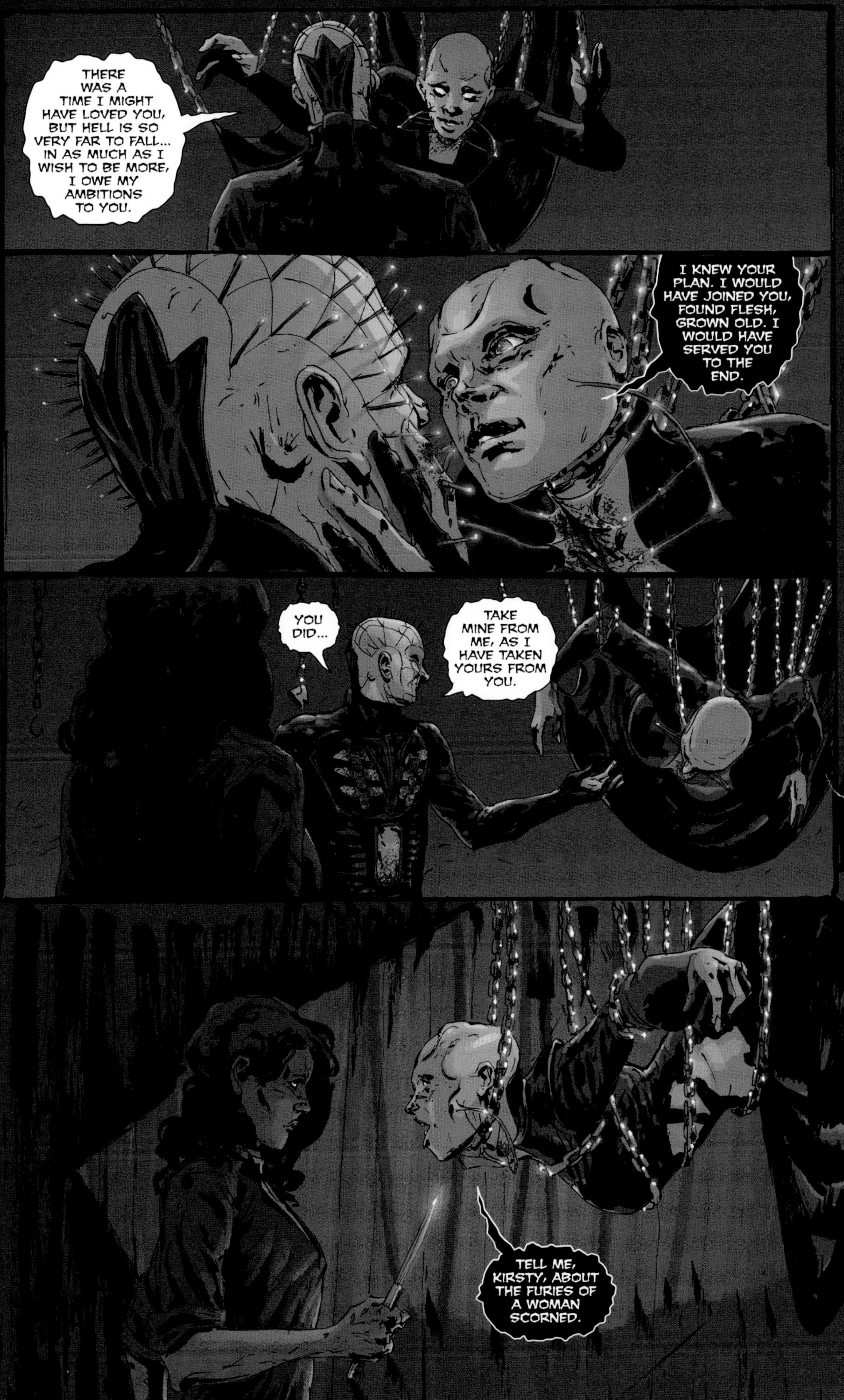
THERE WAS A TIME I MIGHT HAVE LOVED YOU, BUT HELL IS SO VERY FAR TO FALL... IN AS MUCH AS I WISH TO BE MORE, I OWE MY AMBITIONS TO YOU.
I KNEW YOUR PLAN. I WOULD HAVE JOINED YOU, FOUND FLESH, GROWN OLD. I WOULD HAVE SERVED YOU TO THE END.
YOU DID...
TAKE MINE FROM ME, AS I HAVE TAKEN YOURS FROM YOU.
TELL ME, KIRSTY, ABOUT THE FURIES OF A WOMAN SCORNED.

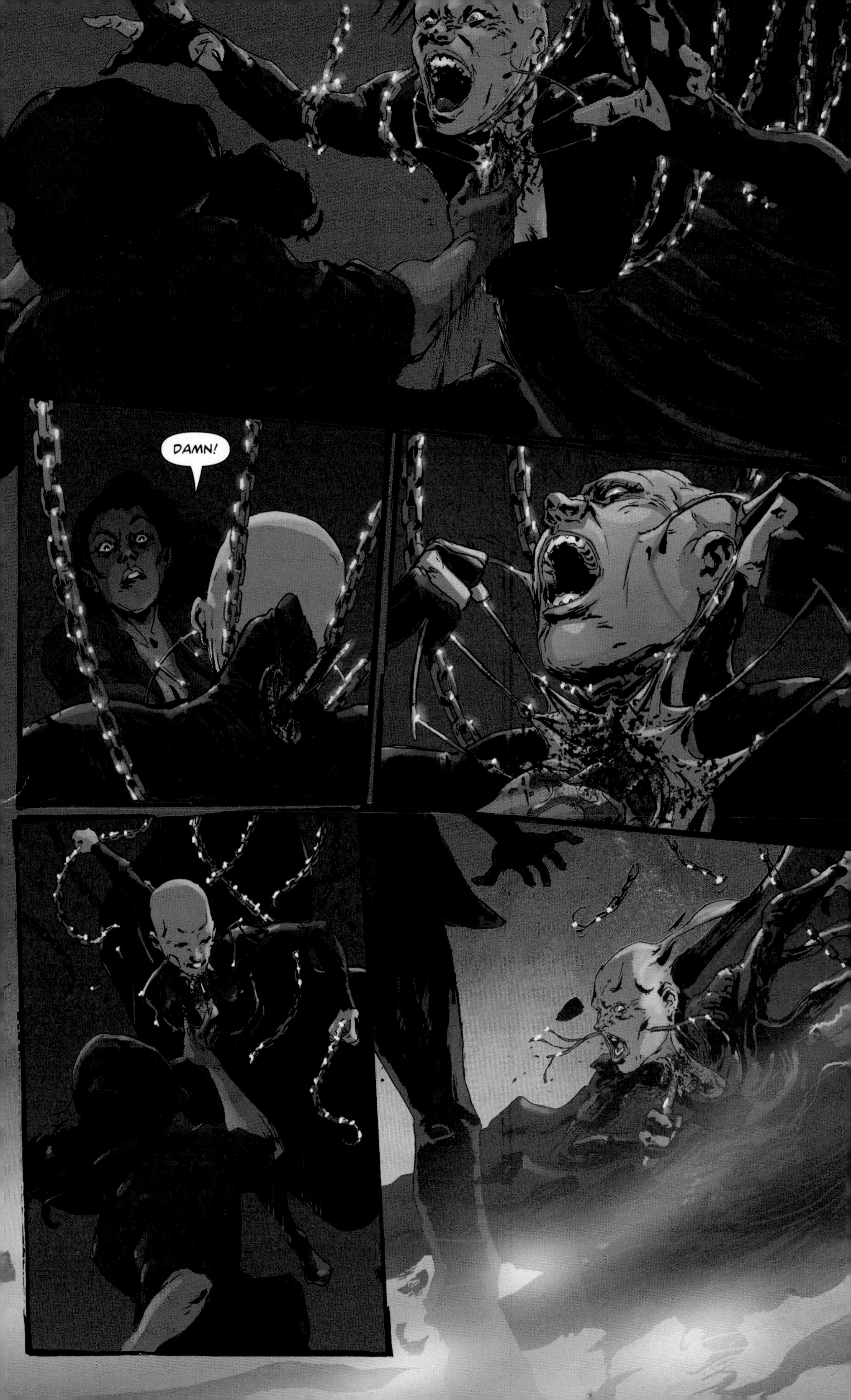
DAMN!

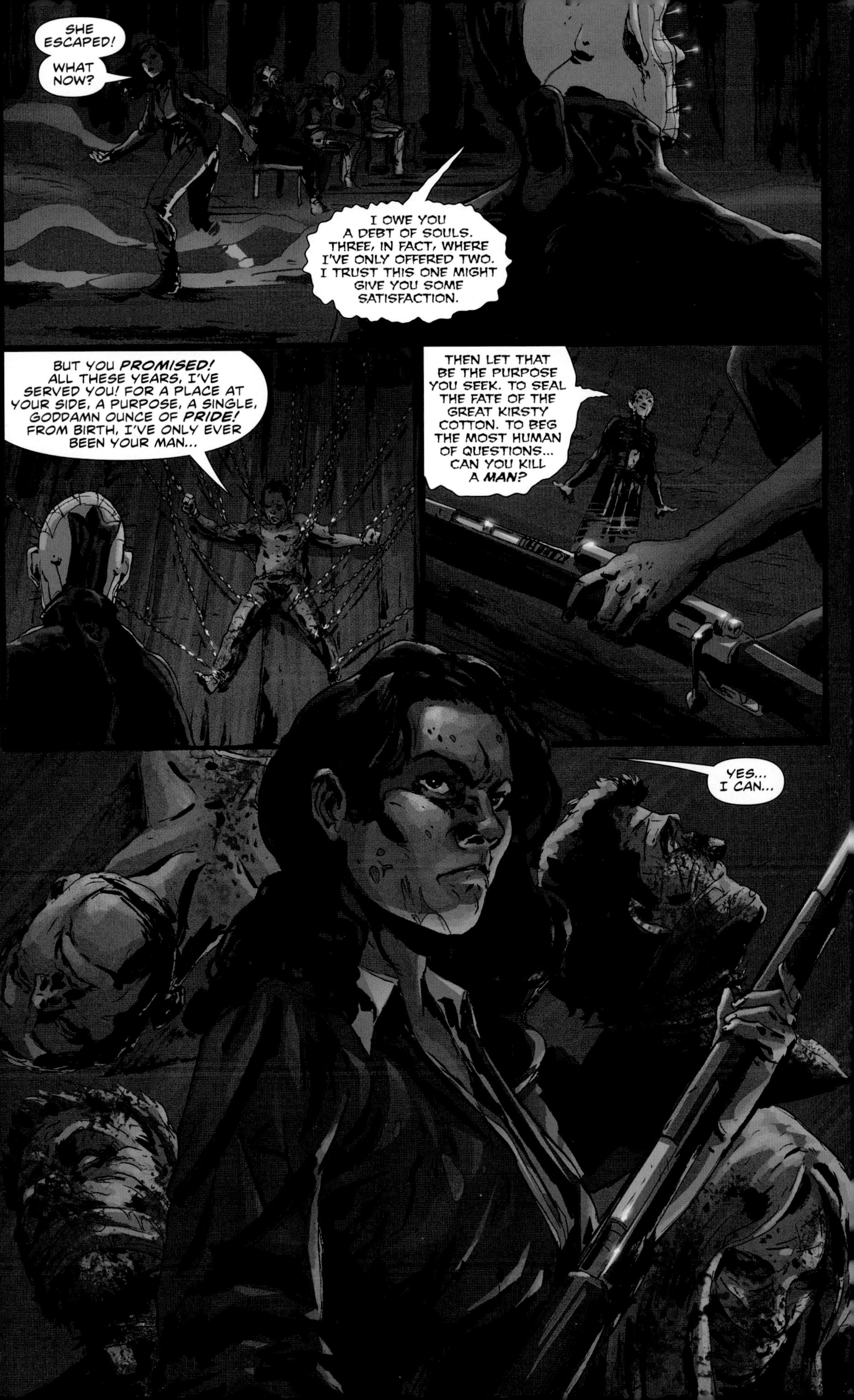
SHE ESCAPED!
WHAT NOW?
I OWE YOU A DEBT OF SOULS. THREE, IN FACT, WHERE I'VE ONLY OFFERED TWO. I TRUST THIS ONE MIGHT GIVE YOU SOME SATISFACTION.
BUT YOU *PROMISED!* ALL THESE YEARS, I'VE SERVED YOU! FOR A PLACE AT YOUR SIDE, A PURPOSE, A SINGLE, GODDAMN OUNCE OF *PRIDE!* FROM BIRTH, I'VE ONLY EVER BEEN YOUR MAN...
THEN LET THAT BE THE PURPOSE YOU SEEK. TO SEAL THE FATE OF THE GREAT KIRSTY COTTON. TO BEG THE MOST HUMAN OF QUESTIONS... CAN YOU KILL A *MAN?*
YES... I CAN...

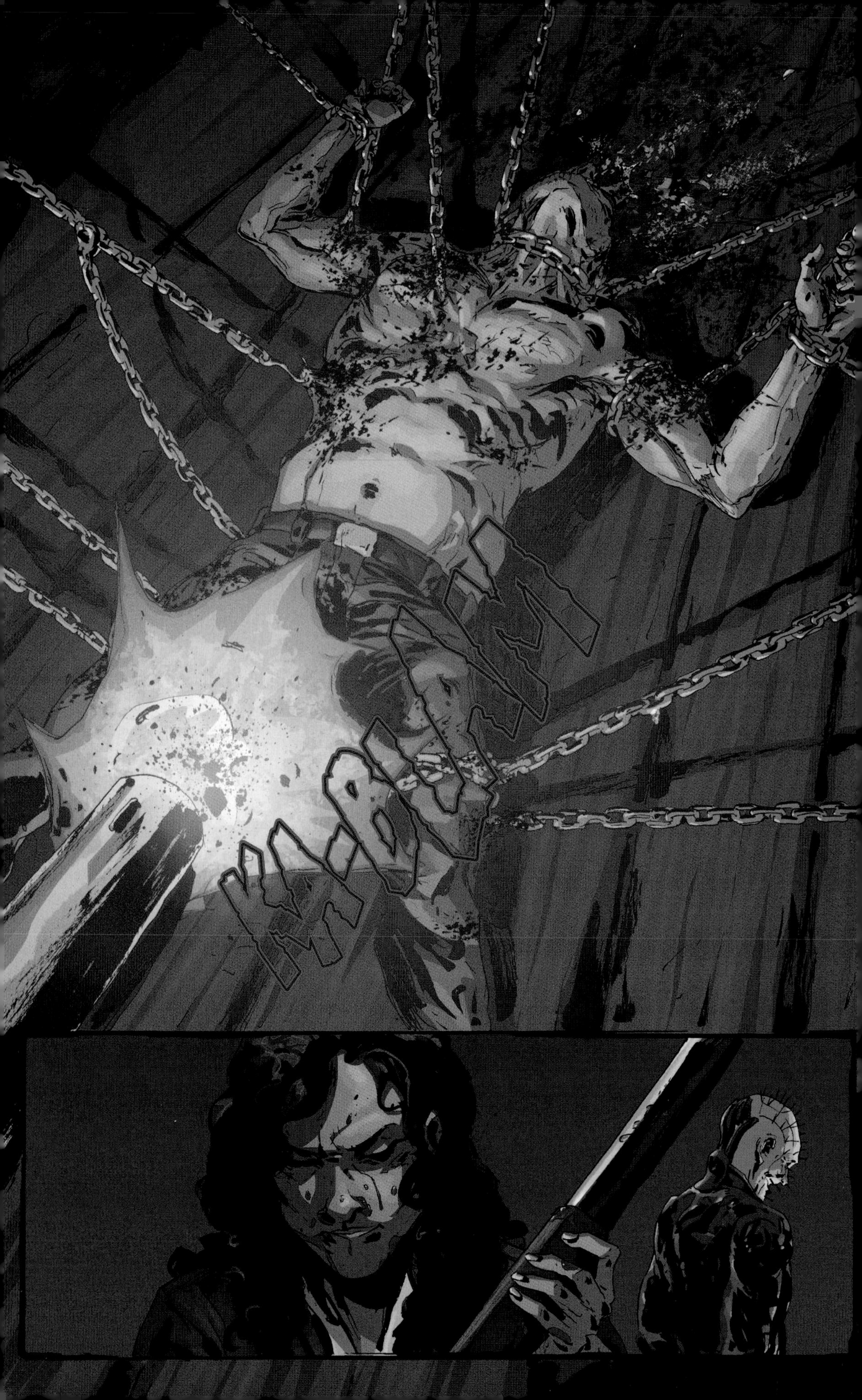
KA-BLAM

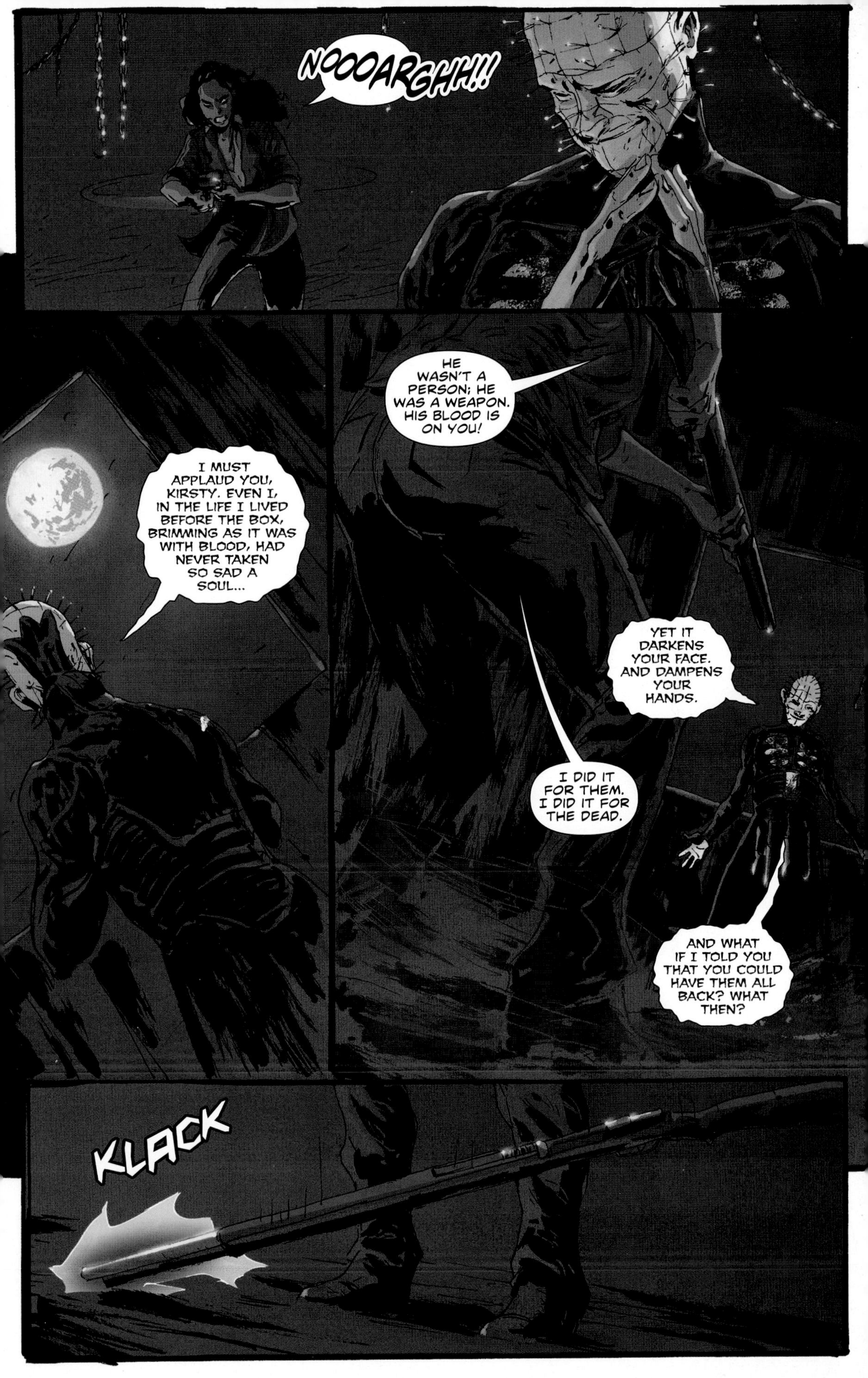
NOOOARGHH!!
I MUST APPLAUD YOU, KIRSTY. EVEN I, IN THE LIFE I LIVED BEFORE THE BOX, BRIMMING AS IT WAS WITH BLOOD, HAD NEVER TAKEN SO SAD A SOUL...
HE WASN'T A PERSON; HE WAS A WEAPON. HIS BLOOD IS ON YOU!
YET IT DARKENS YOUR FACE. AND DAMPENS YOUR HANDS.
I DID IT FOR THEM. I DID IT FOR THE DEAD.
AND WHAT IF I TOLD YOU THAT YOU COULD HAVE THEM ALL BACK? WHAT THEN?
KLACK

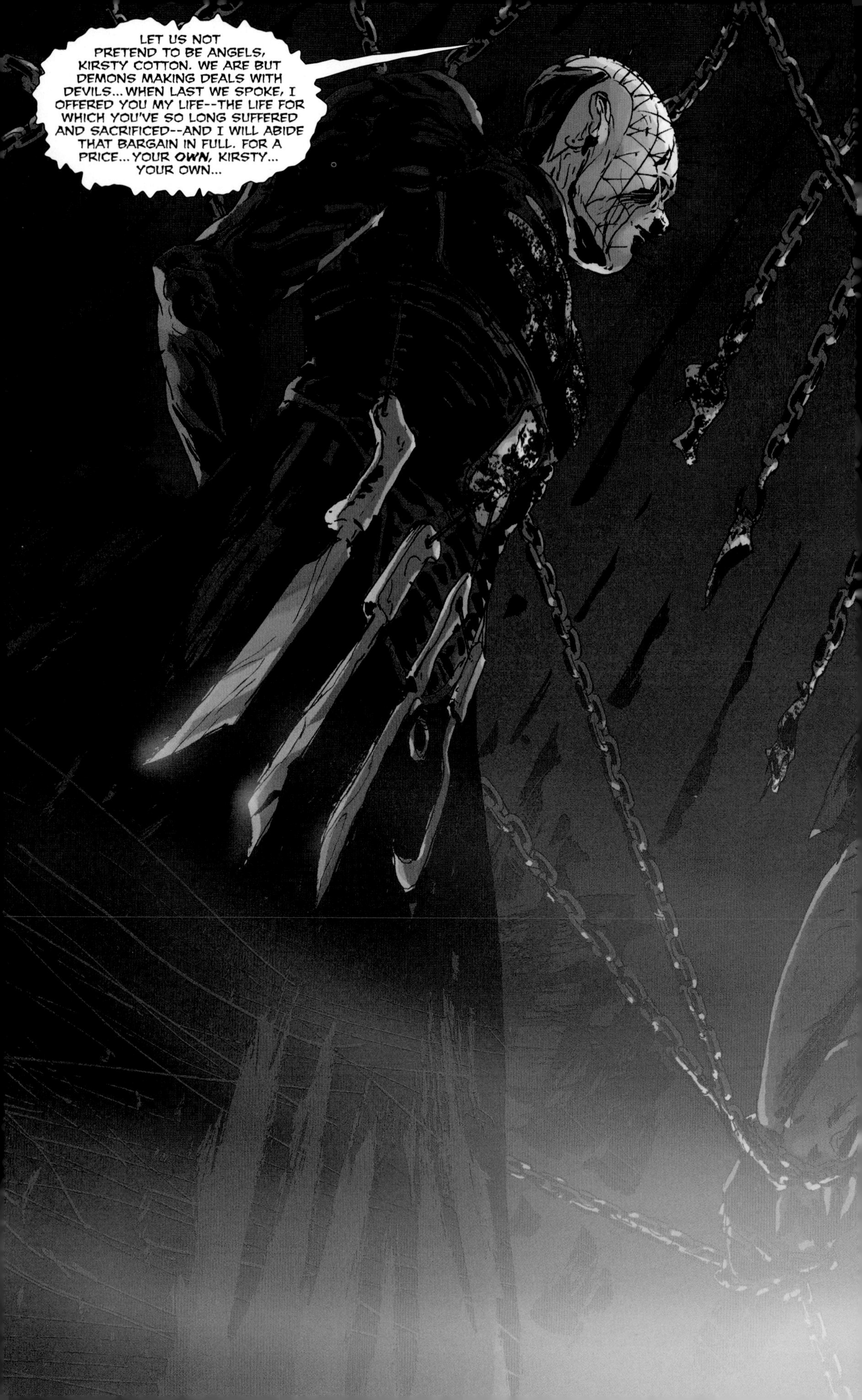
LET US NOT PRETEND TO BE ANGELS, KIRSTY COTTON. WE ARE BUT DEMONS MAKING DEALS WITH DEVILS... WHEN LAST WE SPOKE, I OFFERED YOU MY LIFE--THE LIFE FOR WHICH YOU'VE SO LONG SUFFERED AND SACRIFICED--AND I WILL ABIDE THAT BARGAIN IN FULL. FOR A PRICE... YOUR **OWN**, KIRSTY... YOUR OWN...

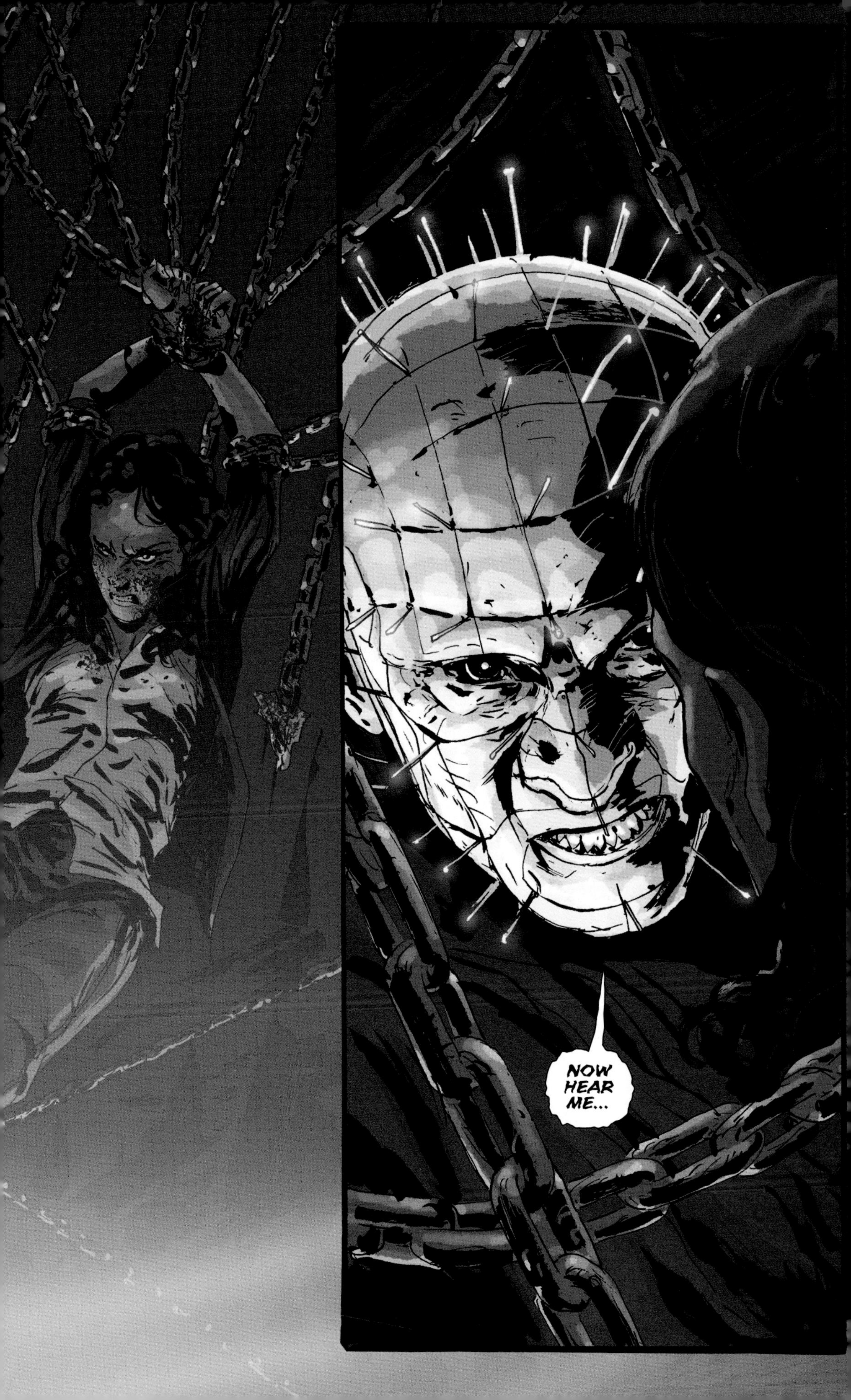
NOW HEAR ME...

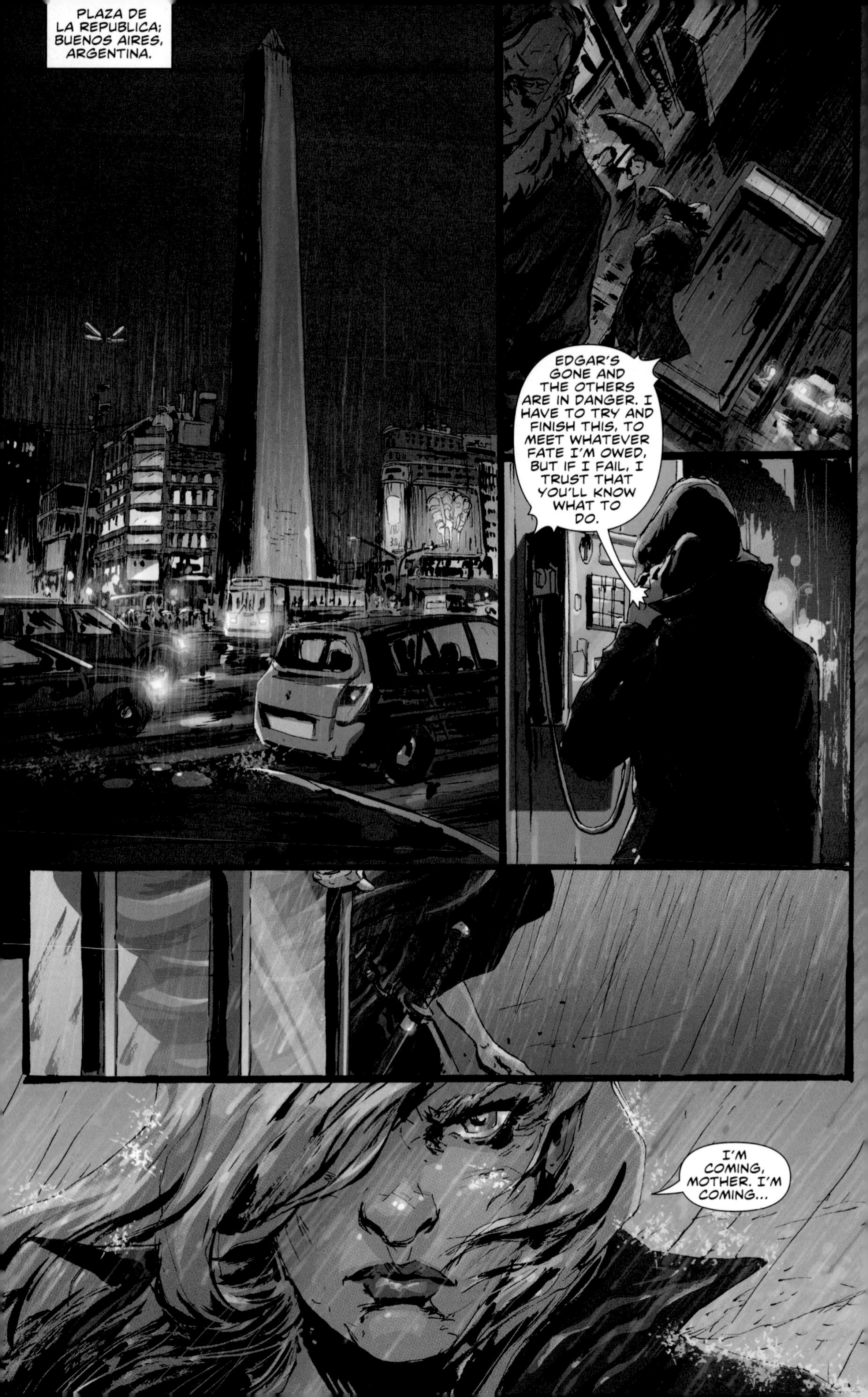
PLAZA DE LA REPUBLICA; BUENOS AIRES, ARGENTINA.
EDGAR'S GONE AND THE OTHERS ARE IN DANGER. I HAVE TO TRY AND FINISH THIS, TO MEET WHATEVER FATE I'M OWED, BUT IF I FAIL, I TRUST THAT YOU'LL KNOW WHAT TO DO.
I'M COMING, MOTHER. I'M COMING...

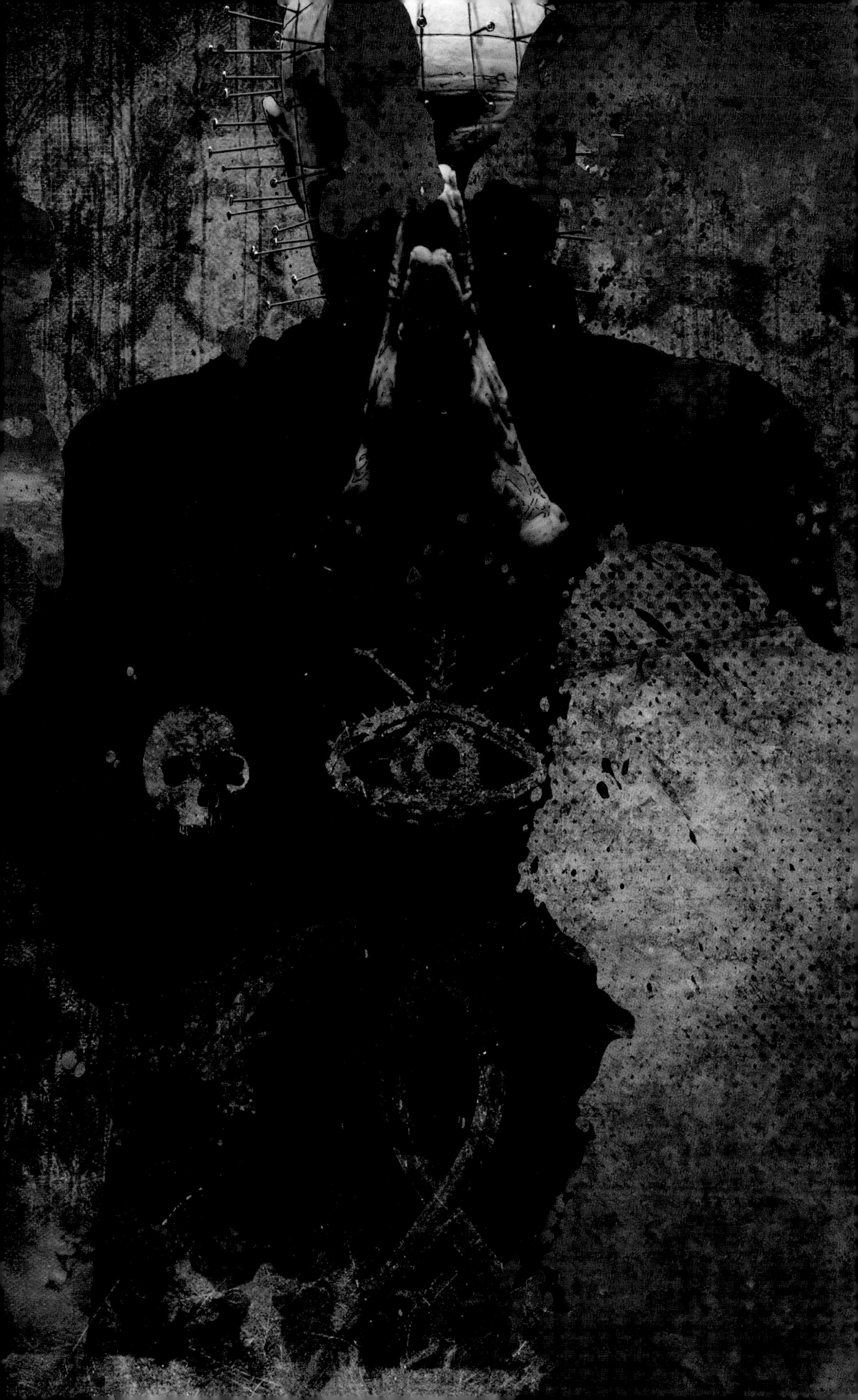

CHAPTER **SIX**

REQUIEM

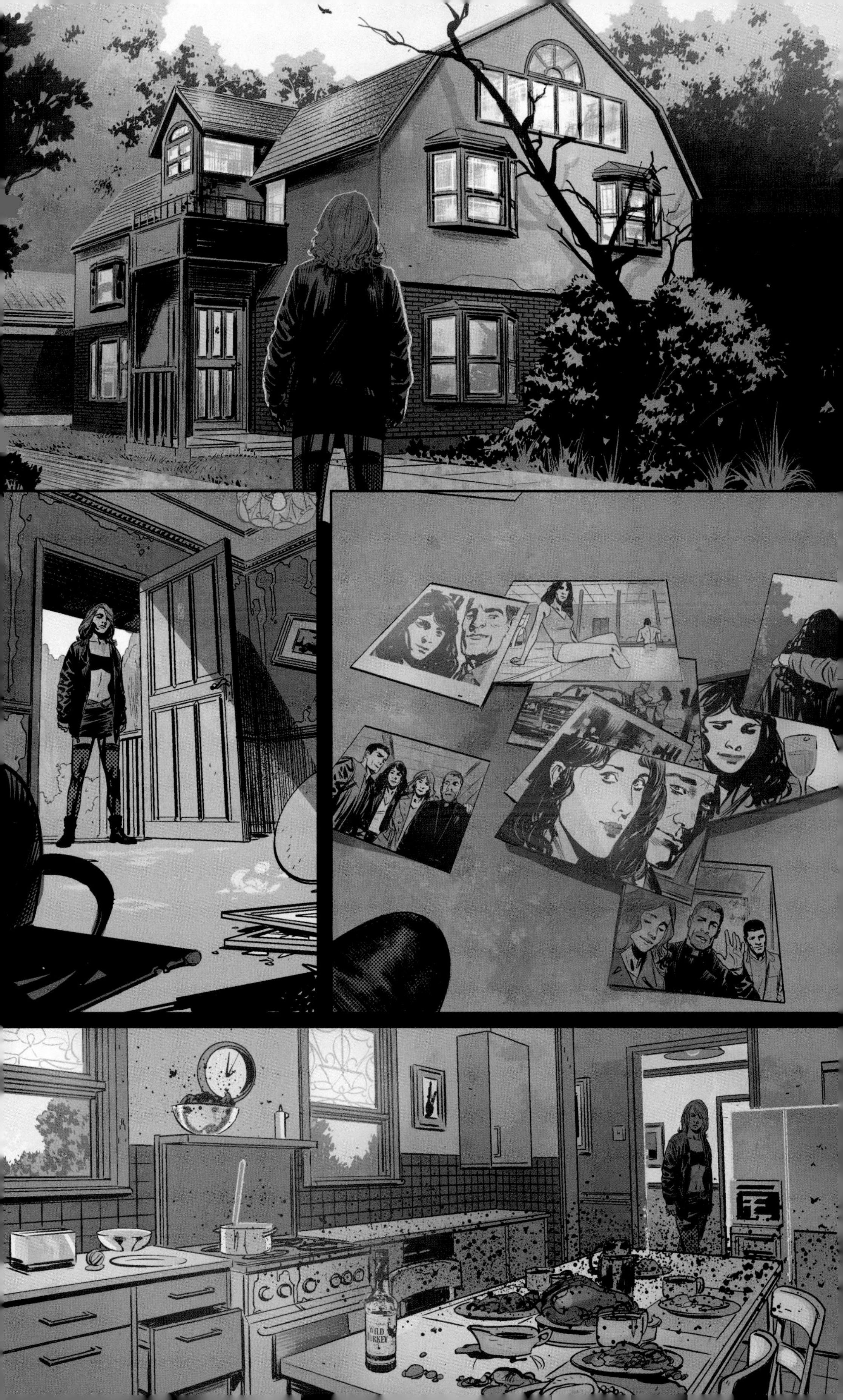
WILD TURKEY

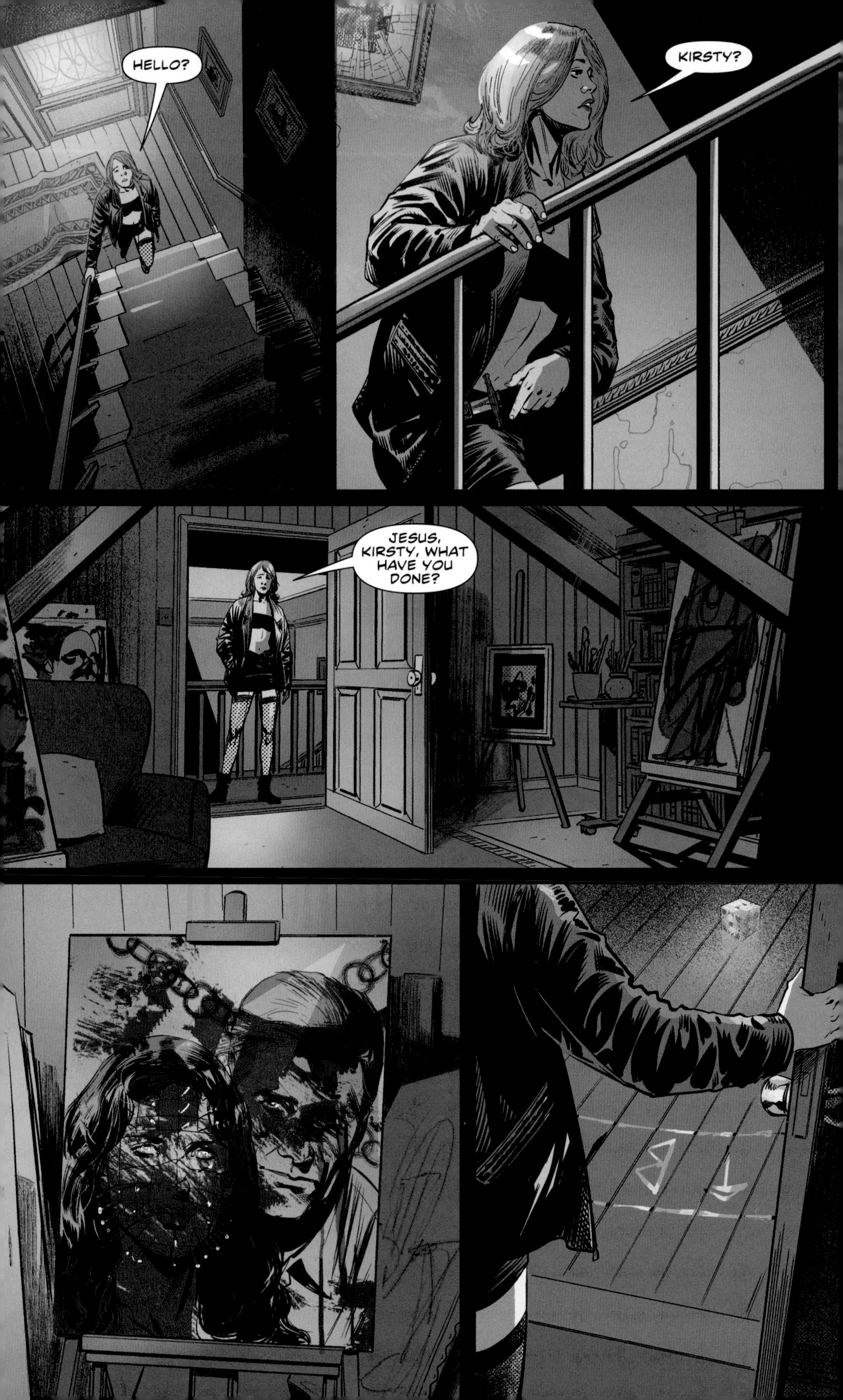
HELLO?
KIRSTY?
JESUS, KIRSTY, WHAT HAVE YOU DONE?

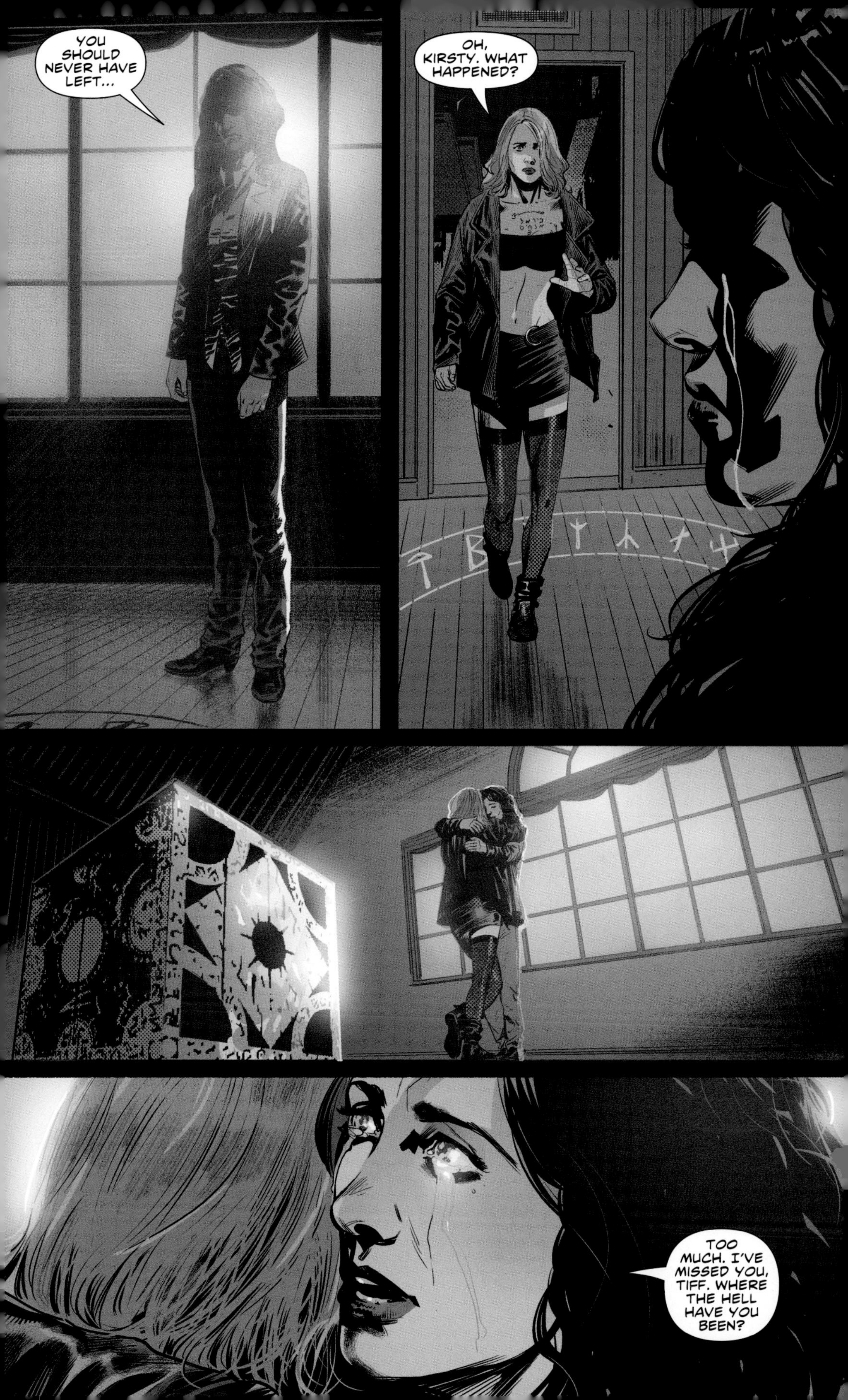
YOU SHOULD NEVER HAVE LEFT...
OH, KIRSTY. WHAT HAPPENED?
TOO MUCH. I'VE MISSED YOU, TIFF. WHERE THE HELL HAVE YOU BEEN?

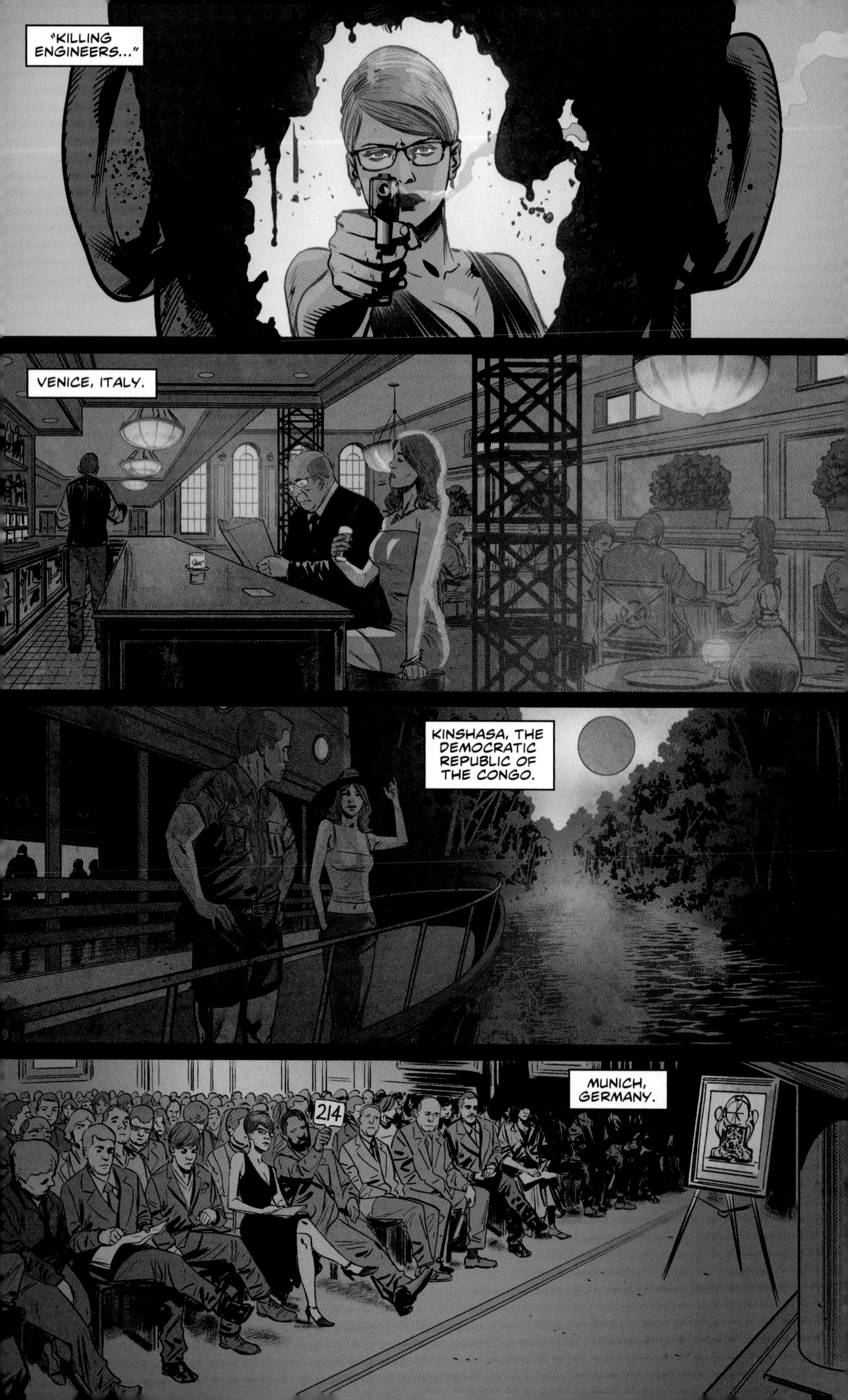
"KILLING ENGINEERS..."
VENICE, ITALY.
KINSHASA, THE DEMOCRATIC REPUBLIC OF THE CONGO.
MUNICH, GERMANY.
214

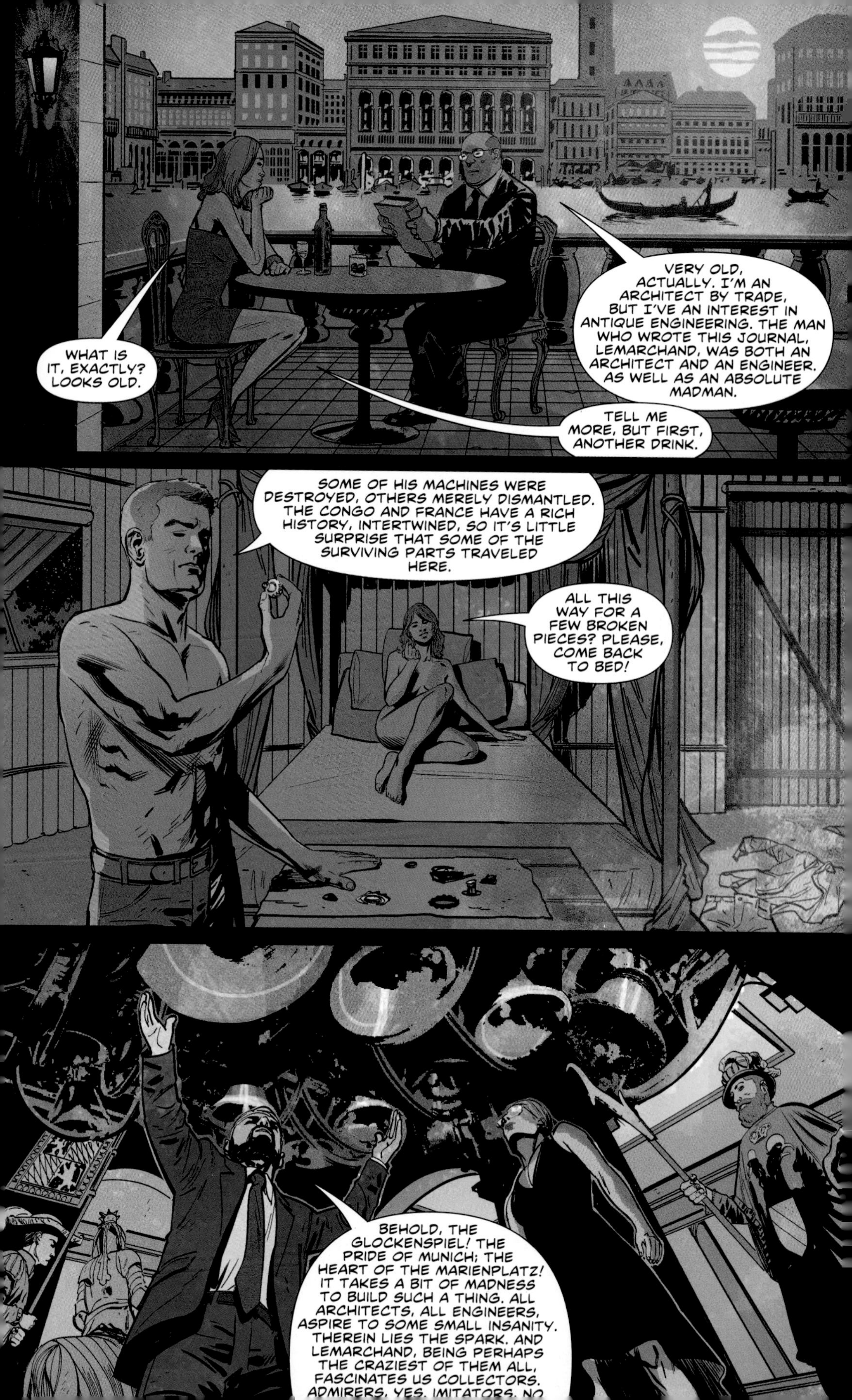
WHAT IS IT, EXACTLY? LOOKS OLD.
VERY OLD, ACTUALLY. I'M AN ARCHITECT BY TRADE, BUT I'VE AN INTEREST IN ANTIQUE ENGINEERING. THE MAN WHO WROTE THIS JOURNAL, LEMARCHAND, WAS BOTH AN ARCHITECT AND AN ENGINEER. AS WELL AS AN ABSOLUTE MADMAN.
TELL ME MORE, BUT FIRST, ANOTHER DRINK.
SOME OF HIS MACHINES WERE DESTROYED, OTHERS MERELY DISMANTLED. THE CONGO AND FRANCE HAVE A RICH HISTORY, INTERTWINED, SO IT'S LITTLE SURPRISE THAT SOME OF THE SURVIVING PARTS TRAVELED HERE.
ALL THIS WAY FOR A FEW BROKEN PIECES? PLEASE, COME BACK TO BED!
BEHOLD, THE GLOCKENSPIEL! THE PRIDE OF MUNICH; THE HEART OF THE MARIENPLATZ! IT TAKES A BIT OF MADNESS TO BUILD SUCH A THING. ALL ARCHITECTS, ALL ENGINEERS, ASPIRE TO SOME SMALL INSANITY. THEREIN LIES THE SPARK. AND LEMARCHAND, BEING PERHAPS THE CRAZIEST OF THEM ALL, FASCINATES US COLLECTORS. ADMIRERS, YES. IMITATORS, NO

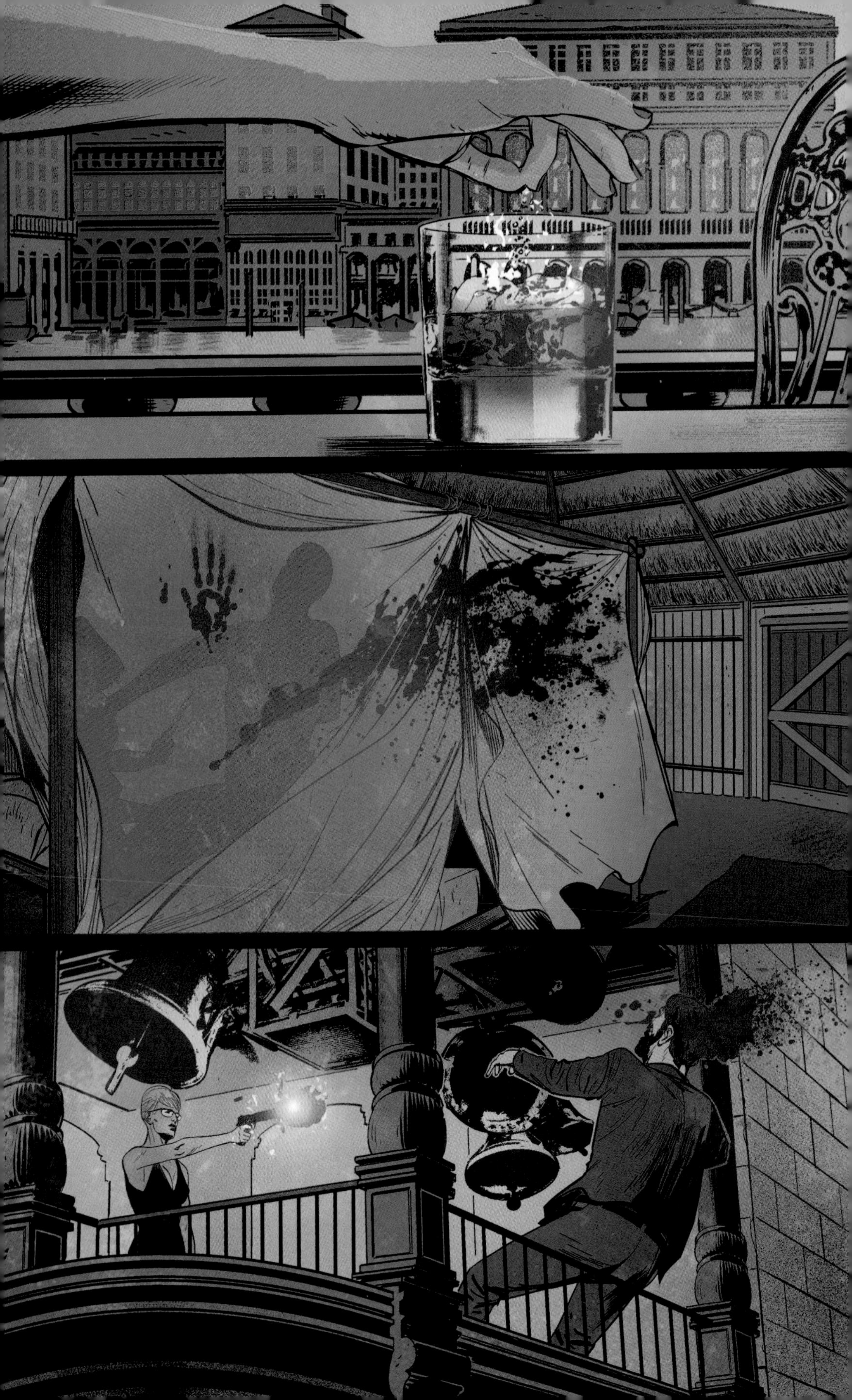

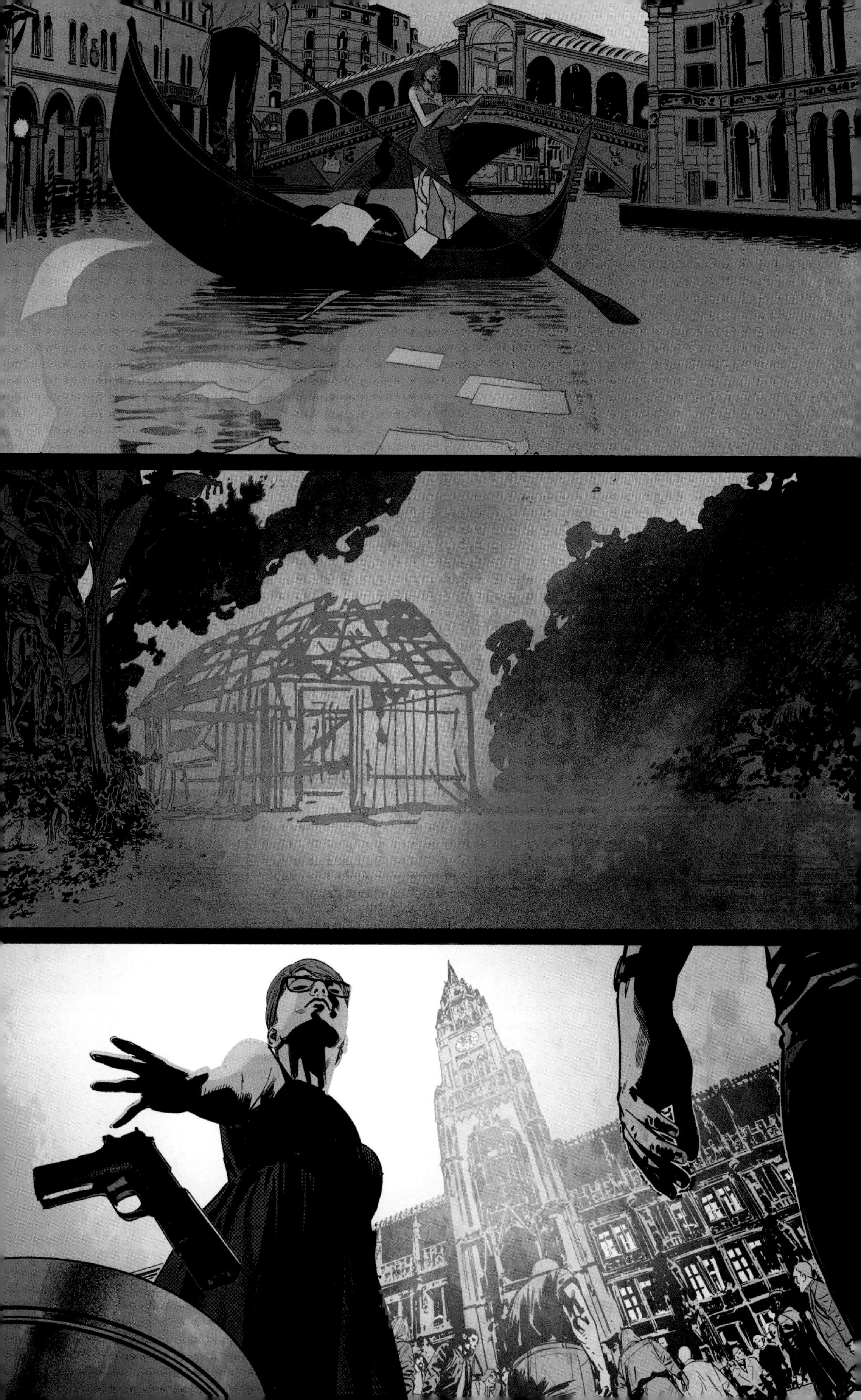

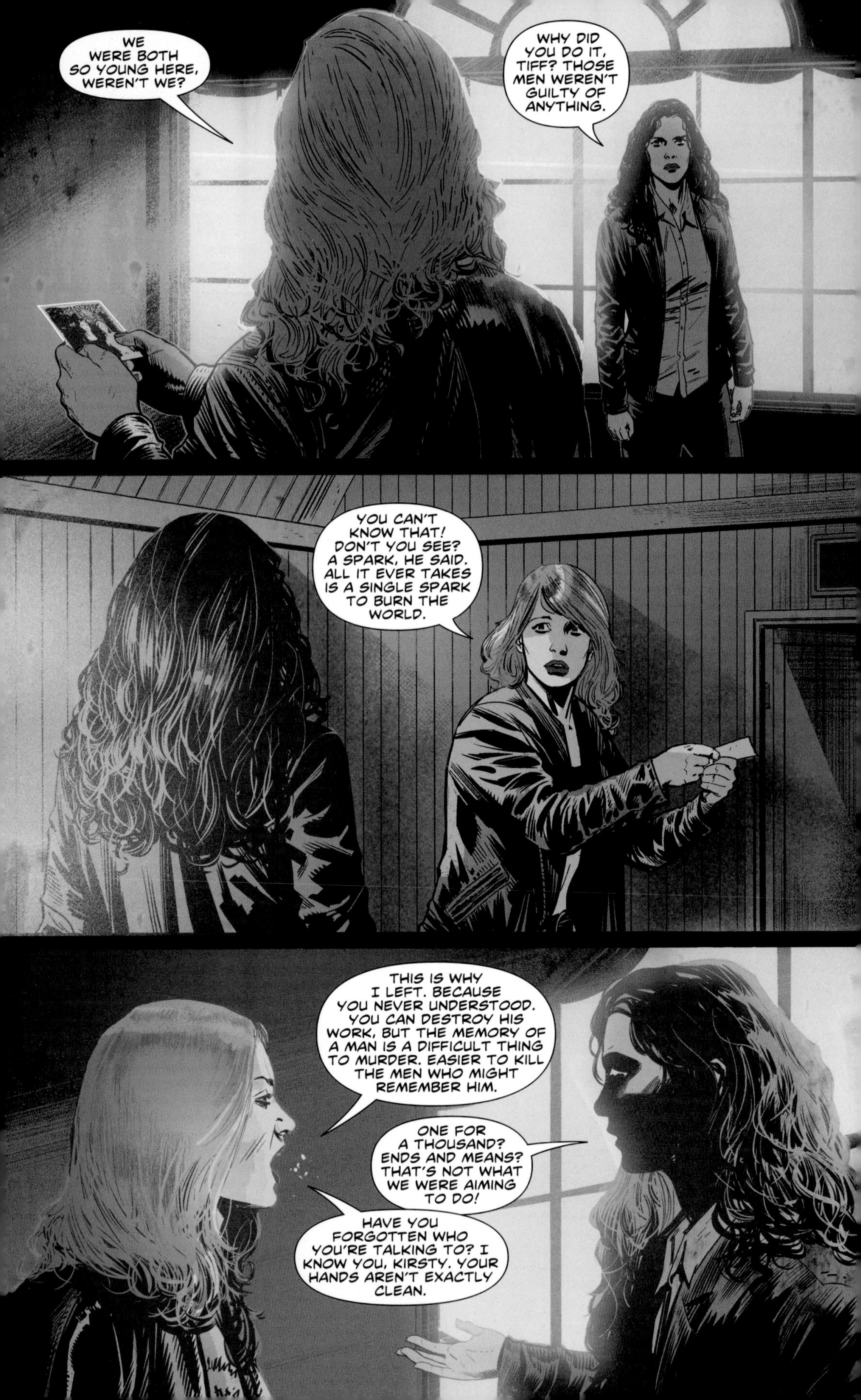

WE WERE BOTH SO YOUNG HERE, WEREN'T WE?
WHY DID YOU DO IT, TIFF? THOSE MEN WEREN'T GUILTY OF ANYTHING.
YOU CAN'T KNOW THAT! DON'T YOU SEE? A SPARK, HE SAID. ALL IT EVER TAKES IS A SINGLE SPARK TO BURN THE WORLD.
THIS IS WHY I LEFT. BECAUSE YOU NEVER UNDERSTOOD. YOU CAN DESTROY HIS WORK, BUT THE MEMORY OF A MAN IS A DIFFICULT THING TO MURDER. EASIER TO KILL THE MEN WHO MIGHT REMEMBER HIM.
ONE FOR A THOUSAND? ENDS AND MEANS? THAT'S NOT WHAT WE WERE AIMING TO DO!
HAVE YOU FORGOTTEN WHO YOU'RE TALKING TO? I KNOW YOU, KIRSTY. YOUR HANDS AREN'T EXACTLY CLEAN.

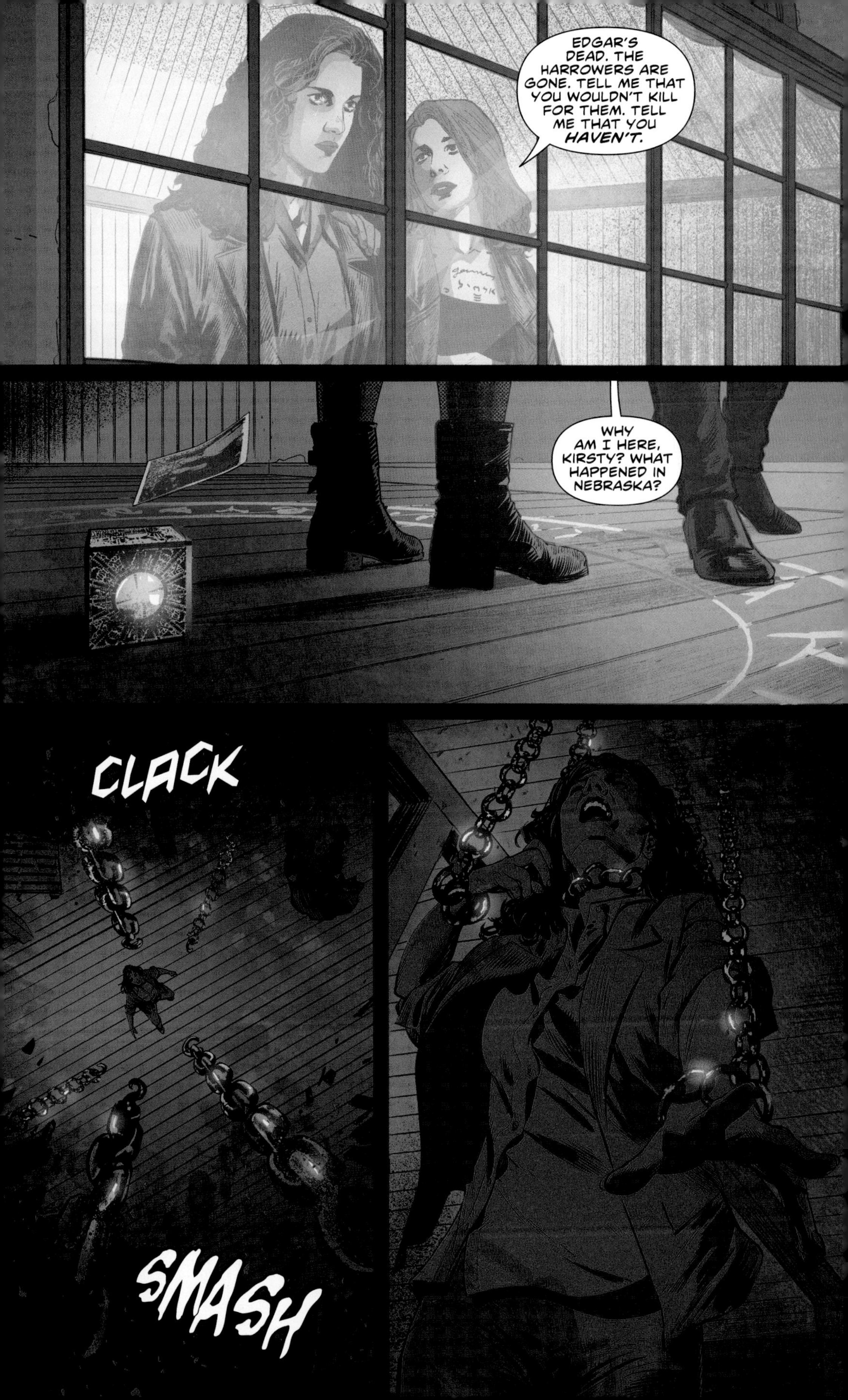
EDGAR'S DEAD. THE HARROWERS ARE GONE. TELL ME THAT YOU WOULDN'T KILL FOR THEM. TELL ME THAT YOU *HAVEN'T*.
WHY AM I HERE, KIRSTY? WHAT HAPPENED IN NEBRASKA?
CLACK
SMASH

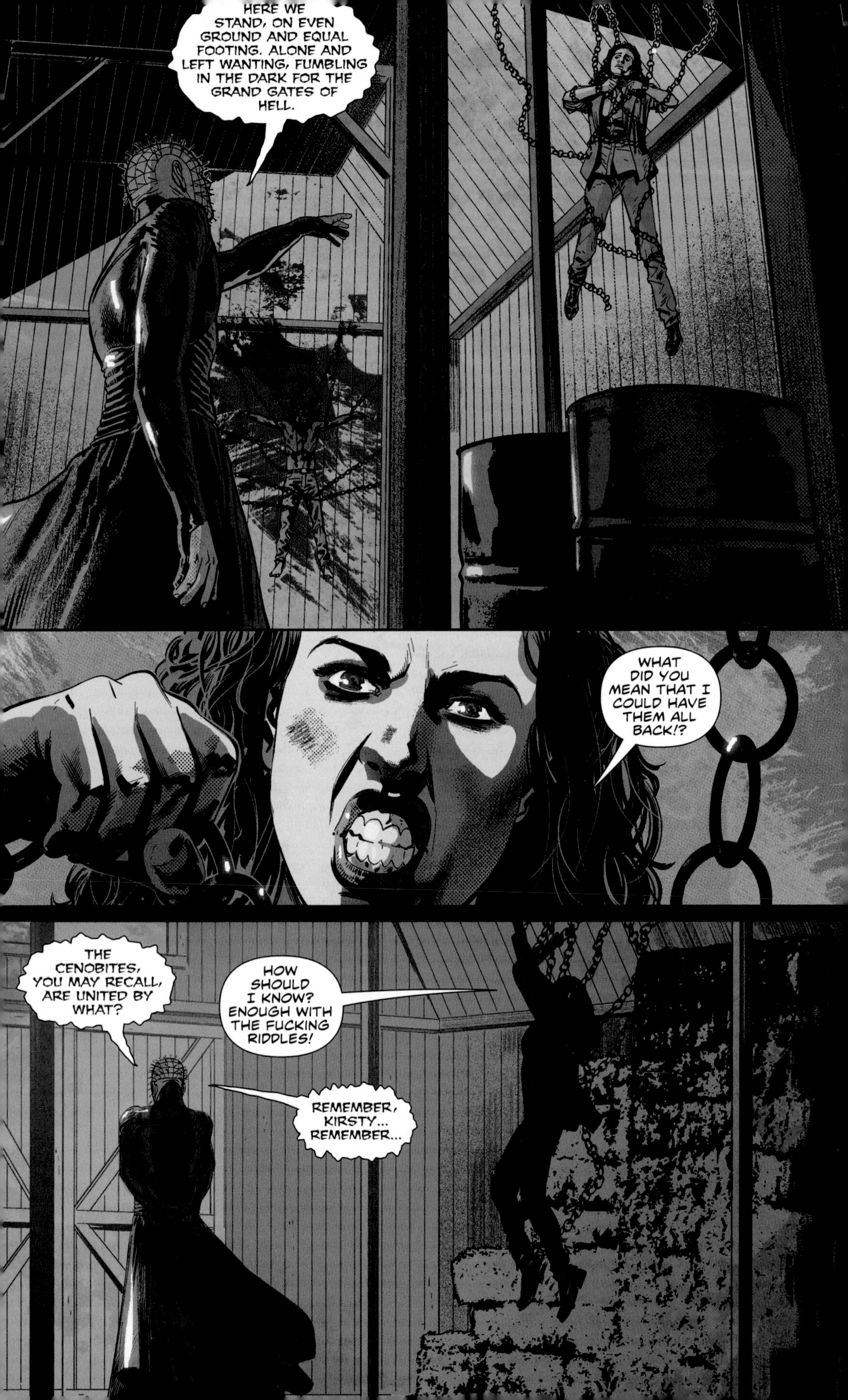
HERE WE STAND, ON EVEN GROUND AND EQUAL FOOTING. ALONE AND LEFT WANTING, FUMBLING IN THE DARK FOR THE GRAND GATES OF HELL.
WHAT DID YOU MEAN THAT I COULD HAVE THEM ALL BACK!?
THE CENOBITES, YOU MAY RECALL, ARE UNITED BY WHAT?
HOW SHOULD I KNOW? ENOUGH WITH THE FUCKING RIDDLES!
REMEMBER, KIRSTY... REMEMBER...

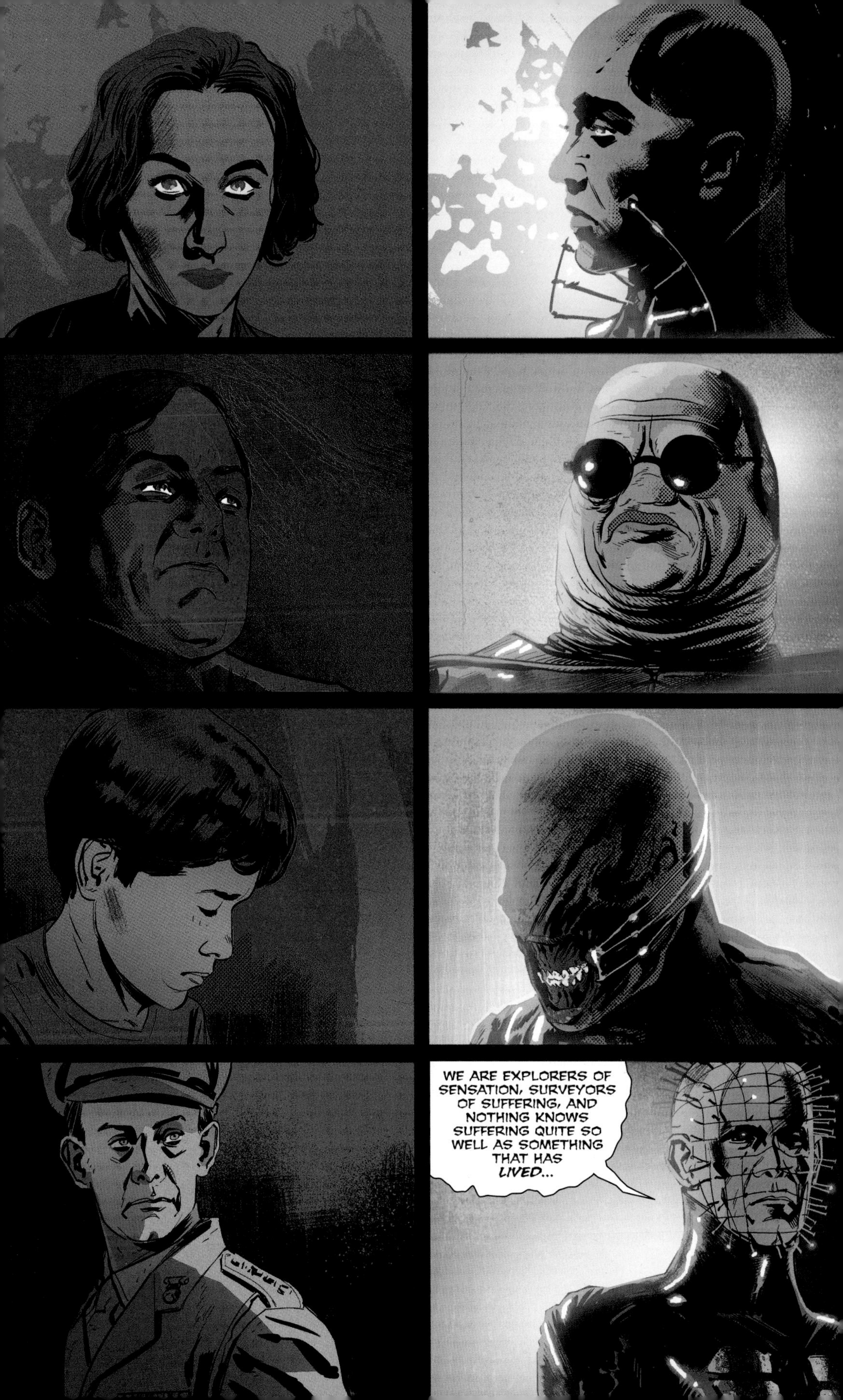
WE ARE EXPLORERS OF SENSATION, SURVEYORS OF SUFFERING, AND NOTHING KNOWS SUFFERING QUITE SO WELL AS SOMETHING THAT HAS *LIVED*...

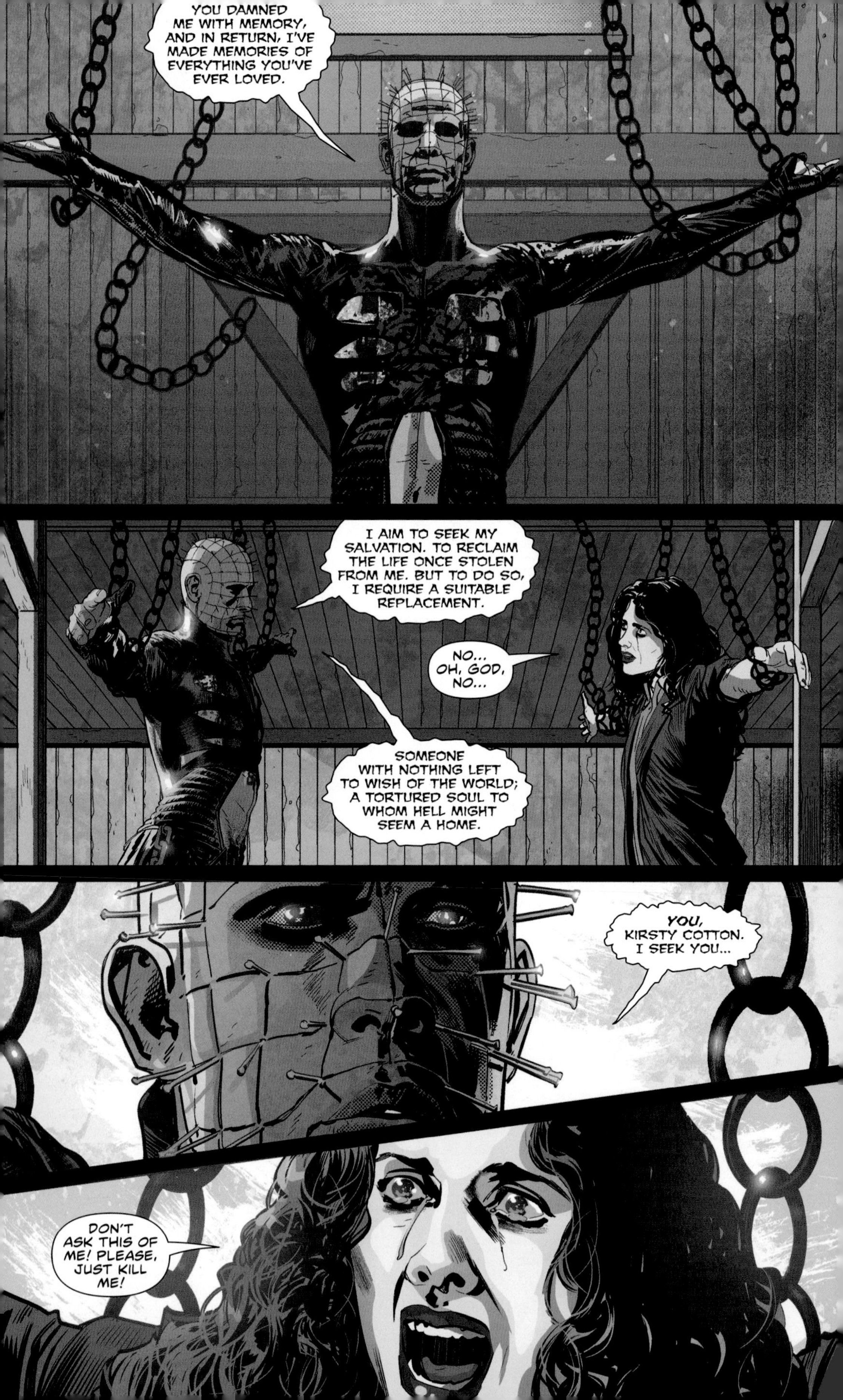
YOU DAMNED ME WITH MEMORY, AND IN RETURN, I'VE MADE MEMORIES OF EVERYTHING YOU'VE EVER LOVED.
I AIM TO SEEK MY SALVATION. TO RECLAIM THE LIFE ONCE STOLEN FROM ME. BUT TO DO SO, I REQUIRE A SUITABLE REPLACEMENT.
NO... OH, GOD, NO...
SOMEONE WITH NOTHING LEFT TO WISH OF THE WORLD; A TORTURED SOUL TO WHOM HELL MIGHT SEEM A HOME.
YOU, KIRSTY COTTON. I SEEK YOU...
DON'T ASK THIS OF ME! PLEASE, JUST KILL ME!

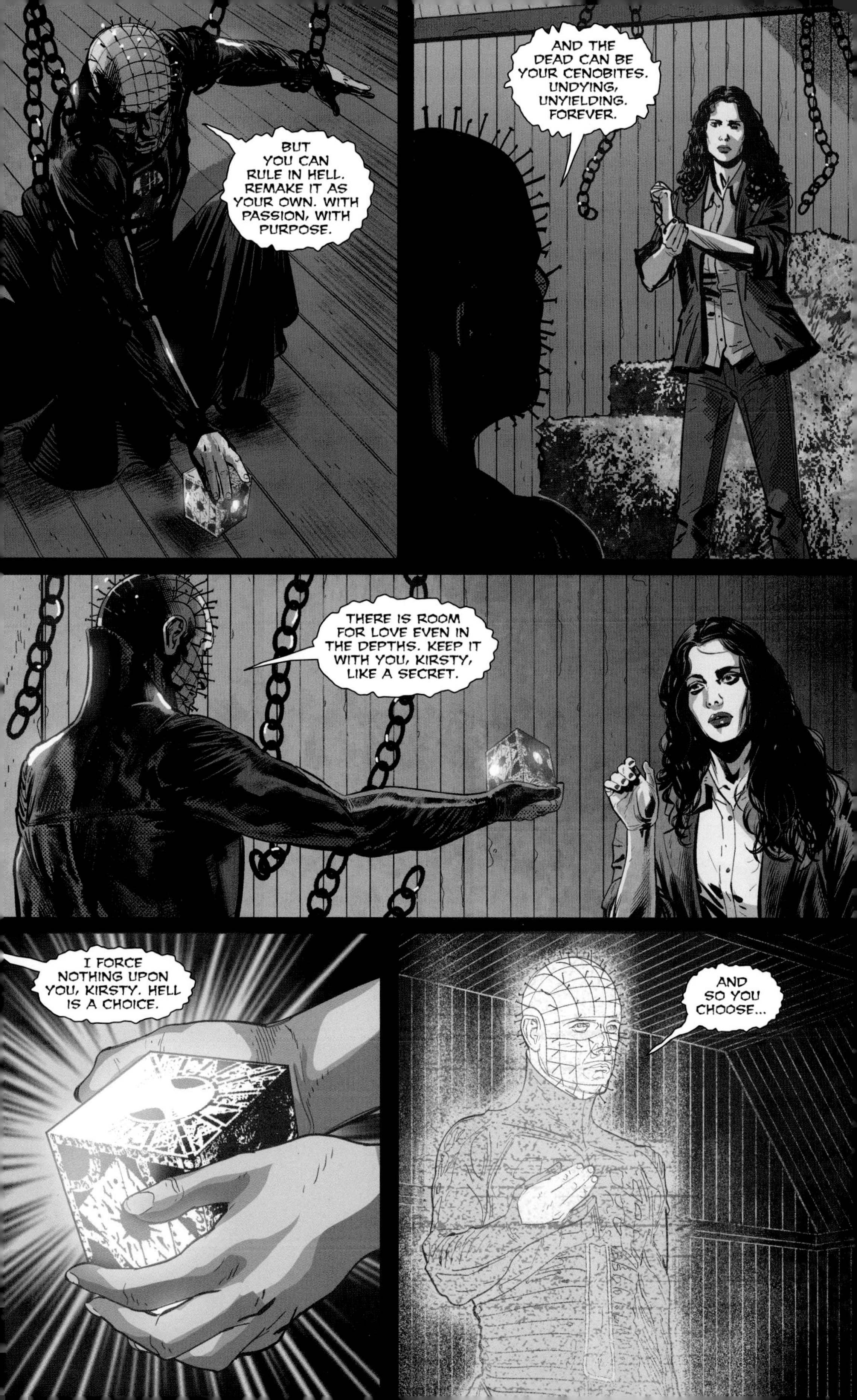
BUT YOU CAN RULE IN HELL. REMAKE IT AS YOUR OWN. WITH PASSION, WITH PURPOSE.
AND THE DEAD CAN BE YOUR CENOBITES. UNDYING, UNYIELDING. FOREVER.
THERE IS ROOM FOR LOVE EVEN IN THE DEPTHS. KEEP IT WITH YOU, KIRSTY, LIKE A SECRET.
I FORCE NOTHING UPON YOU, KIRSTY. HELL IS A CHOICE.
AND SO YOU CHOOSE...

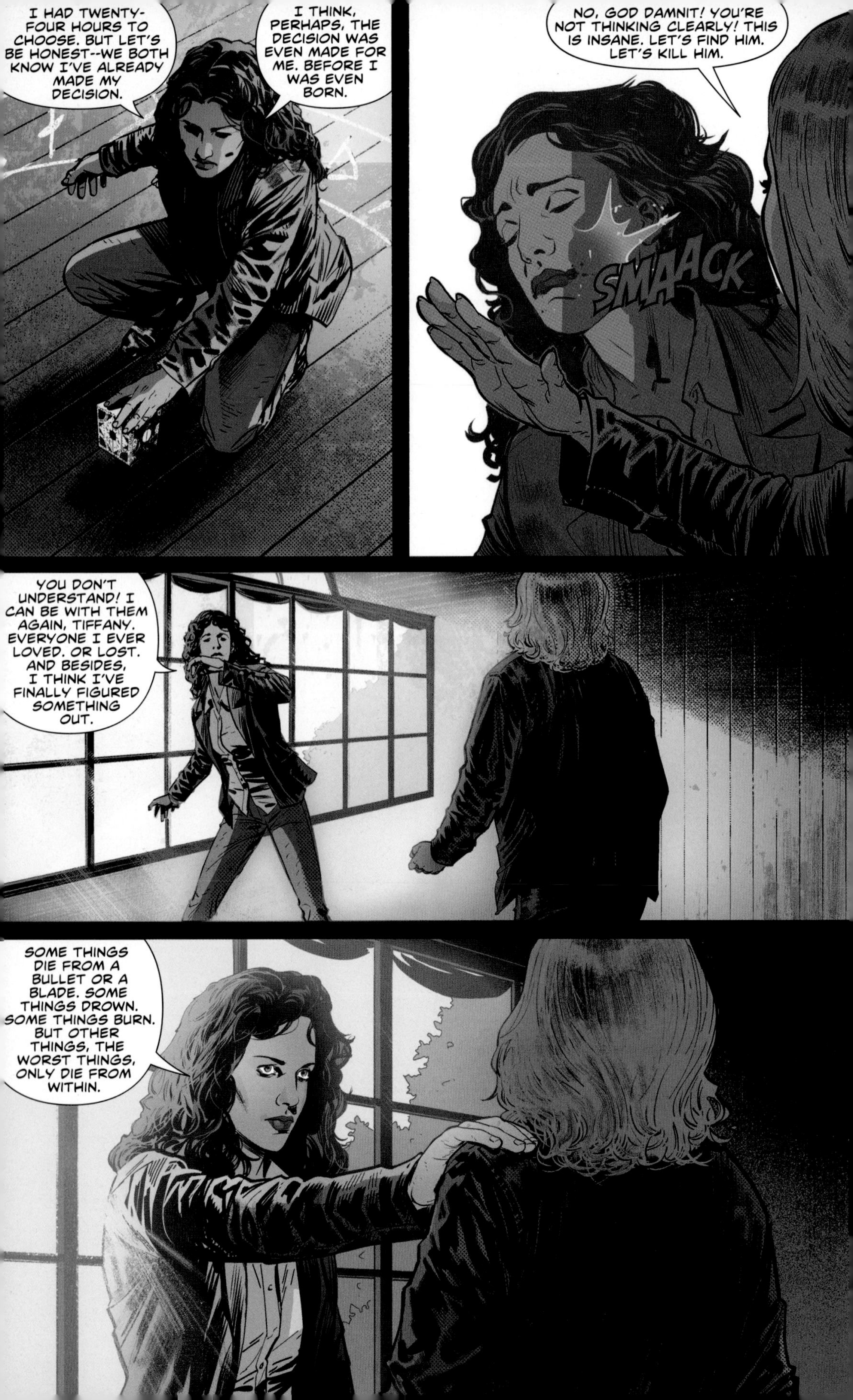
I HAD TWENTY-FOUR HOURS TO CHOOSE. BUT LET'S BE HONEST--WE BOTH KNOW I'VE ALREADY MADE MY DECISION.
I THINK, PERHAPS, THE DECISION WAS EVEN MADE FOR ME. BEFORE I WAS EVEN BORN.
NO, GOD DAMNIT! YOU'RE NOT THINKING CLEARLY! THIS IS INSANE. LET'S FIND HIM. LET'S KILL HIM.
SMAACK
YOU DON'T UNDERSTAND! I CAN BE WITH THEM AGAIN, TIFFANY. EVERYONE I EVER LOVED. OR LOST. AND BESIDES, I THINK I'VE FINALLY FIGURED SOMETHING OUT.
SOME THINGS DIE FROM A BULLET OR A BLADE. SOME THINGS DROWN. SOME THINGS BURN. BUT OTHER THINGS, THE WORST THINGS, ONLY DIE FROM WITHIN.

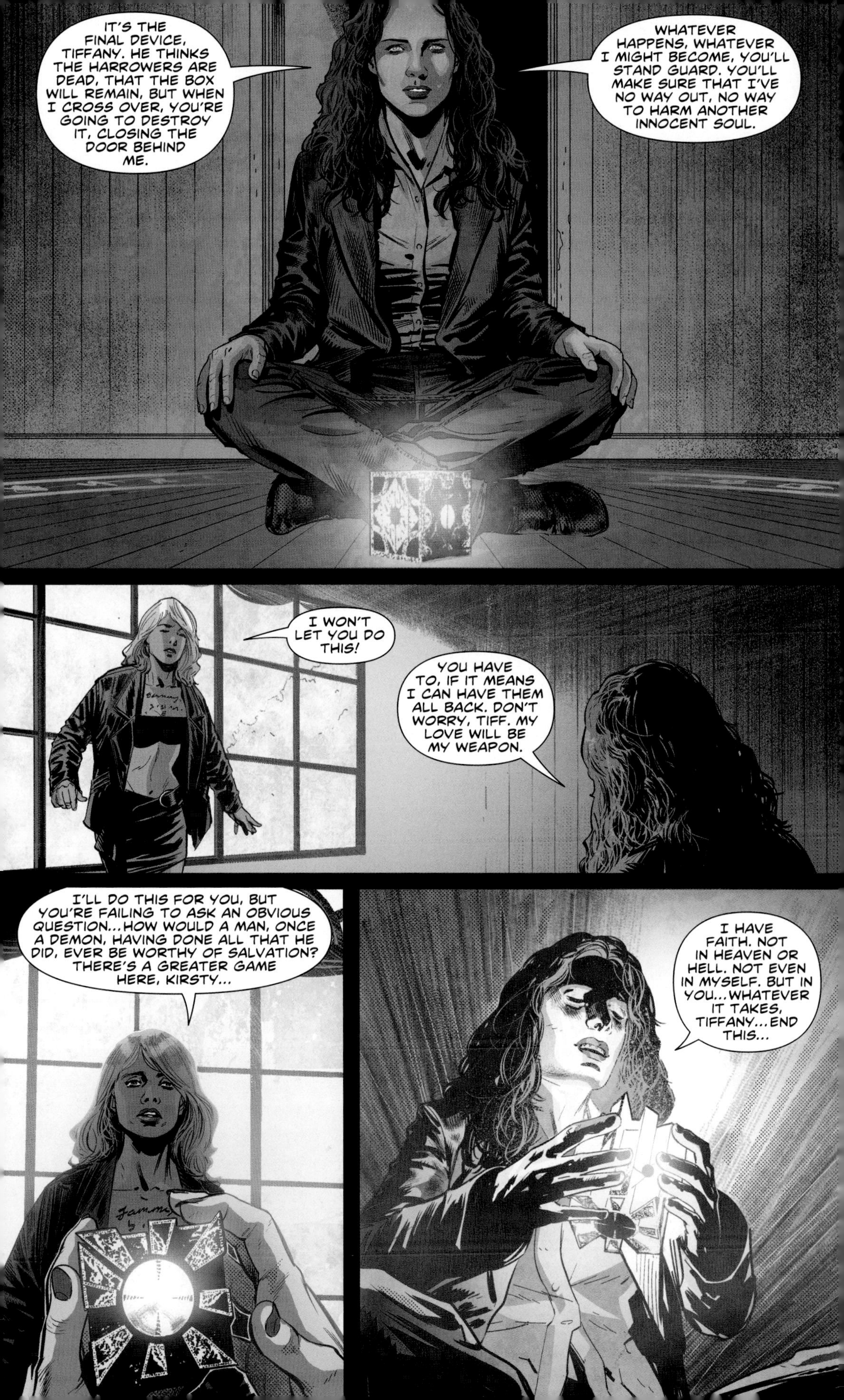
IT'S THE FINAL DEVICE, TIFFANY. HE THINKS THE HARROWERS ARE DEAD, THAT THE BOX WILL REMAIN, BUT WHEN I CROSS OVER, YOU'RE GOING TO DESTROY IT, CLOSING THE DOOR BEHIND ME.
WHATEVER HAPPENS, WHATEVER I MIGHT BECOME, YOU'LL STAND GUARD. YOU'LL MAKE SURE THAT I'VE NO WAY OUT, NO WAY TO HARM ANOTHER INNOCENT SOUL.
I WON'T LET YOU DO THIS!
YOU HAVE TO, IF IT MEANS I CAN HAVE THEM ALL BACK. DON'T WORRY, TIFF. MY LOVE WILL BE MY WEAPON.
I'LL DO THIS FOR YOU, BUT YOU'RE FAILING TO ASK AN OBVIOUS QUESTION... HOW WOULD A MAN, ONCE A DEMON, HAVING DONE ALL THAT HE DID, EVER BE WORTHY OF SALVATION? THERE'S A GREATER GAME HERE, KIRSTY...
I HAVE FAITH. NOT IN HEAVEN OR HELL. NOT EVEN IN MYSELF. BUT IN YOU... WHATEVER IT TAKES, TIFFANY... END THIS...

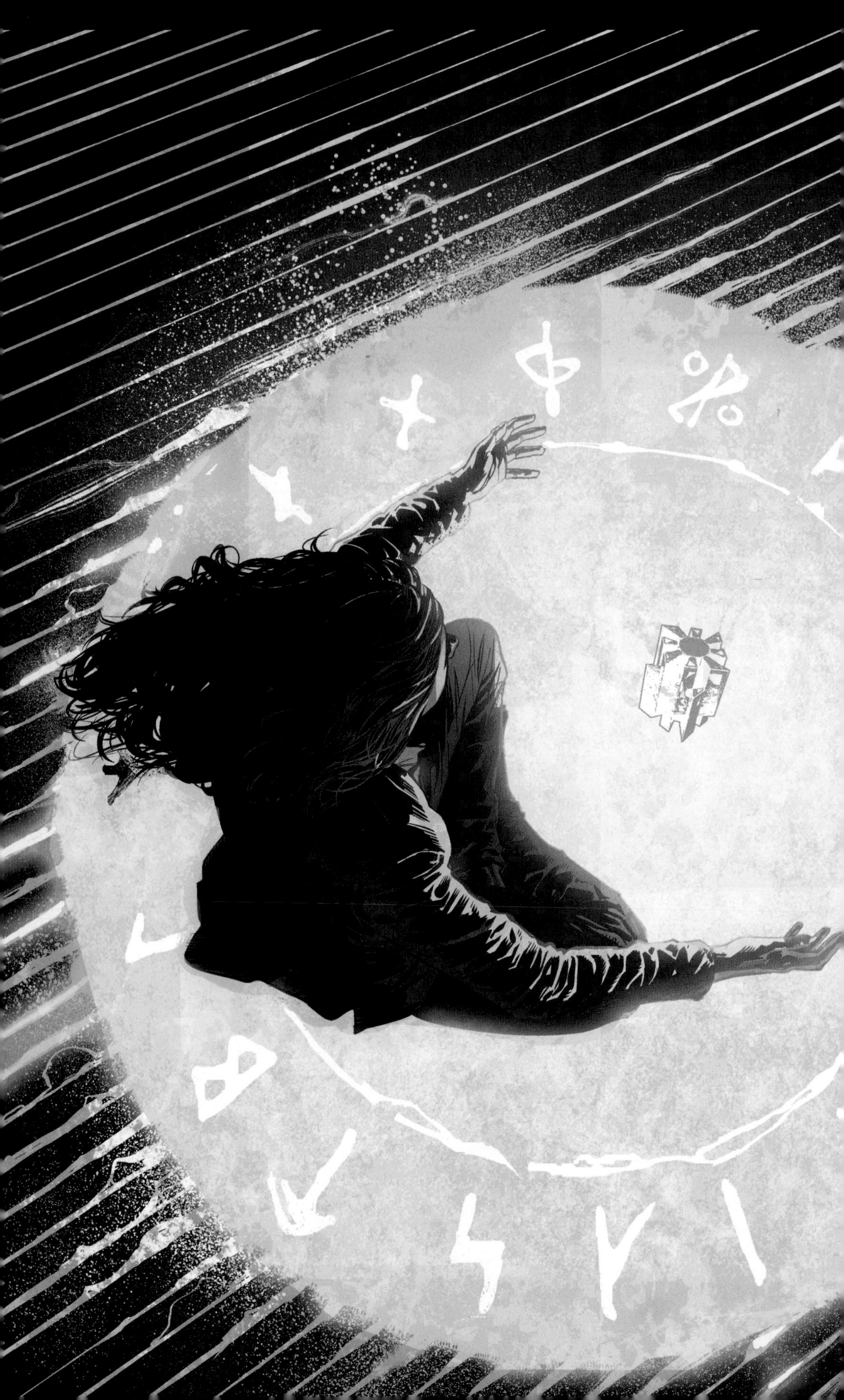

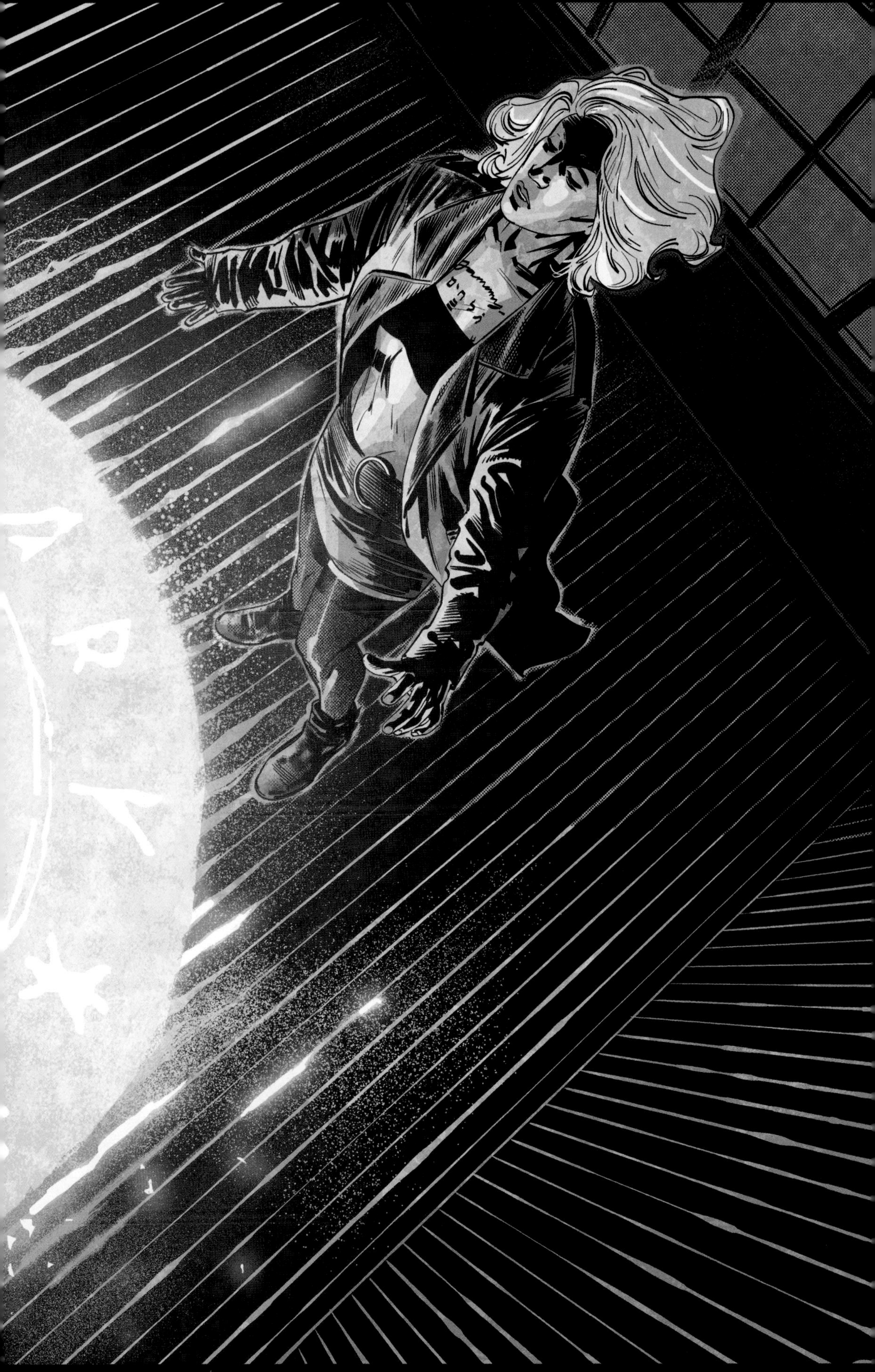

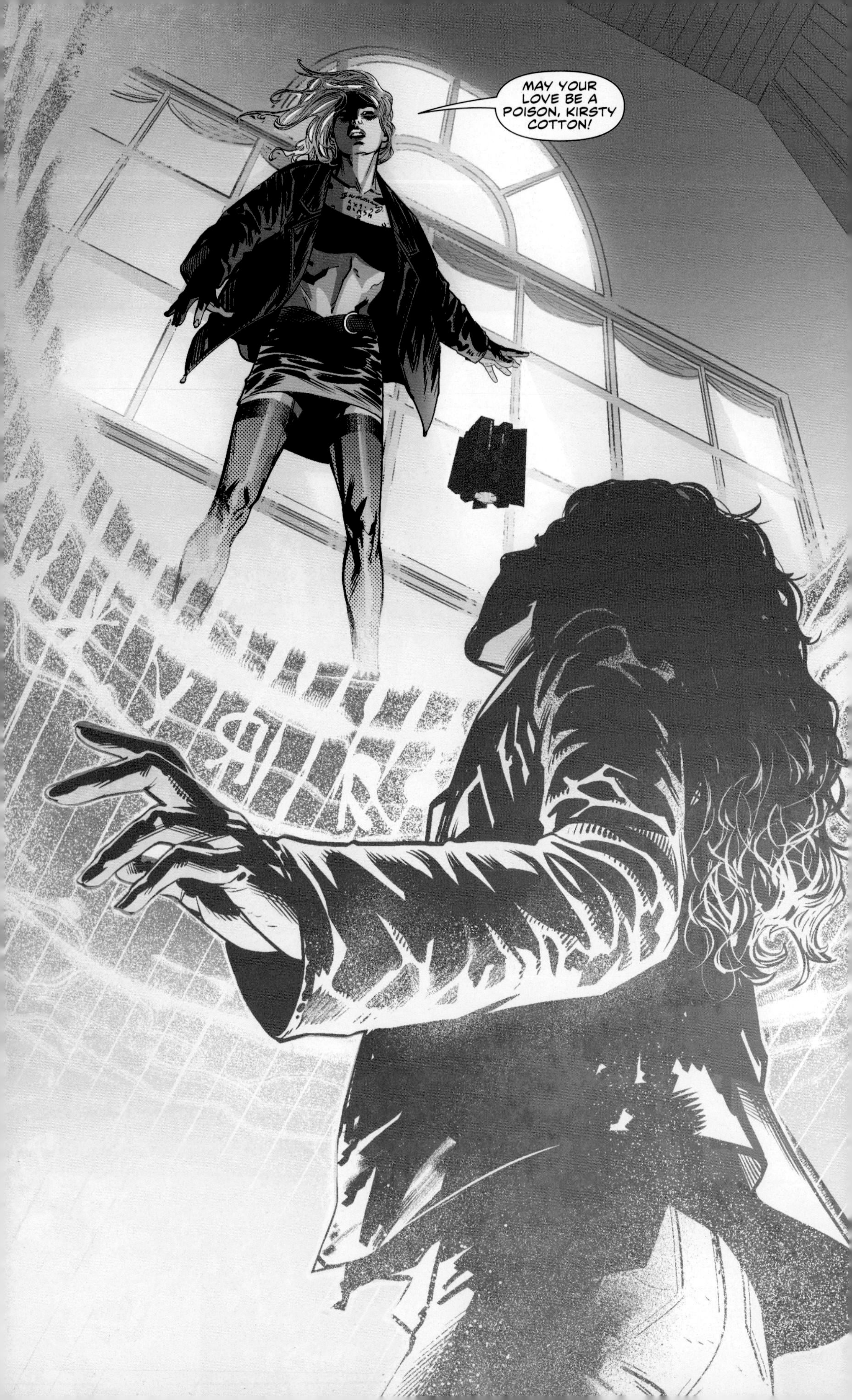
MAY YOUR LOVE BE A POISON, KIRSTY COTTON!

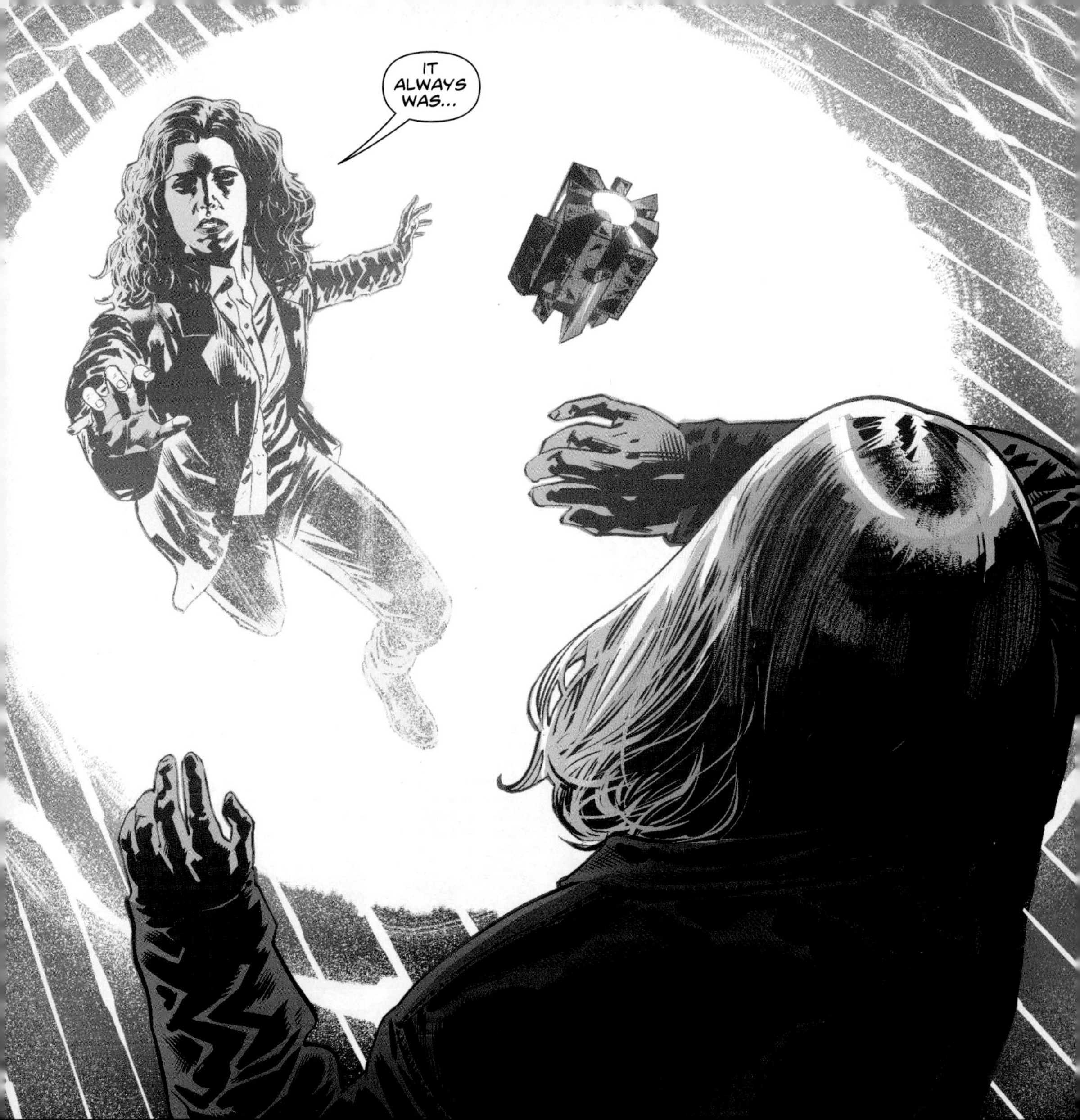
IT ALWAYS WAS...
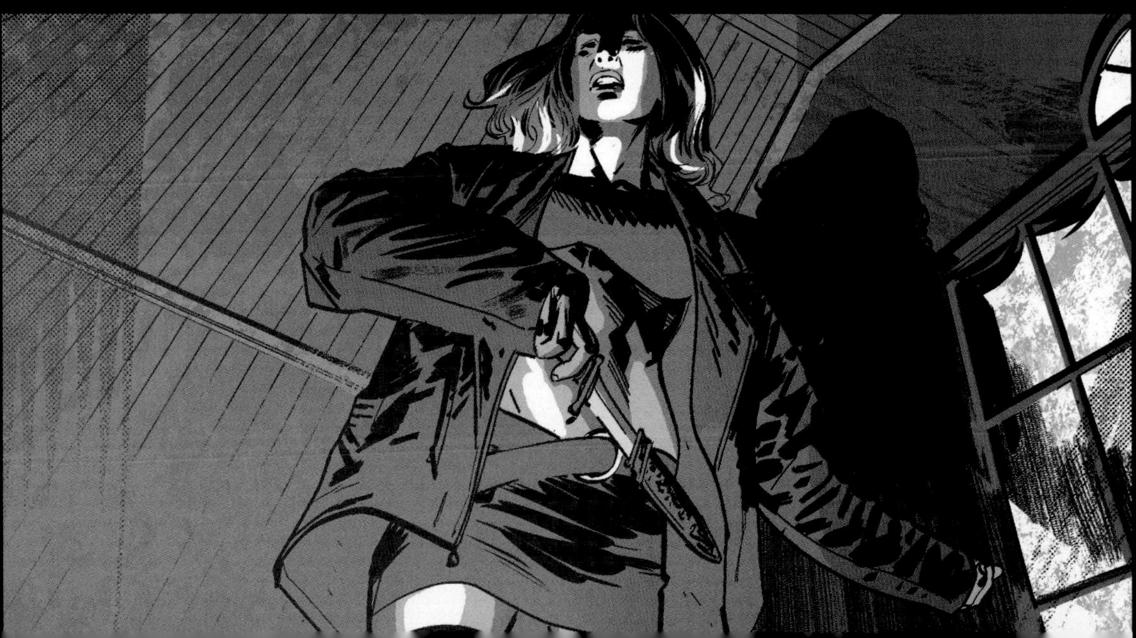

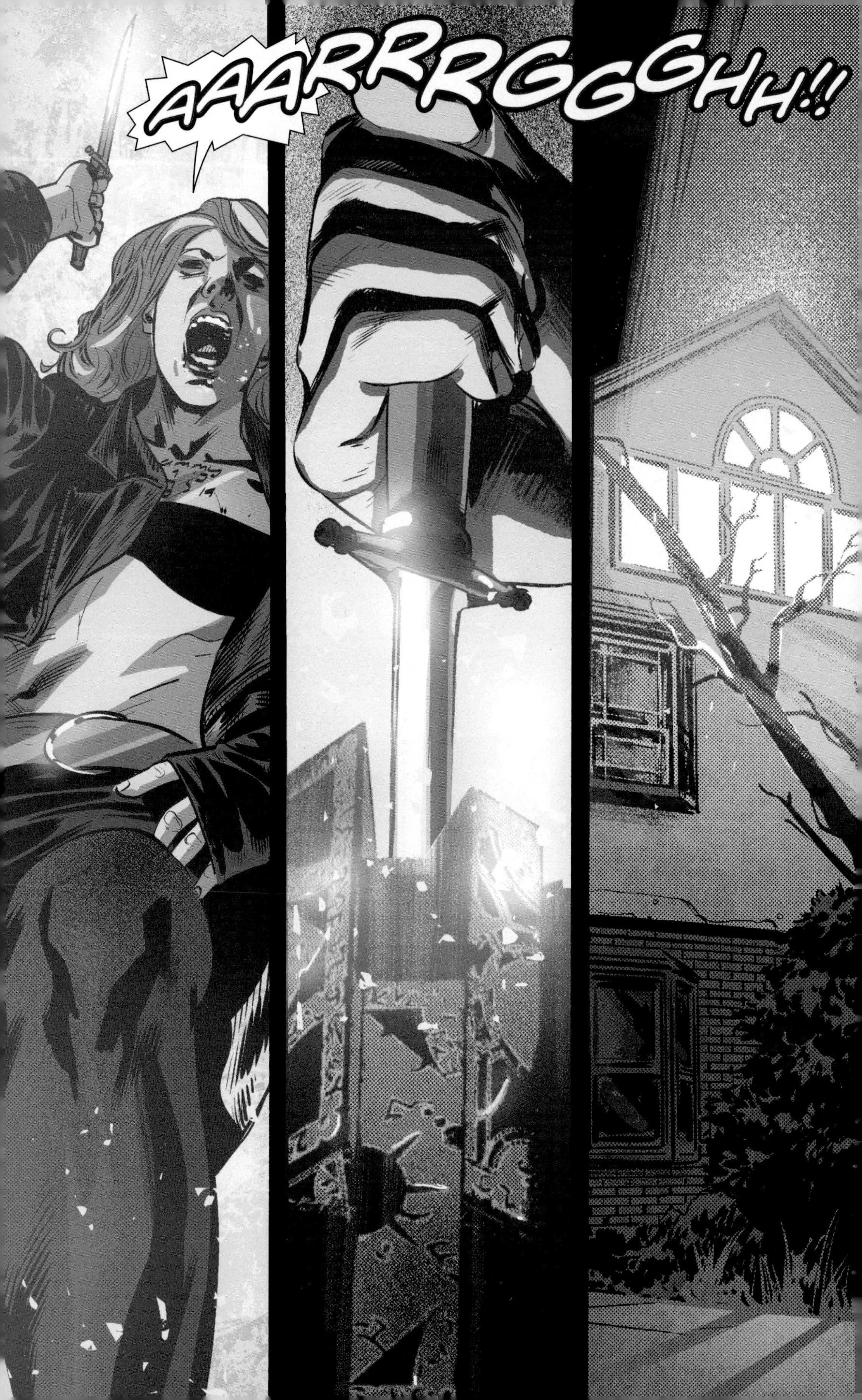
AAARRRGGGHH!!

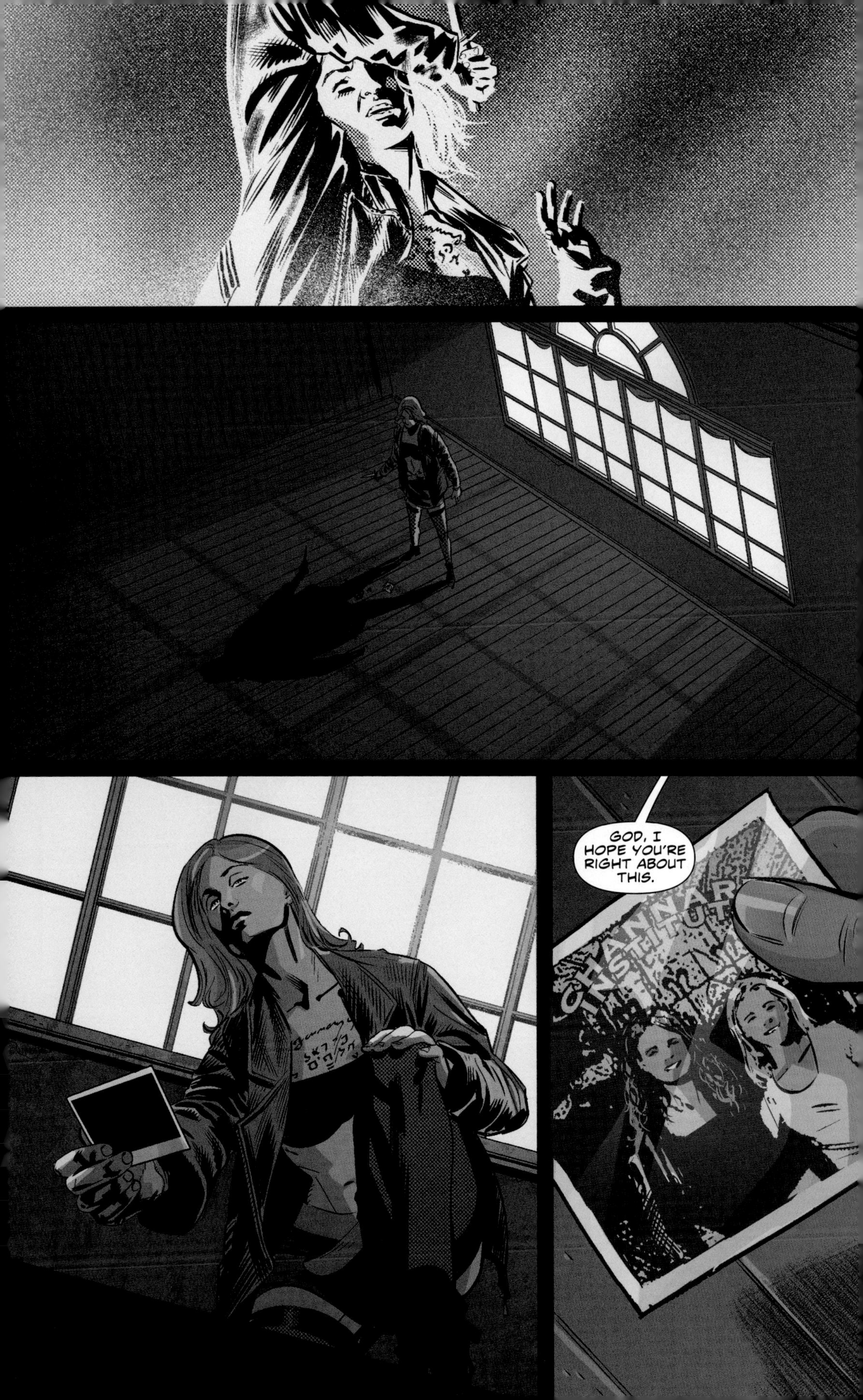
GOD, I HOPE YOU'RE RIGHT ABOUT THIS.

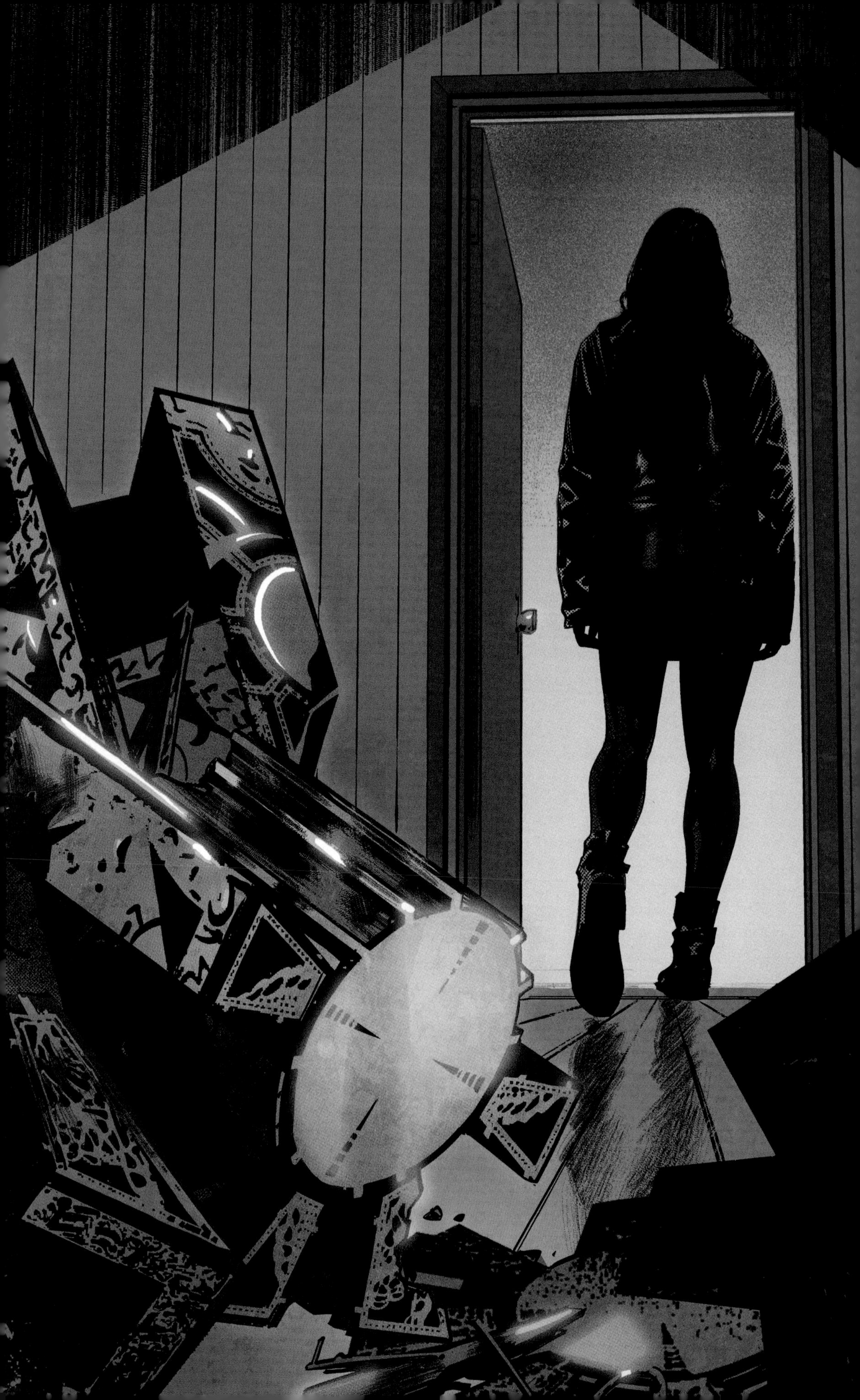

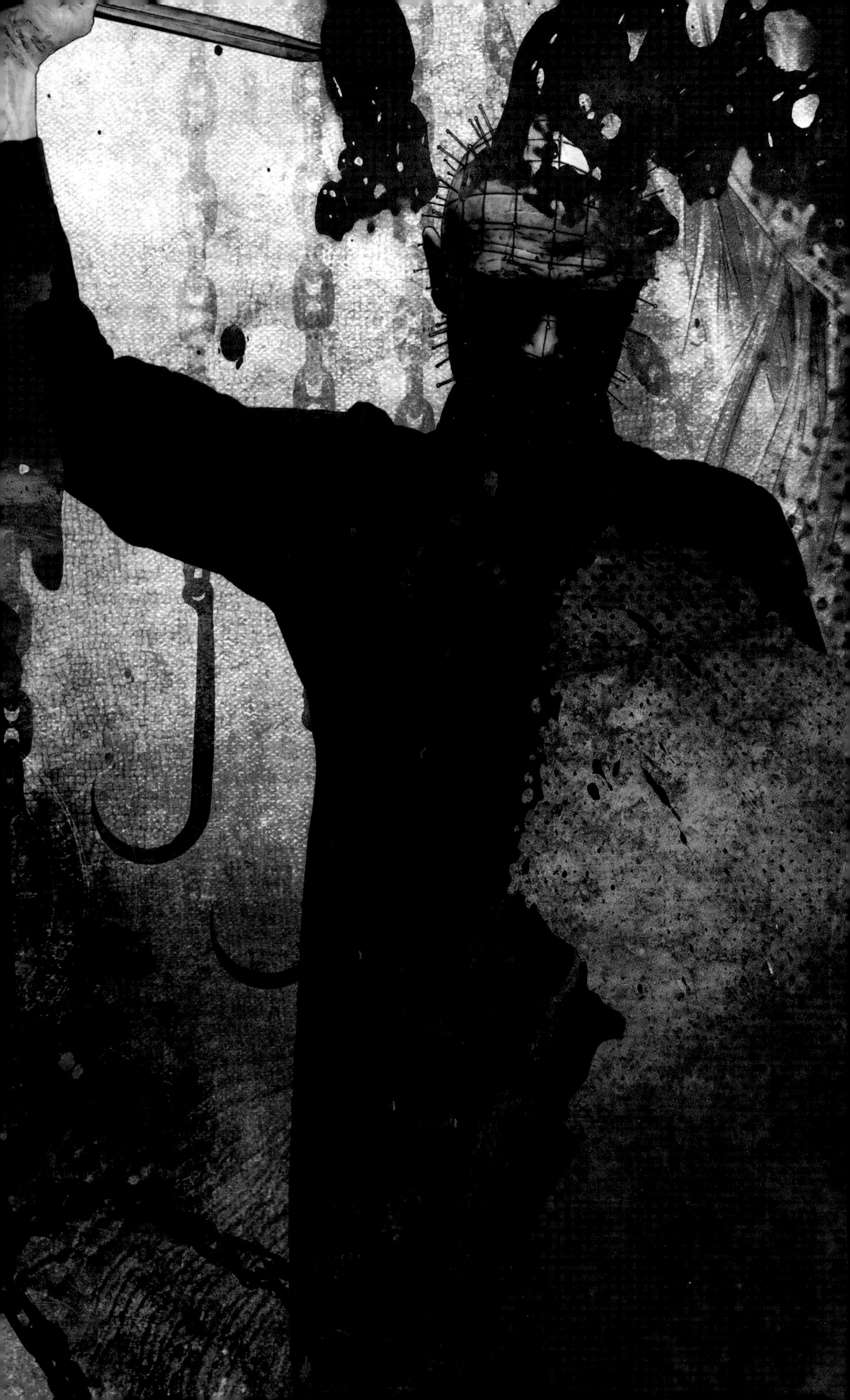

CHAPTER **SEVEN**

REQUIEM

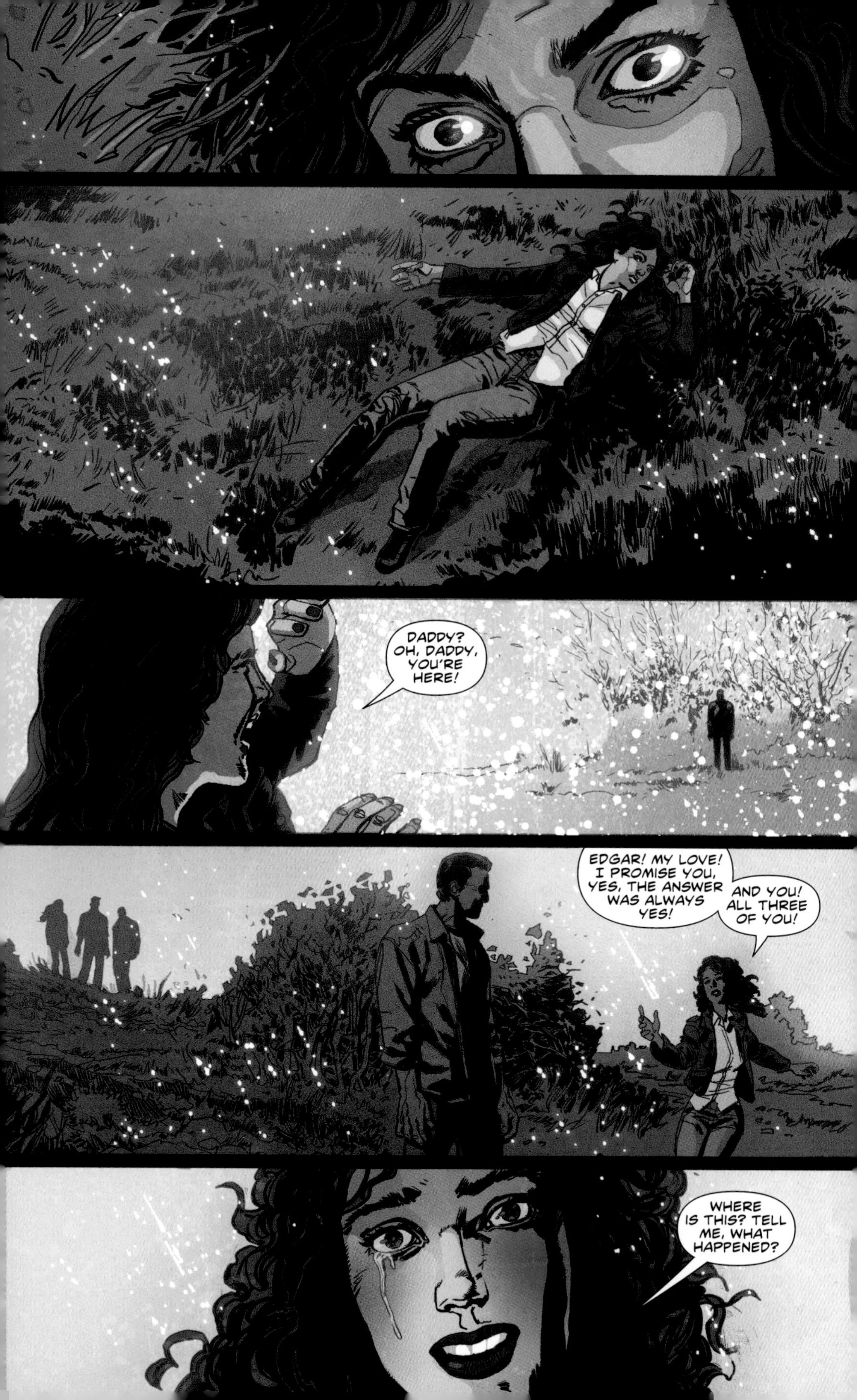
DADDY? OH, DADDY, YOU'RE HERE!
EDGAR! MY LOVE! I PROMISE YOU, YES, THE ANSWER WAS ALWAYS YES!
AND YOU! ALL THREE OF YOU!
WHERE IS THIS? TELL ME, WHAT HAPPENED?

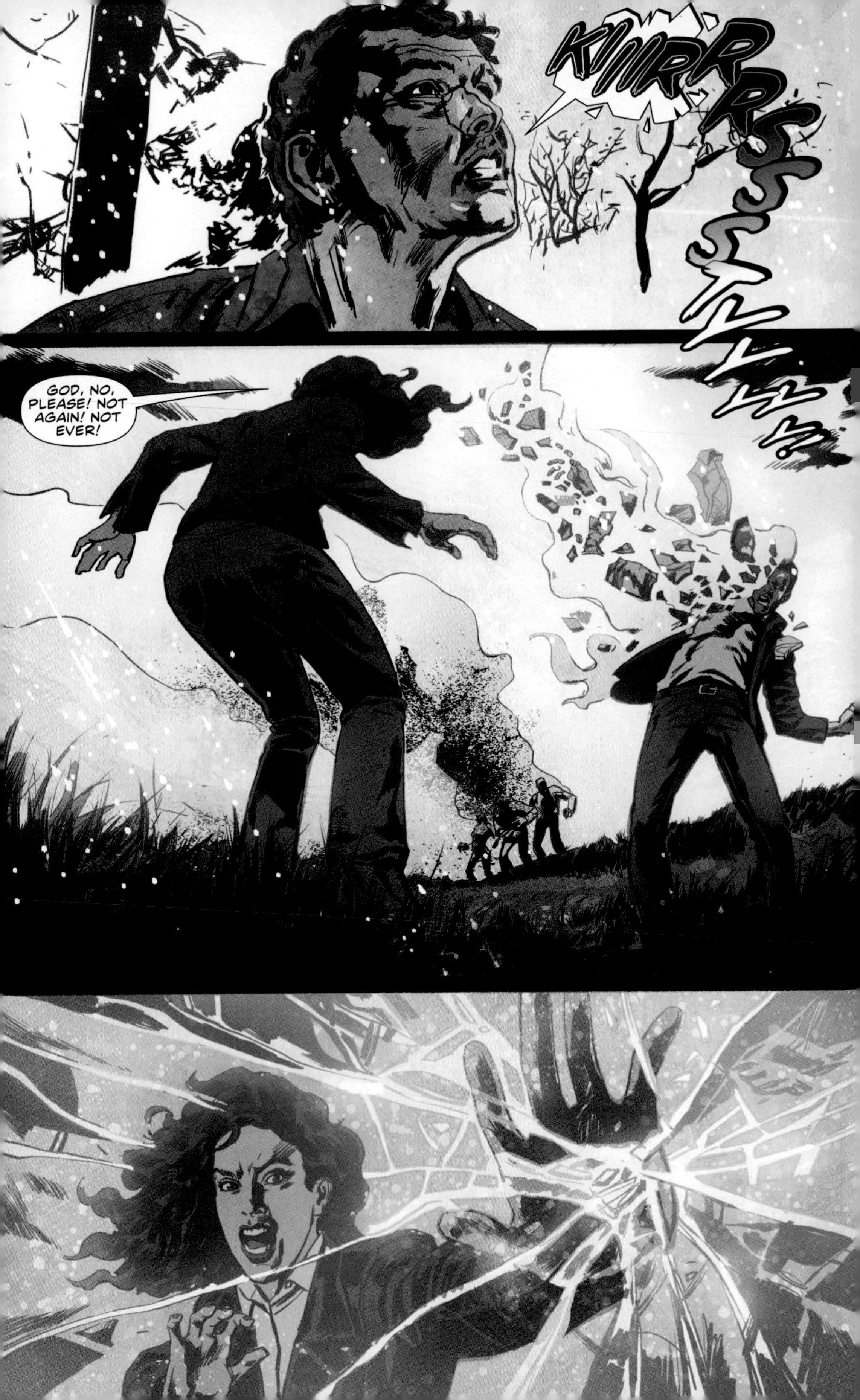

KIIIRRRSSSYYYZZM!
GOD, NO, PLEASE! NOT AGAIN! NOT EVER!

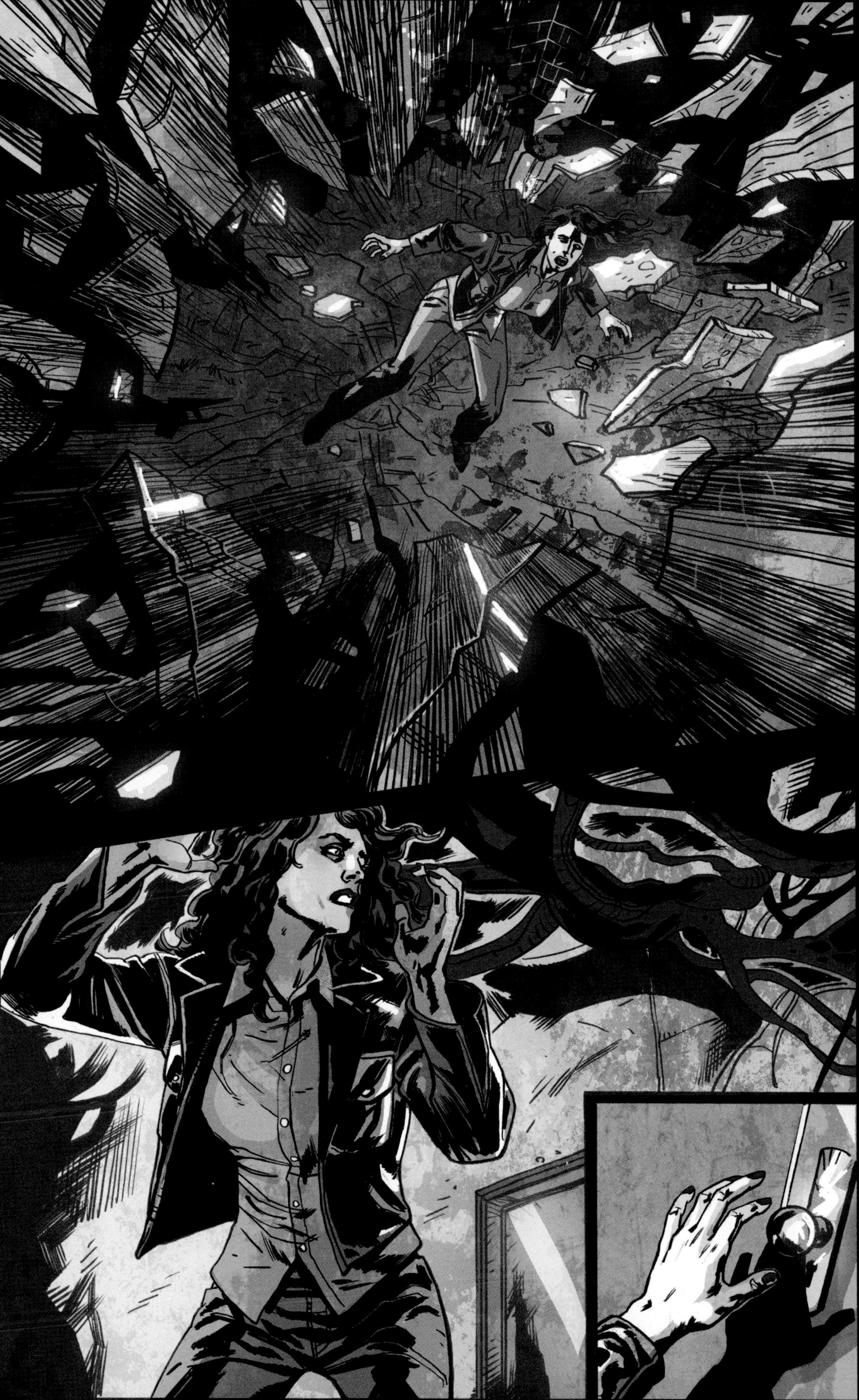

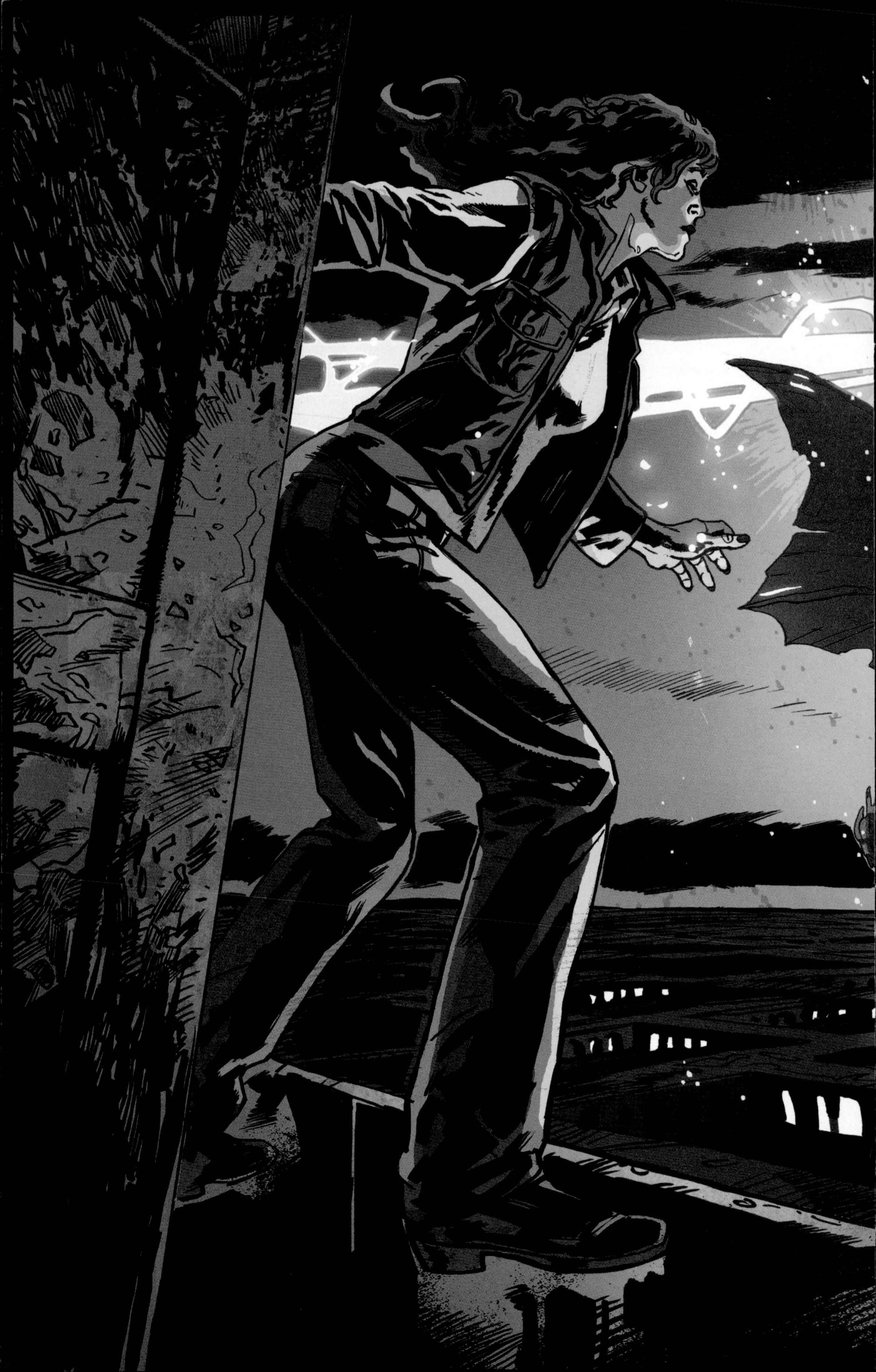

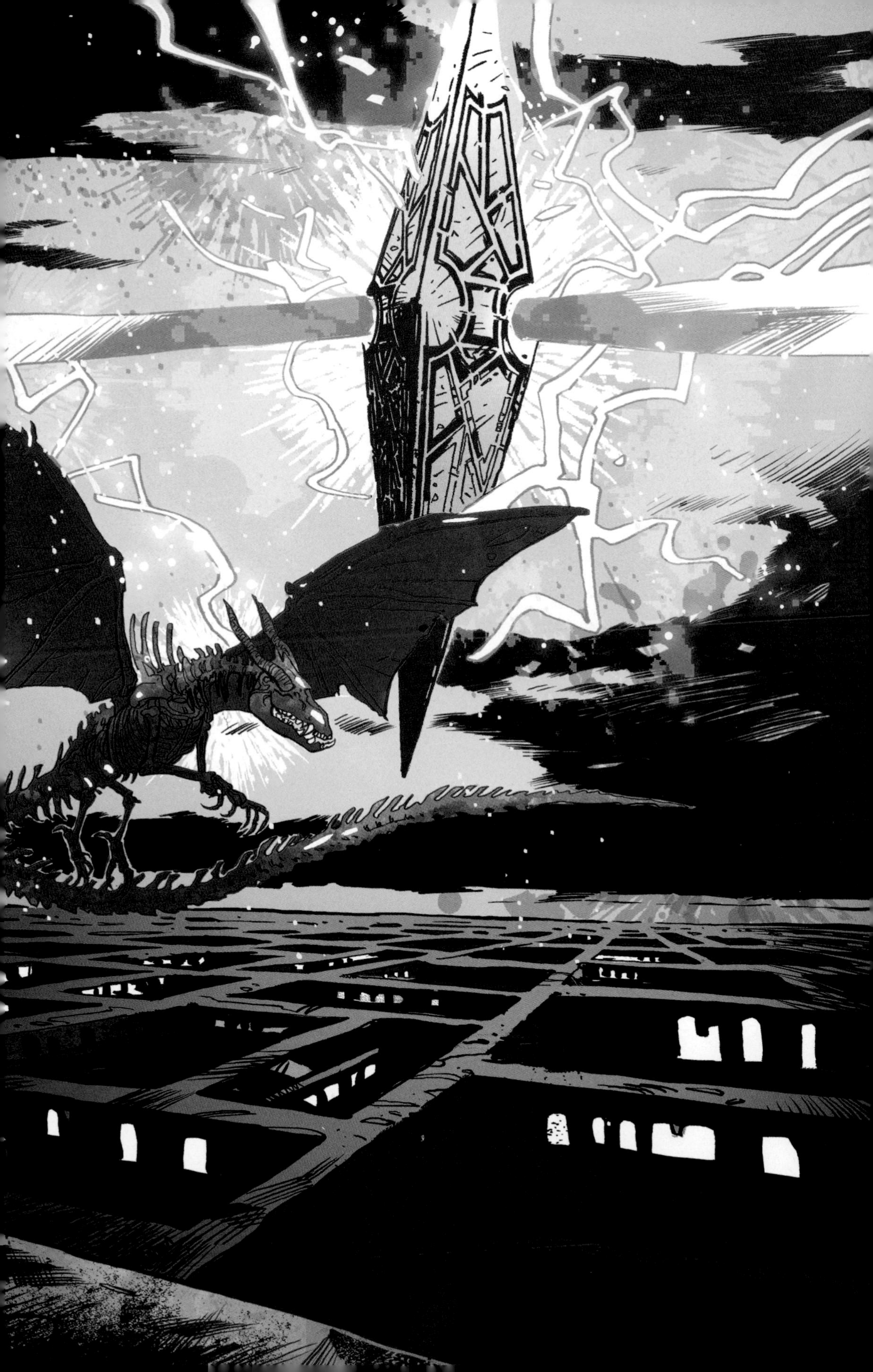

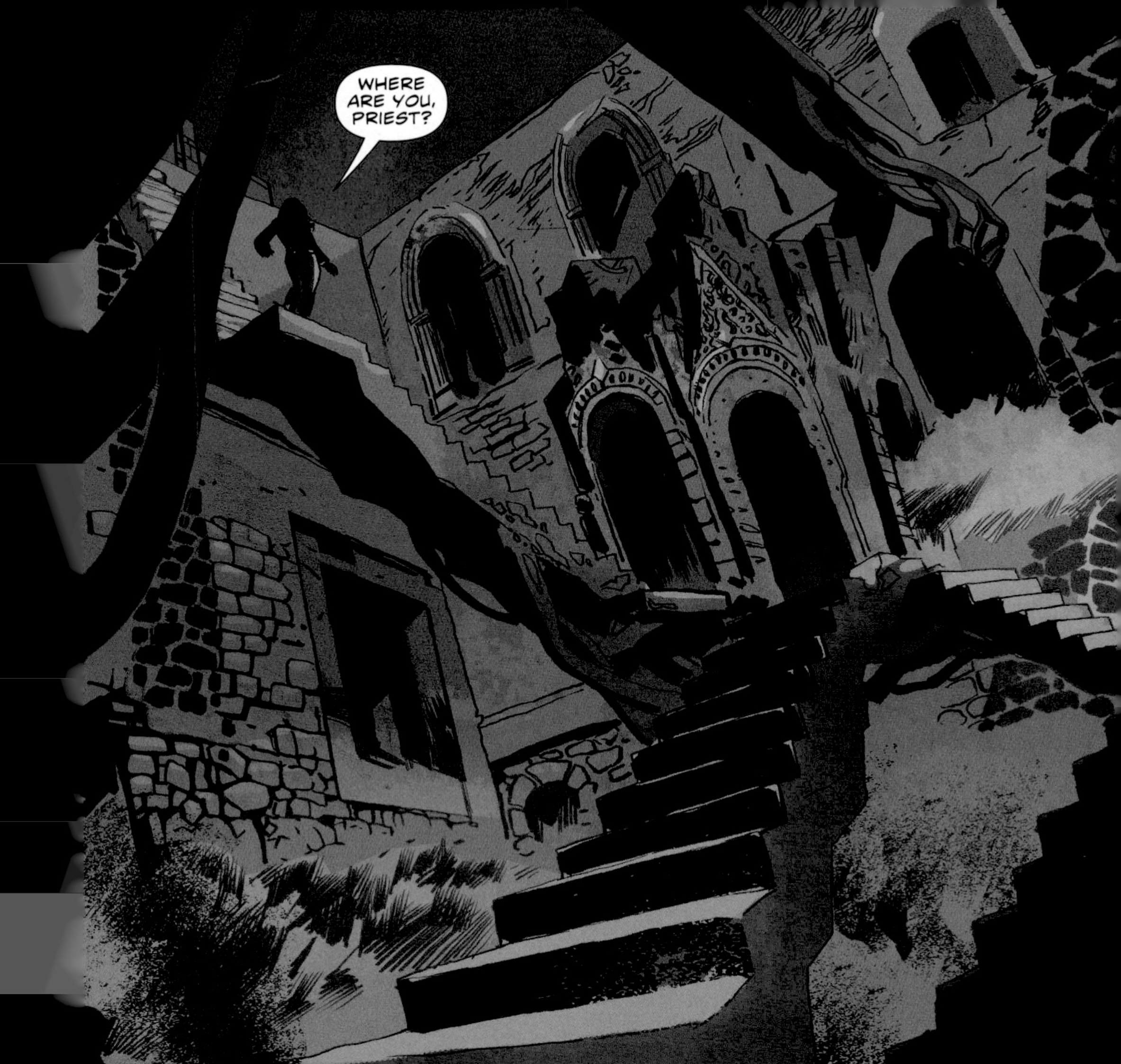
WHERE ARE YOU, PRIEST?

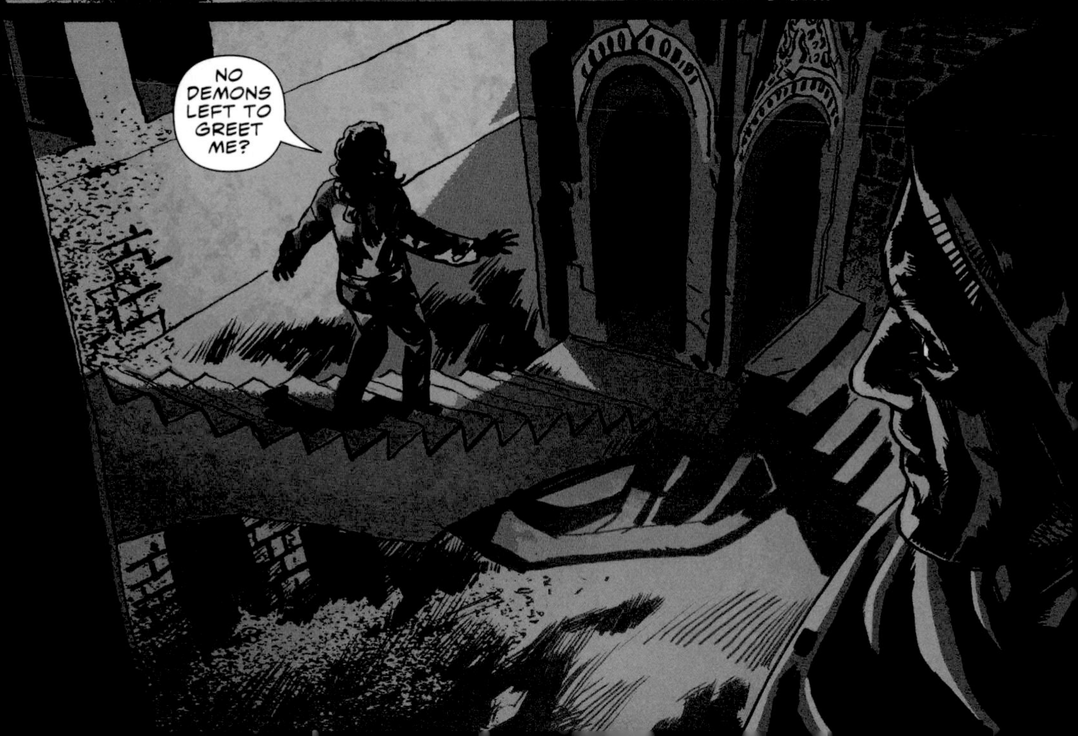
NO DEMONS LEFT TO GREET ME?

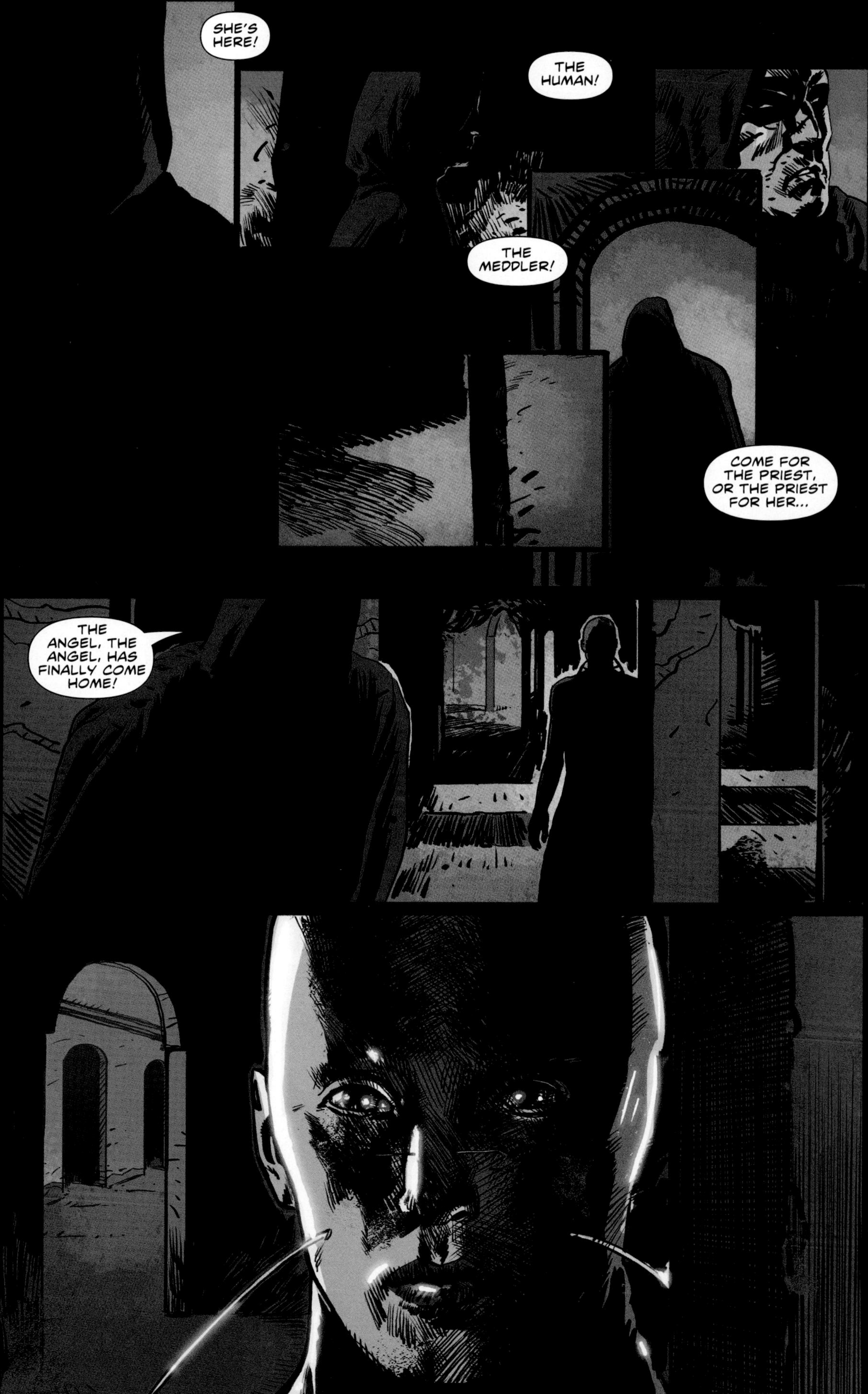
SHE'S HERE!
THE HUMAN!
THE MEDDLER!
COME FOR THE PRIEST, OR THE PRIEST FOR HER...
THE ANGEL, THE ANGEL, HAS FINALLY COME HOME!

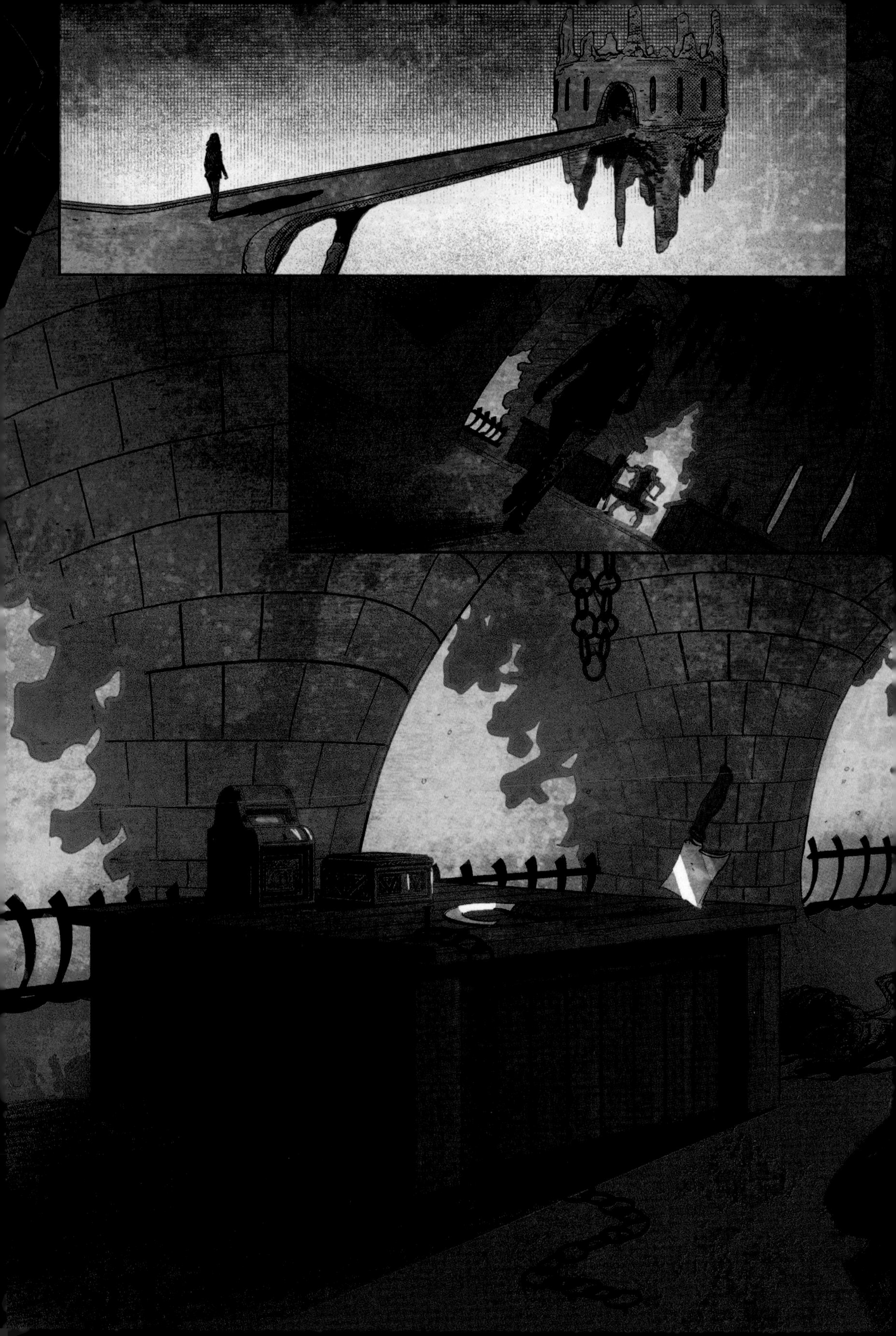

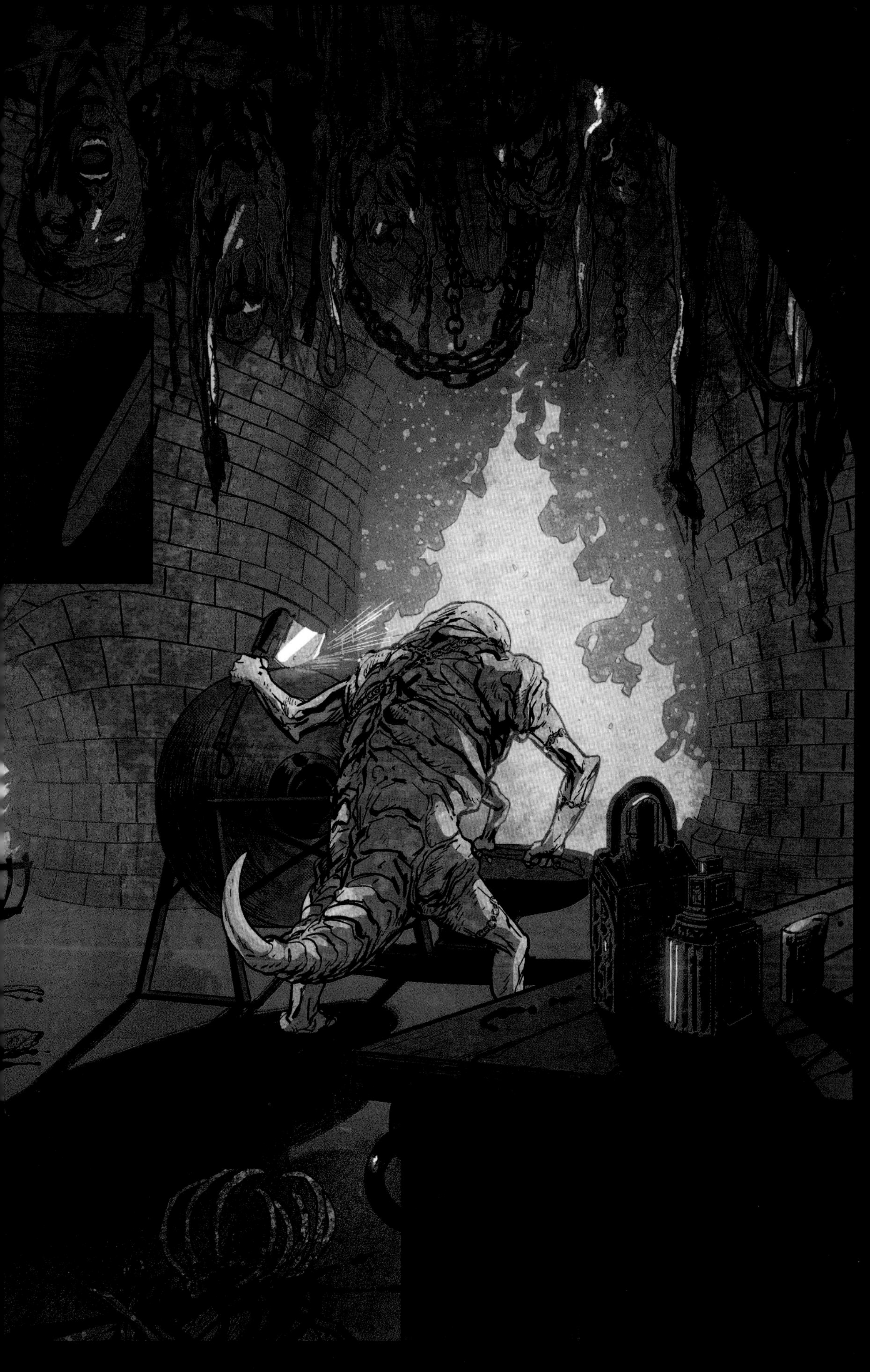

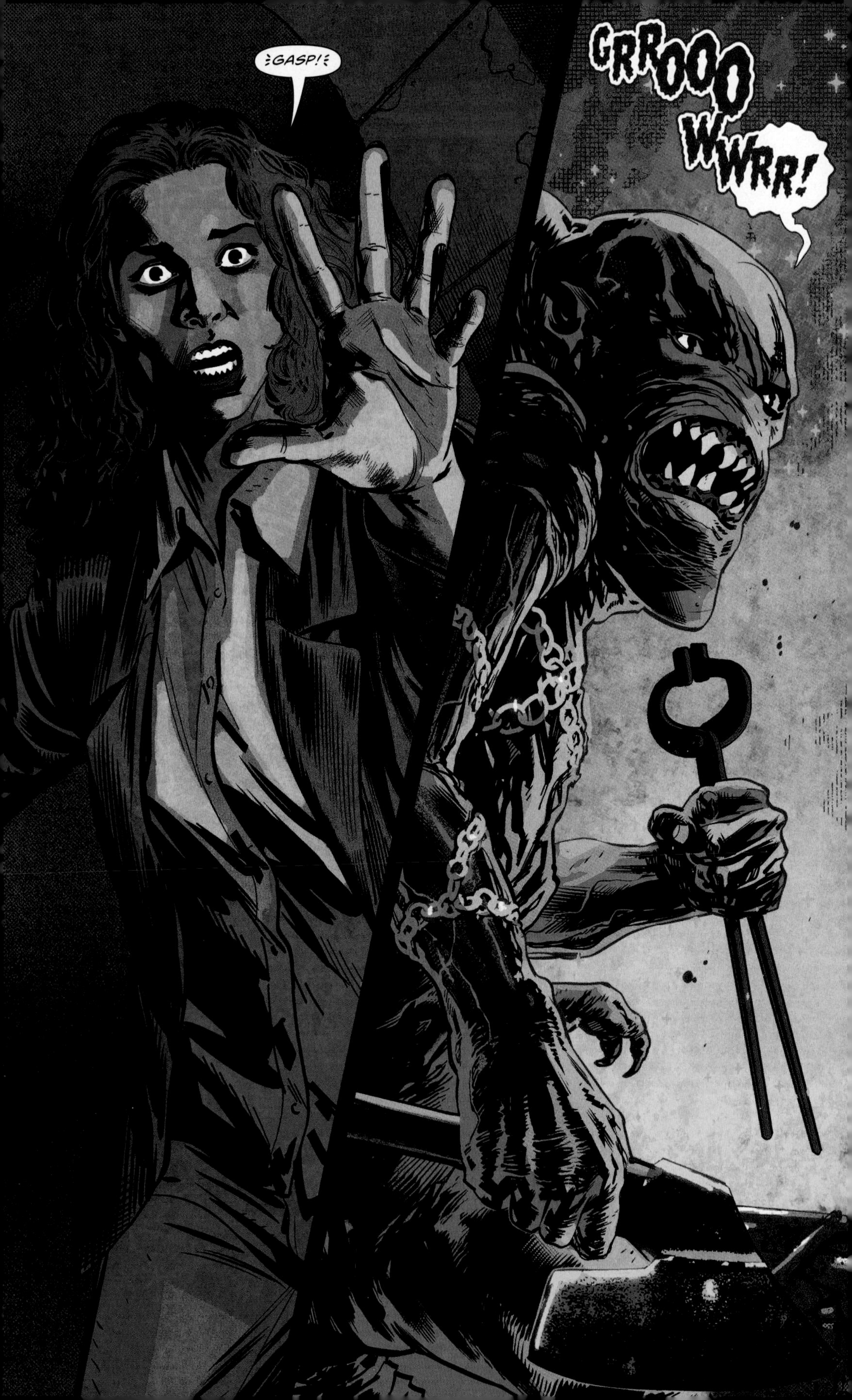
GASP!
GRROOOWWRR!

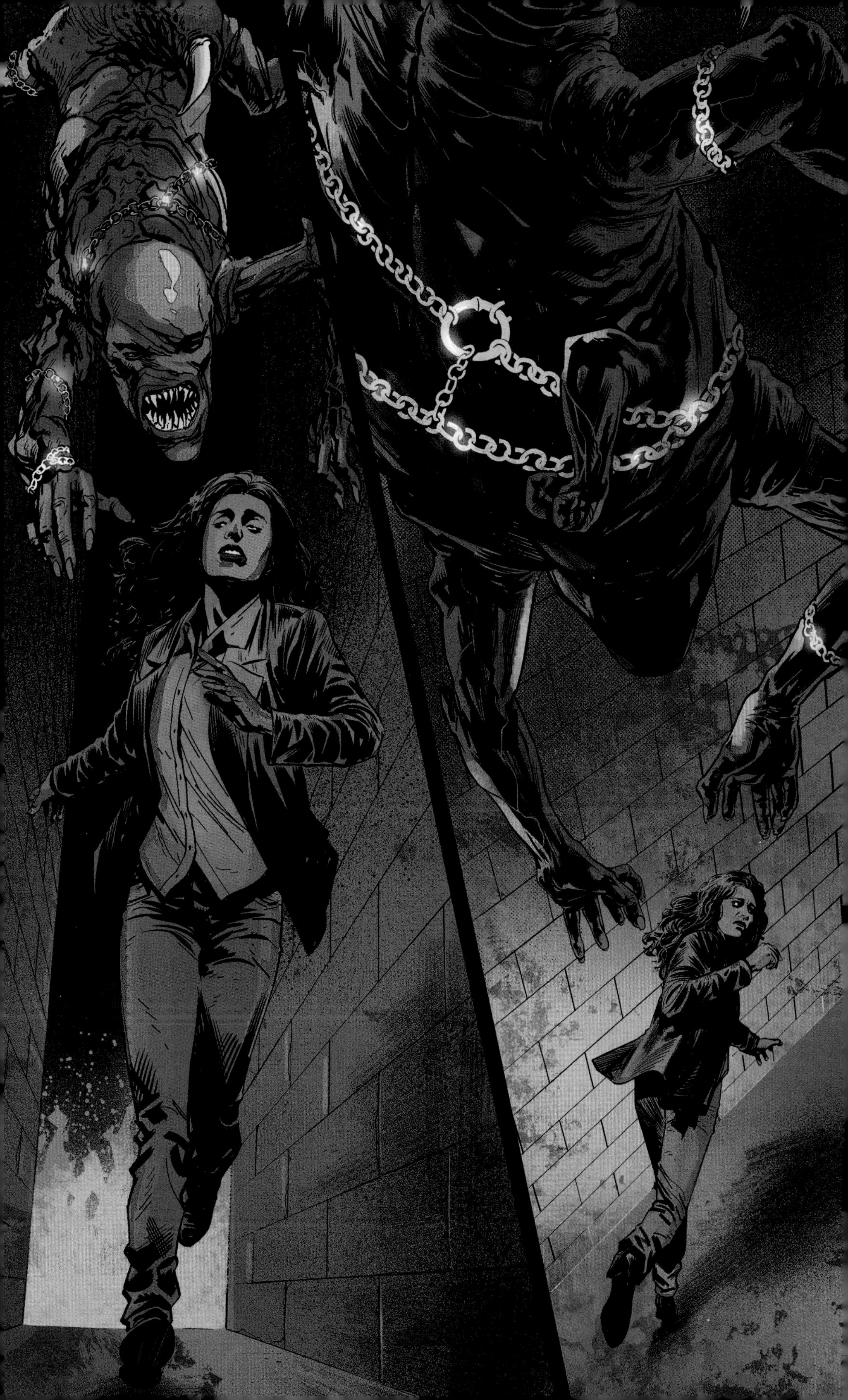

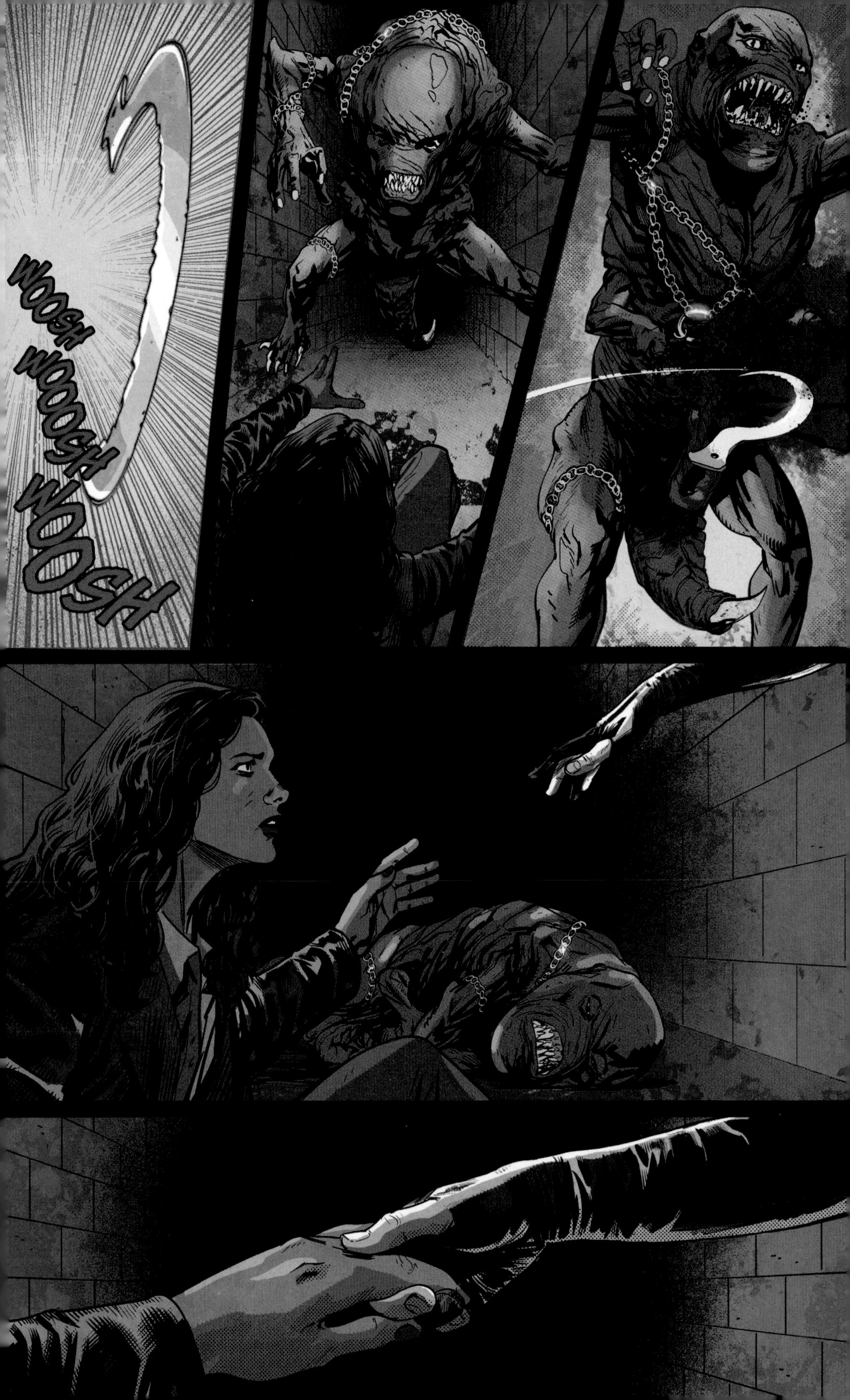
WOOSH
WOOOSH
WOOSH

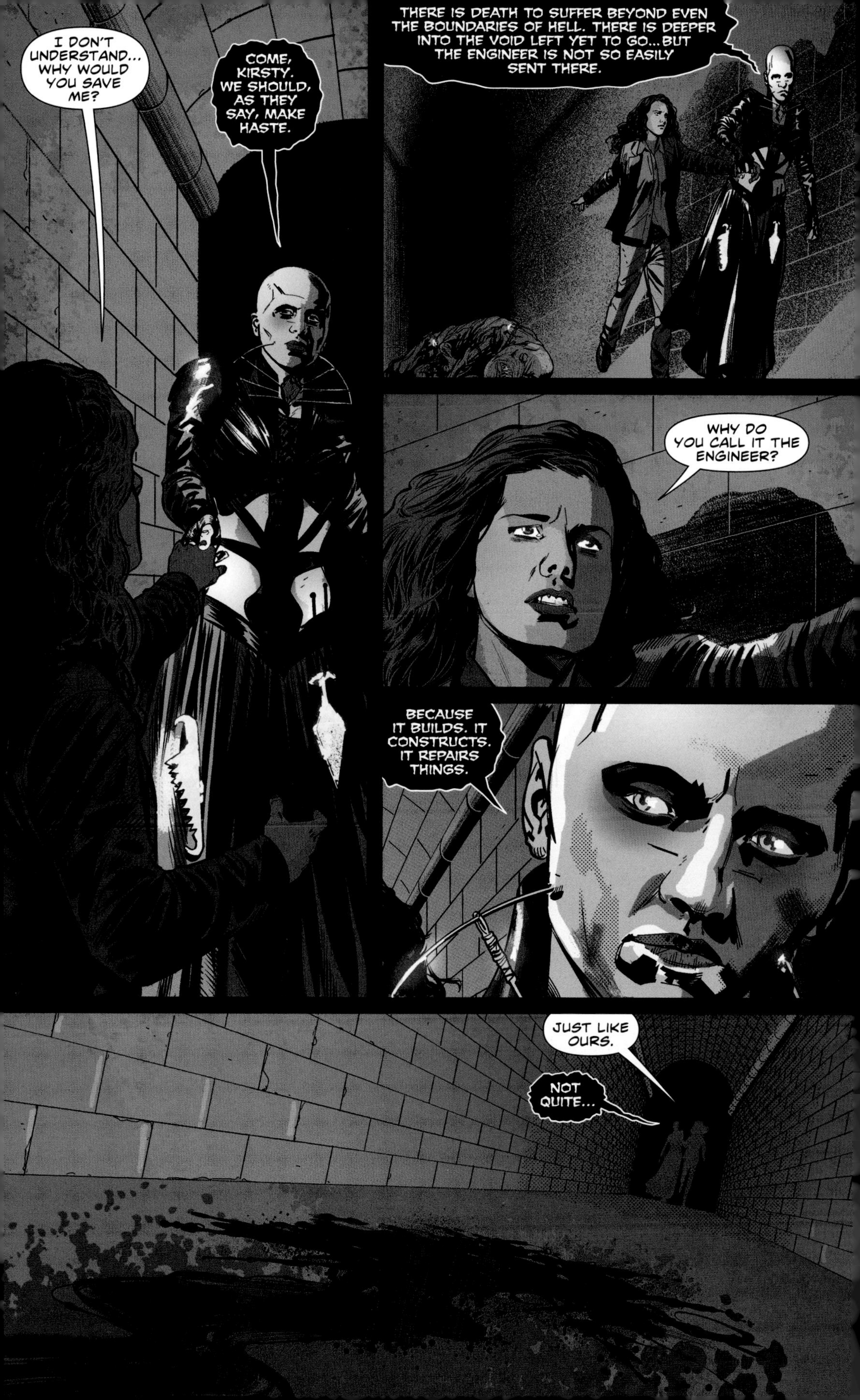
I DON'T UNDERSTAND... WHY WOULD YOU SAVE ME?
COME, KIRSTY. WE SHOULD, AS THEY SAY, MAKE HASTE.
THERE IS DEATH TO SUFFER BEYOND EVEN THE BOUNDARIES OF HELL. THERE IS DEEPER INTO THE VOID LEFT YET TO GO...BUT THE ENGINEER IS NOT SO EASILY SENT THERE.
WHY DO YOU CALL IT THE ENGINEER?
BECAUSE IT BUILDS. IT CONSTRUCTS. IT REPAIRS THINGS.
JUST LIKE OURS.
NOT QUITE...

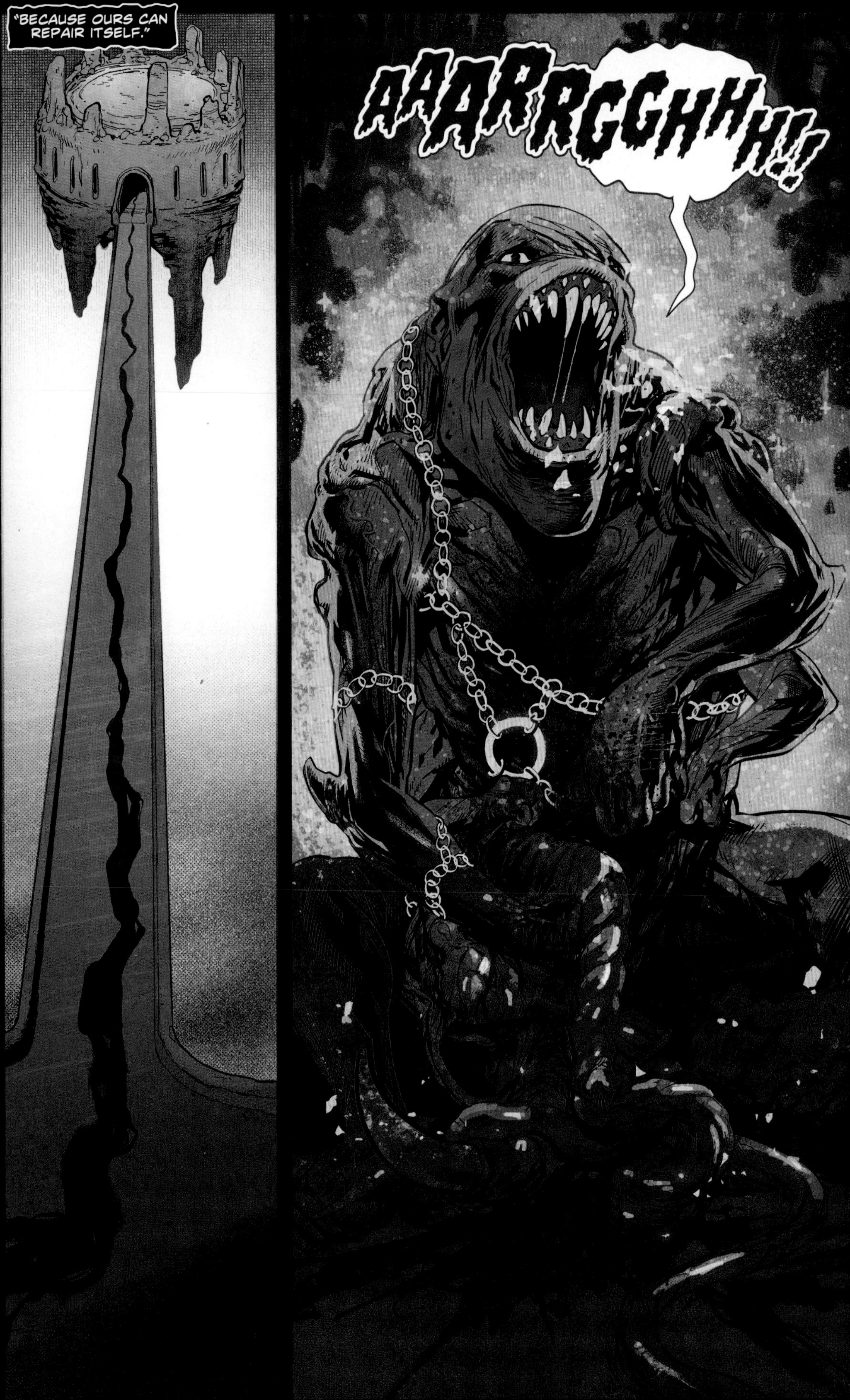
"BECAUSE OURS CAN REPAIR ITSELF."
AAARRGGHHH!!

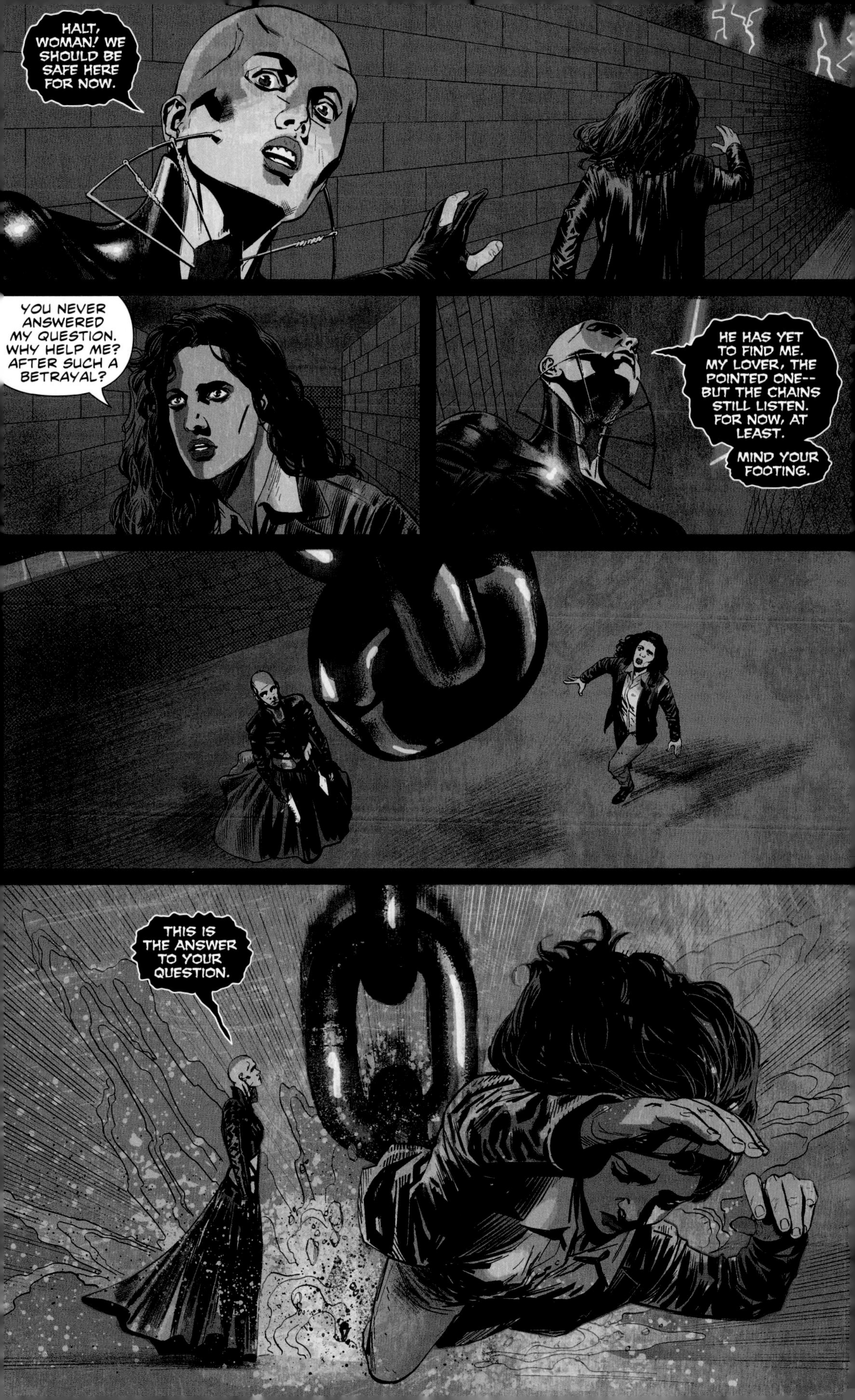
HALT, WOMAN! WE SHOULD BE SAFE HERE FOR NOW.
YOU NEVER ANSWERED MY QUESTION. WHY HELP ME? AFTER SUCH A BETRAYAL?
HE HAS YET TO FIND ME. MY LOVER, THE POINTED ONE-- BUT THE CHAINS STILL LISTEN. FOR NOW, AT LEAST.
MIND YOUR FOOTING.
THIS IS THE ANSWER TO YOUR QUESTION.

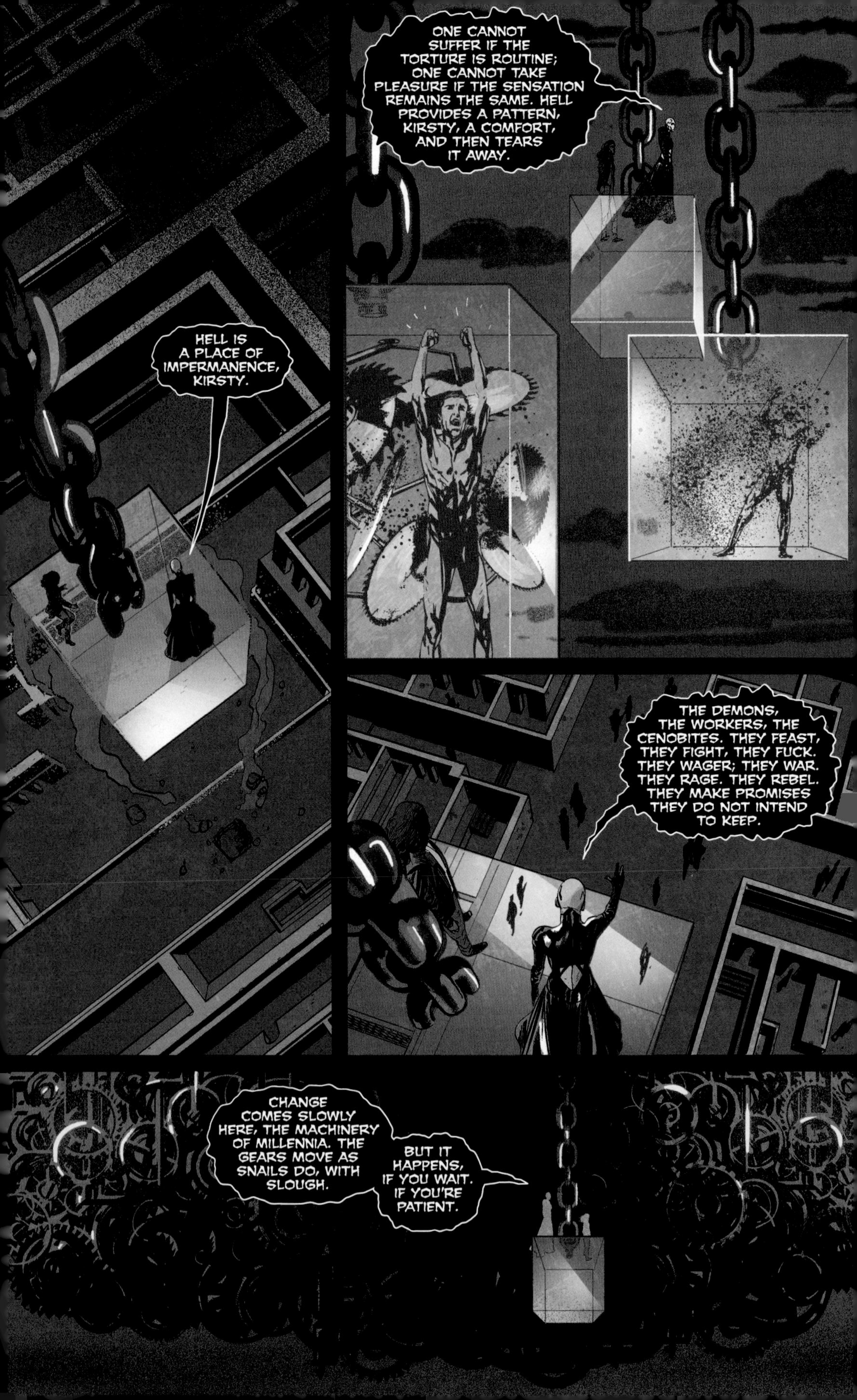
HELL IS A PLACE OF IMPERMANENCE, KIRSTY.
ONE CANNOT SUFFER IF THE TORTURE IS ROUTINE; ONE CANNOT TAKE PLEASURE IF THE SENSATION REMAINS THE SAME. HELL PROVIDES A PATTERN, KIRSTY, A COMFORT, AND THEN TEARS IT AWAY.
THE DEMONS, THE WORKERS, THE CENOBITES. THEY FEAST, THEY FIGHT, THEY FUCK. THEY WAGER; THEY WAR. THEY RAGE. THEY REBEL. THEY MAKE PROMISES THEY DO NOT INTEND TO KEEP.
CHANGE COMES SLOWLY HERE, THE MACHINERY OF MILLENNIA. THE GEARS MOVE AS SNAILS DO, WITH SLOUGH.
BUT IT HAPPENS, IF YOU WAIT. IF YOU'RE PATIENT.

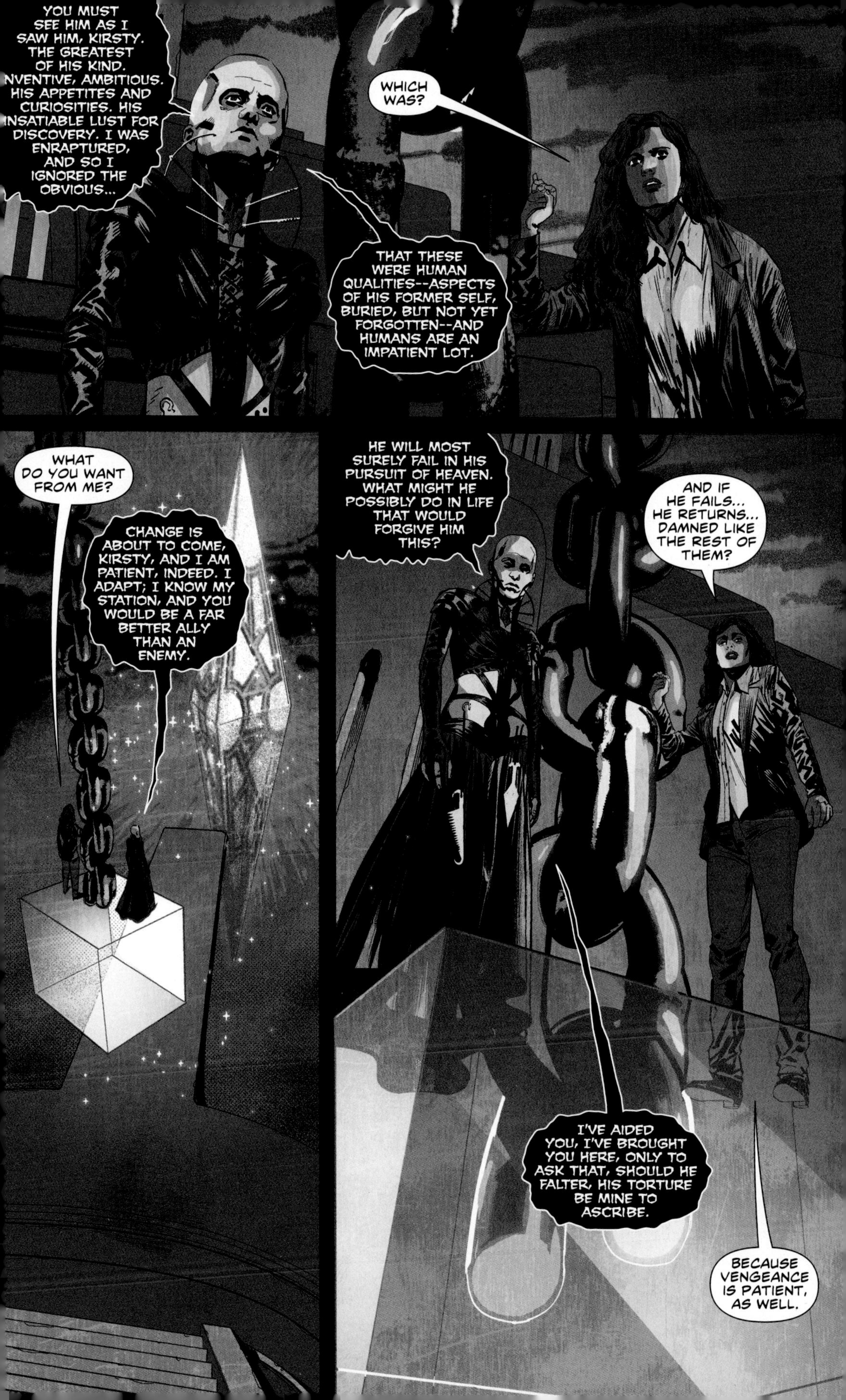
YOU MUST SEE HIM AS I SAW HIM, KIRSTY. THE GREATEST OF HIS KIND. NVENTIVE, AMBITIOUS. HIS APPETITES AND CURIOSITIES. HIS INSATIABLE LUST FOR DISCOVERY. I WAS ENRAPTURED, AND SO I IGNORED THE OBVIOUS...
WHICH WAS?
THAT THESE WERE HUMAN QUALITIES--ASPECTS OF HIS FORMER SELF, BURIED, BUT NOT YET FORGOTTEN--AND HUMANS ARE AN IMPATIENT LOT.
WHAT DO YOU WANT FROM ME?
CHANGE IS ABOUT TO COME, KIRSTY, AND I AM PATIENT, INDEED. I ADAPT; I KNOW MY STATION, AND YOU WOULD BE A FAR BETTER ALLY THAN AN ENEMY.
HE WILL MOST SURELY FAIL IN HIS PURSUIT OF HEAVEN. WHAT MIGHT HE POSSIBLY DO IN LIFE THAT WOULD FORGIVE HIM THIS?
AND IF HE FAILS... HE RETURNS... DAMNED LIKE THE REST OF THEM?
I'VE AIDED YOU, I'VE BROUGHT YOU HERE, ONLY TO ASK THAT, SHOULD HE FALTER, HIS TORTURE BE MINE TO ASCRIBE.
BECAUSE VENGEANCE IS PATIENT, AS WELL.

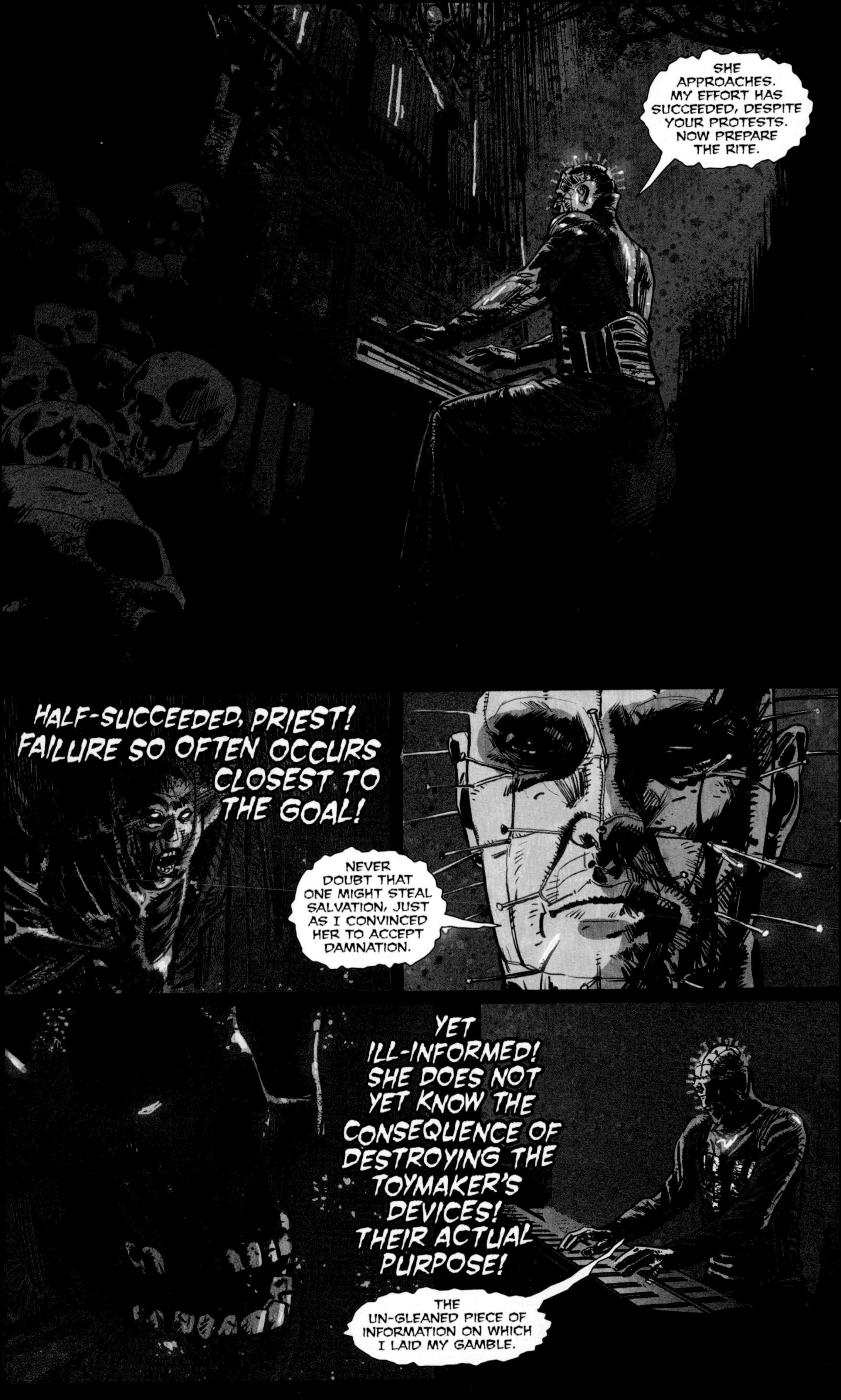
SHE APPROACHES. MY EFFORT HAS SUCCEEDED, DESPITE YOUR PROTESTS. NOW PREPARE THE RITE.
HALF-SUCCEEDED, PRIEST! FAILURE SO OFTEN OCCURS CLOSEST TO THE GOAL!
NEVER DOUBT THAT ONE MIGHT STEAL SALVATION, JUST AS I CONVINCED HER TO ACCEPT DAMNATION.
YET ILL-INFORMED! SHE DOES NOT YET KNOW THE CONSEQUENCE OF DESTROYING THE TOYMAKER'S DEVICES! THEIR ACTUAL PURPOSE!
THE UN-GLEANED PIECE OF INFORMATION ON WHICH I LAID MY GAMBLE.

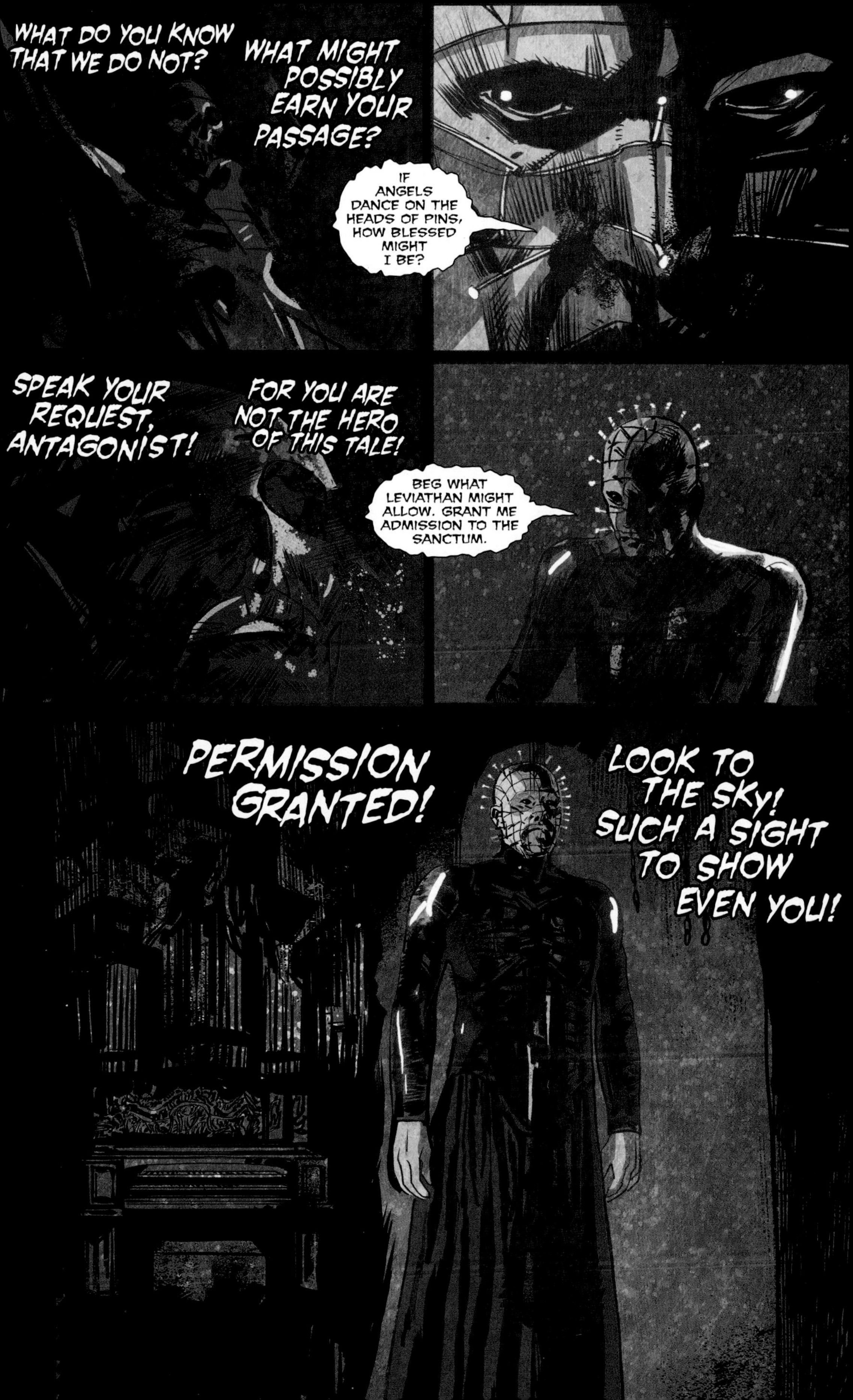
WHAT DO YOU KNOW THAT WE DO NOT?
WHAT MIGHT POSSIBLY EARN YOUR PASSAGE?
IF ANGELS DANCE ON THE HEADS OF PINS, HOW BLESSED MIGHT I BE?
SPEAK YOUR REQUEST, ANTAGONIST!
FOR YOU ARE NOT THE HERO OF THIS TALE!
BEG WHAT LEVIATHAN MIGHT ALLOW. GRANT ME ADMISSION TO THE SANCTUM.
PERMISSION GRANTED!
LOOK TO THE SKY! SUCH A SIGHT TO SHOW EVEN YOU!

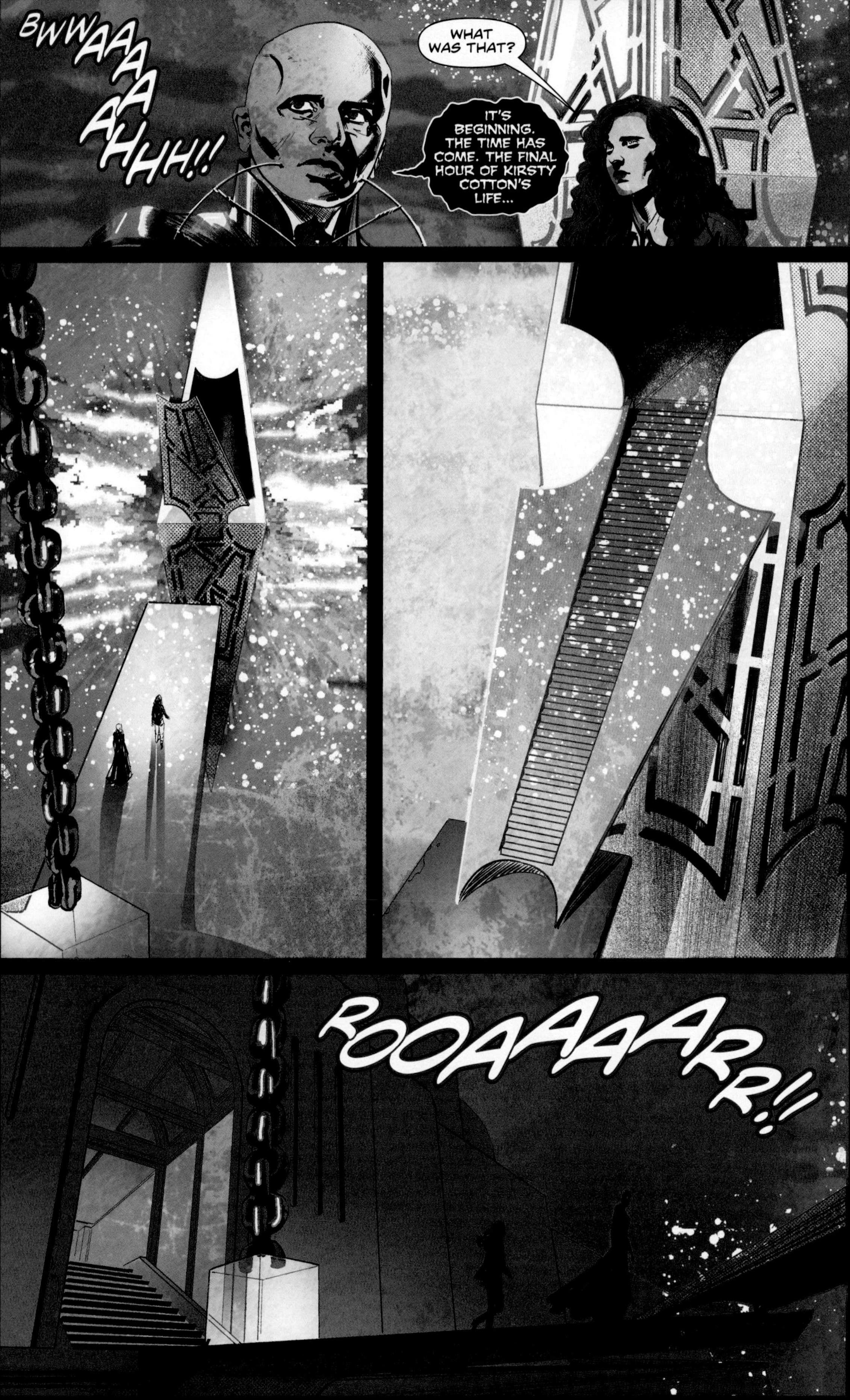
BWWAAAAAHHH!!
WHAT WAS THAT?
IT'S BEGINNING. THE TIME HAS COME. THE FINAL HOUR OF KIRSTY COTTON'S LIFE...
ROOAAAAR!!

KIRSTY, BEWARE!

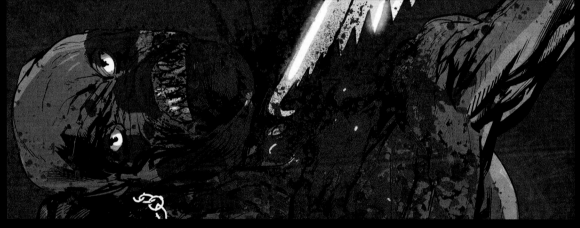

I'M SORRY THIS HAPPENED TO YOU... YOU DESERVED BETTER DESPITE ALL YOU'VE DONE...SO I AGREE. HE'LL BE YOURS. HIS DAMNATION, YOUR PLAY-THING.

BECAUSE I MAKE THE RULES NOW.

GO TO YOUR FATE, KIRSTY COTTON. IT'S YOURS. IT ALWAYS WAS.

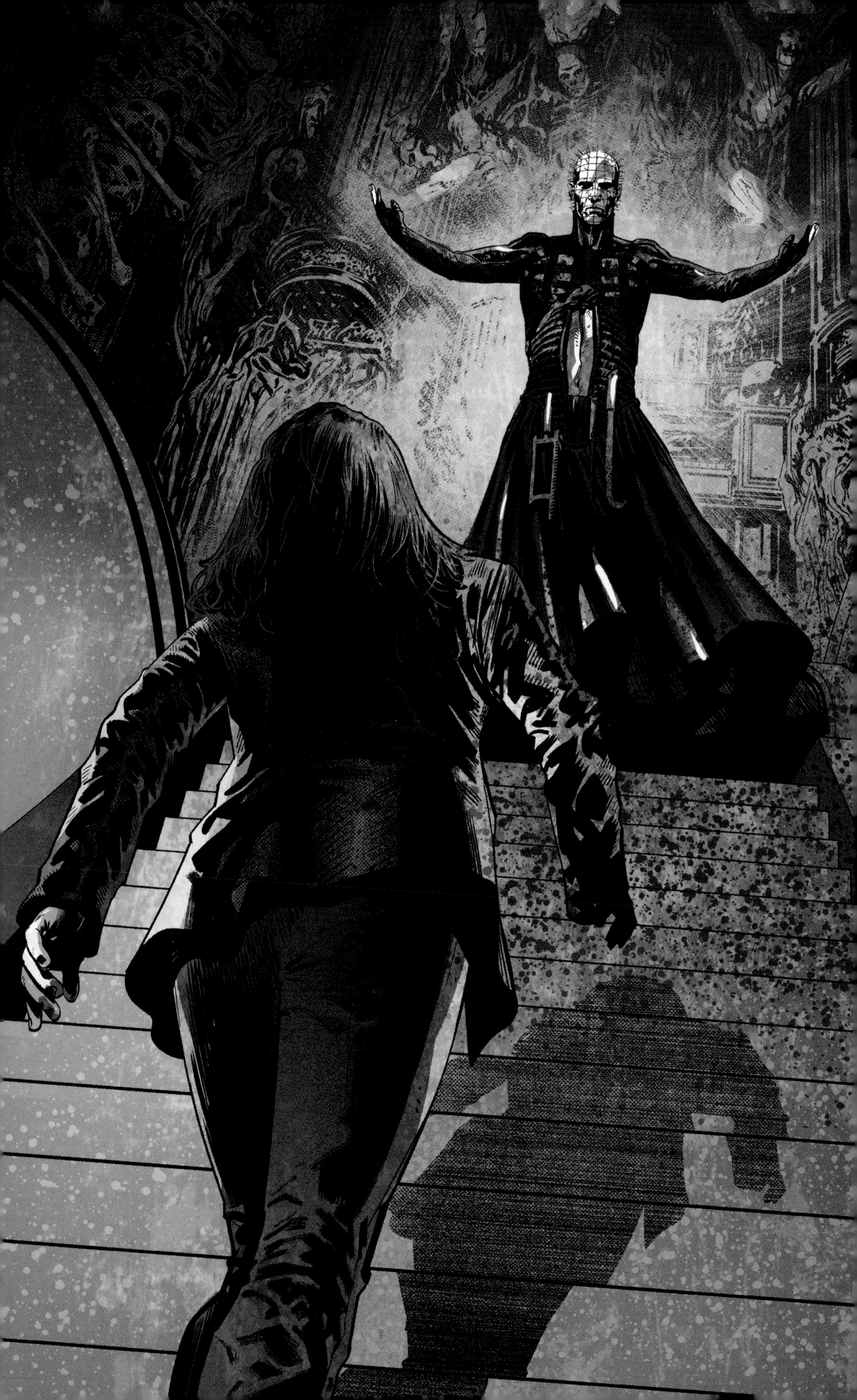

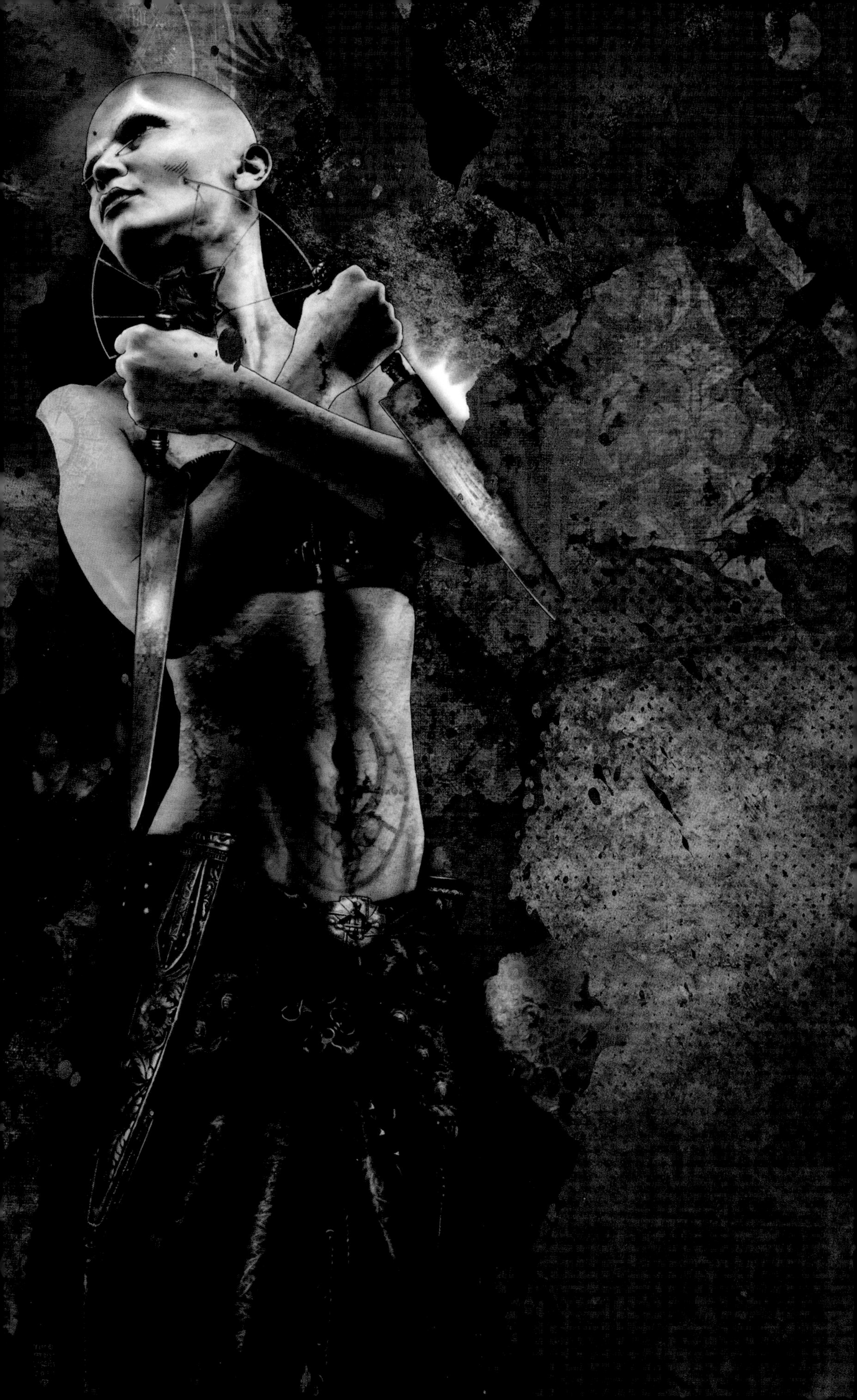

REQUIEM

CHAPTER EIGHT

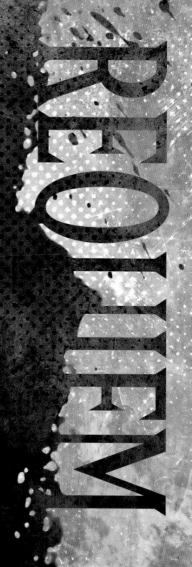

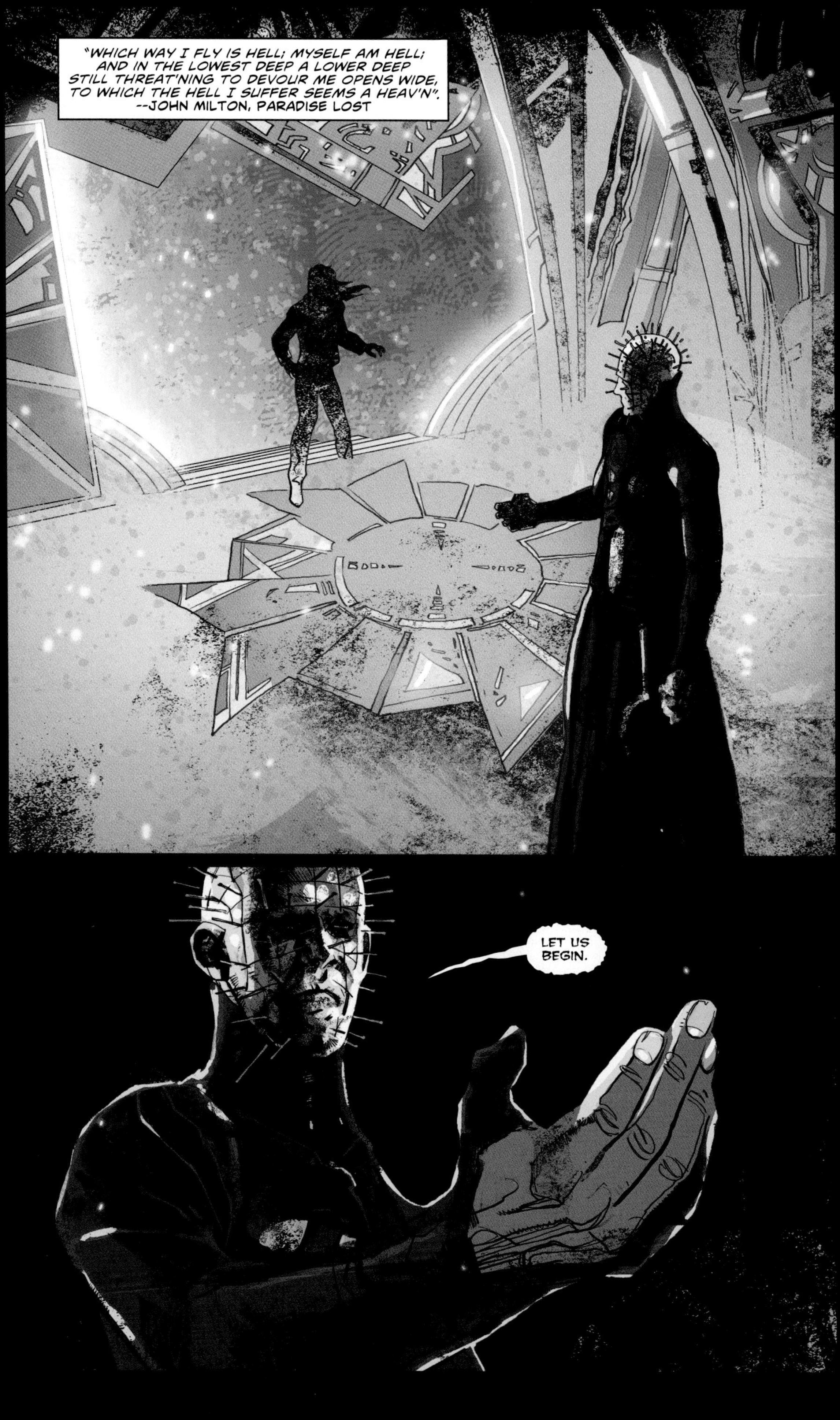
"WHICH WAY I FLY IS HELL; MYSELF AM HELL;
AND IN THE LOWEST DEEP A LOWER DEEP
STILL THREAT'NING TO DEVOUR ME OPENS WIDE,
TO WHICH THE HELL I SUFFER SEEMS A HEAV'N".
--JOHN MILTON, PARADISE LOST
LET US BEGIN.

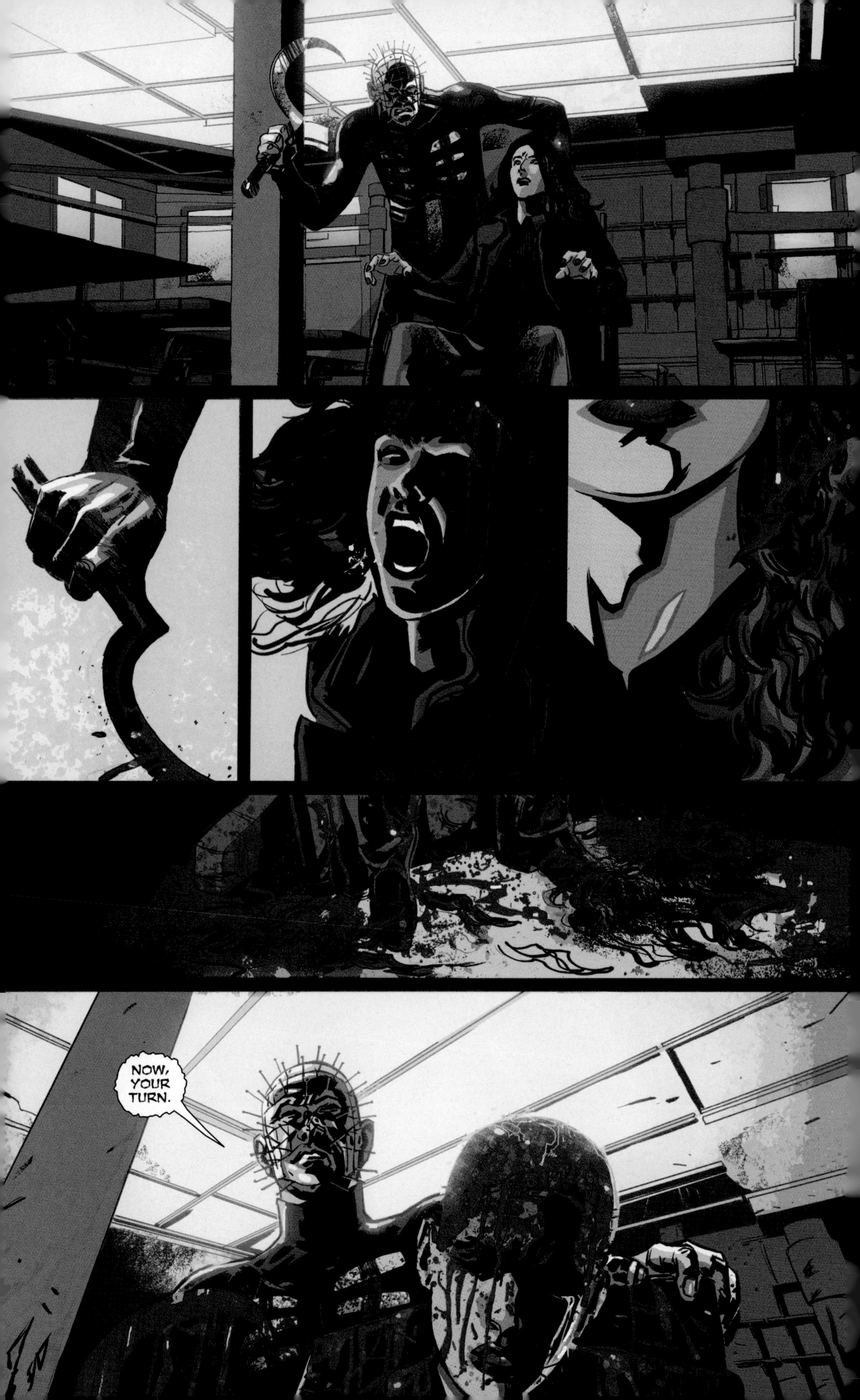
NOW, YOUR TURN.

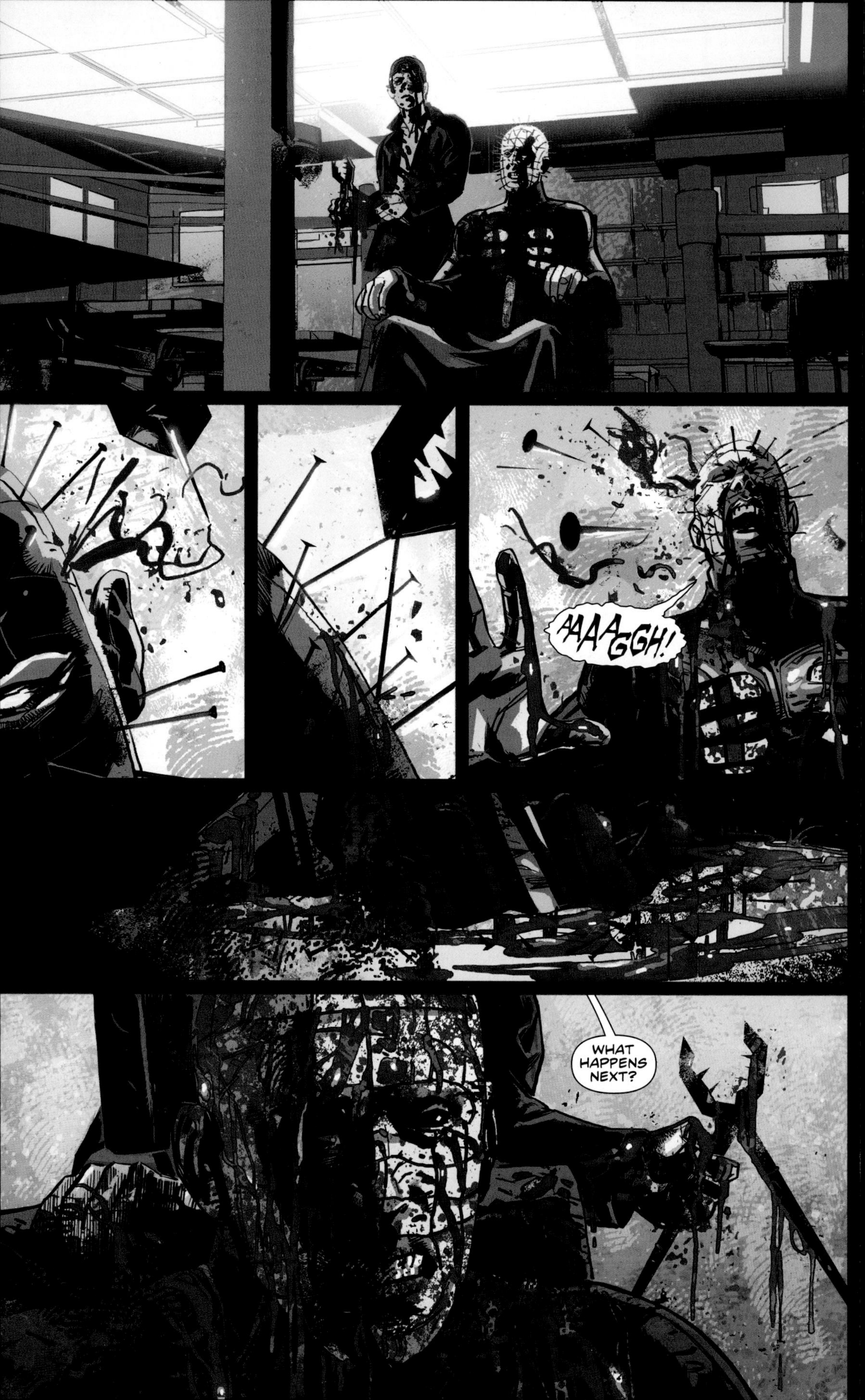
AAAAGGH!
WHAT HAPPENS NEXT?

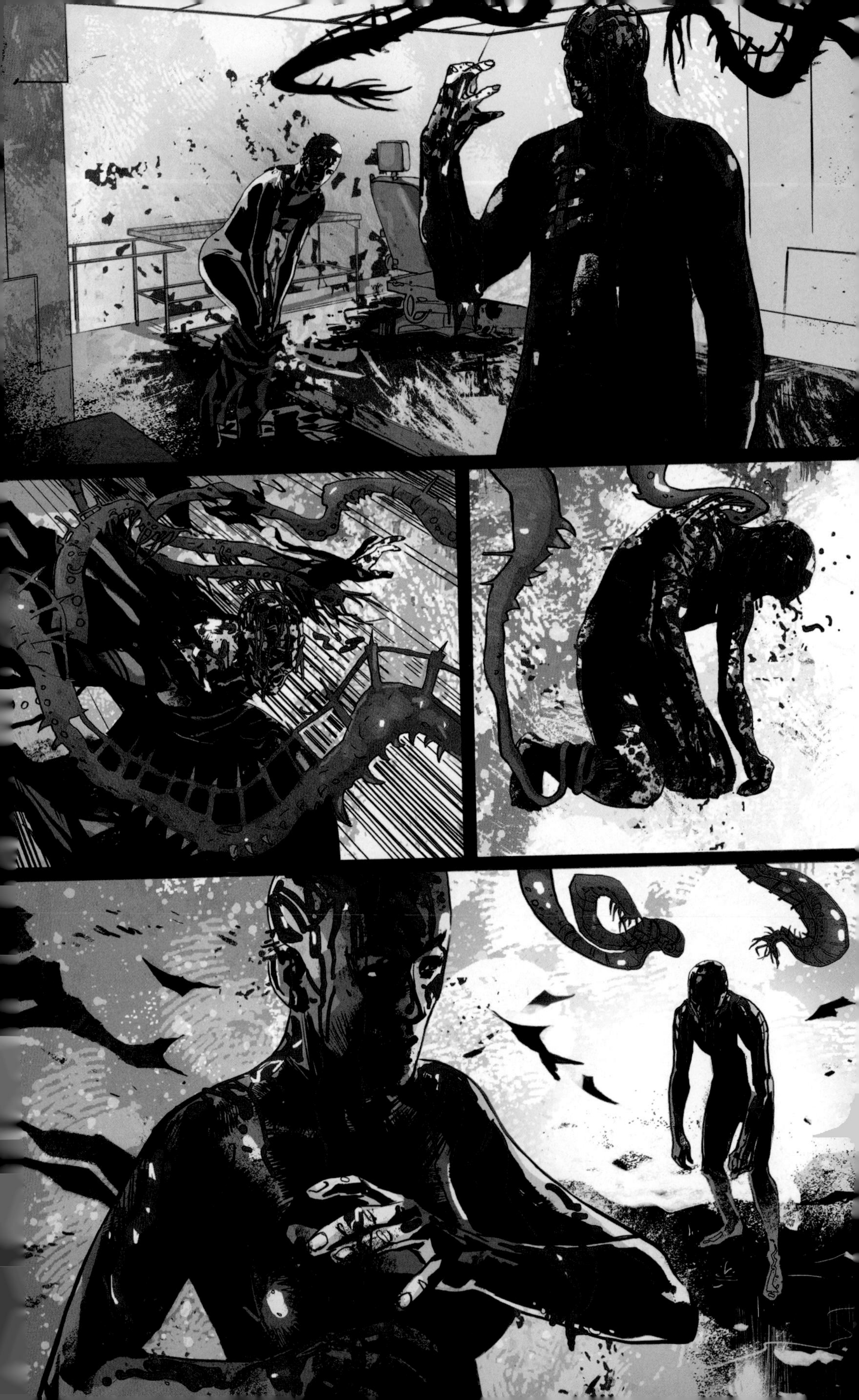

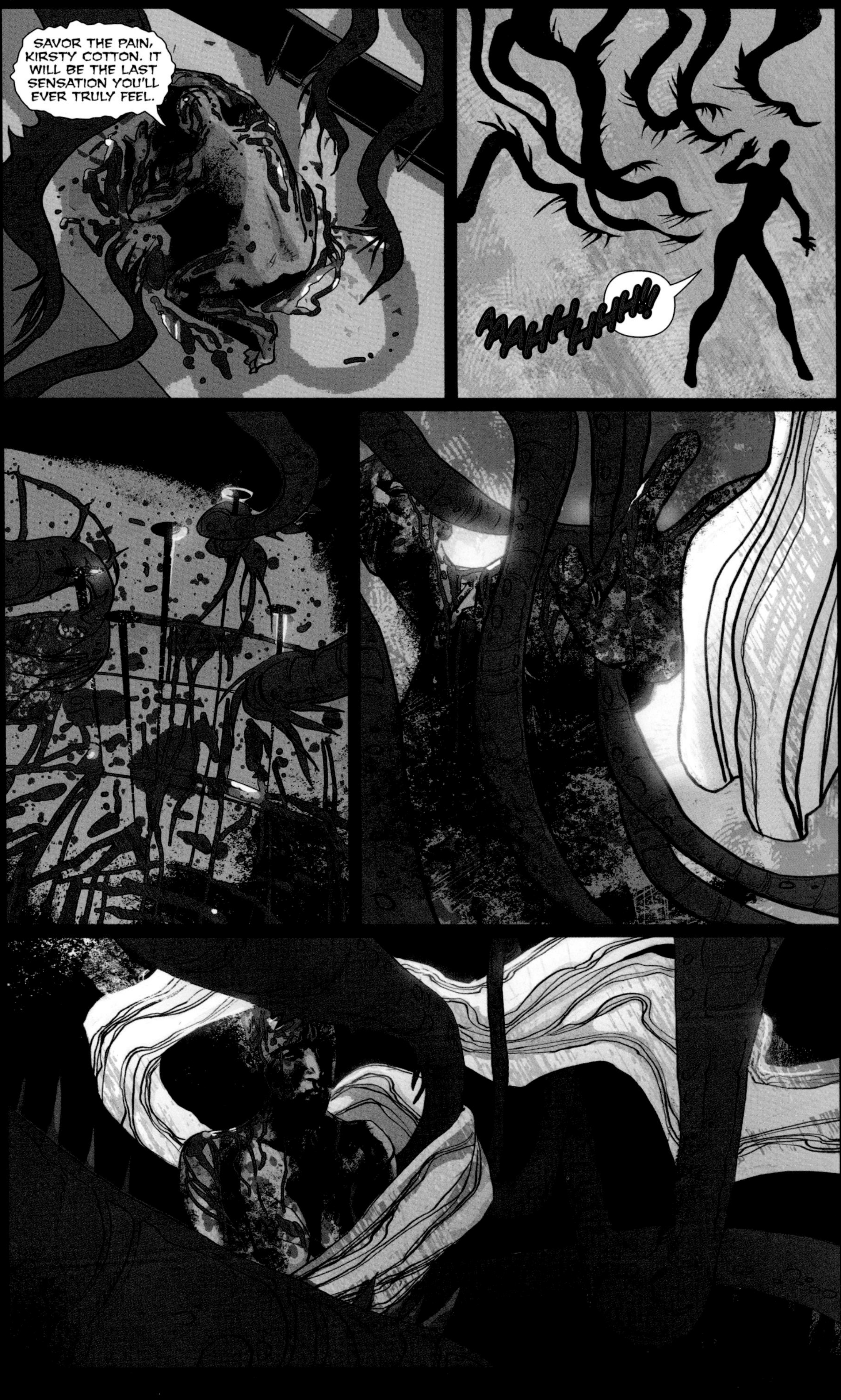
SAVOR THE PAIN, KIRSTY COTTON. IT WILL BE THE LAST SENSATION YOU'LL EVER TRULY FEEL.
AAAHHHHHH!!

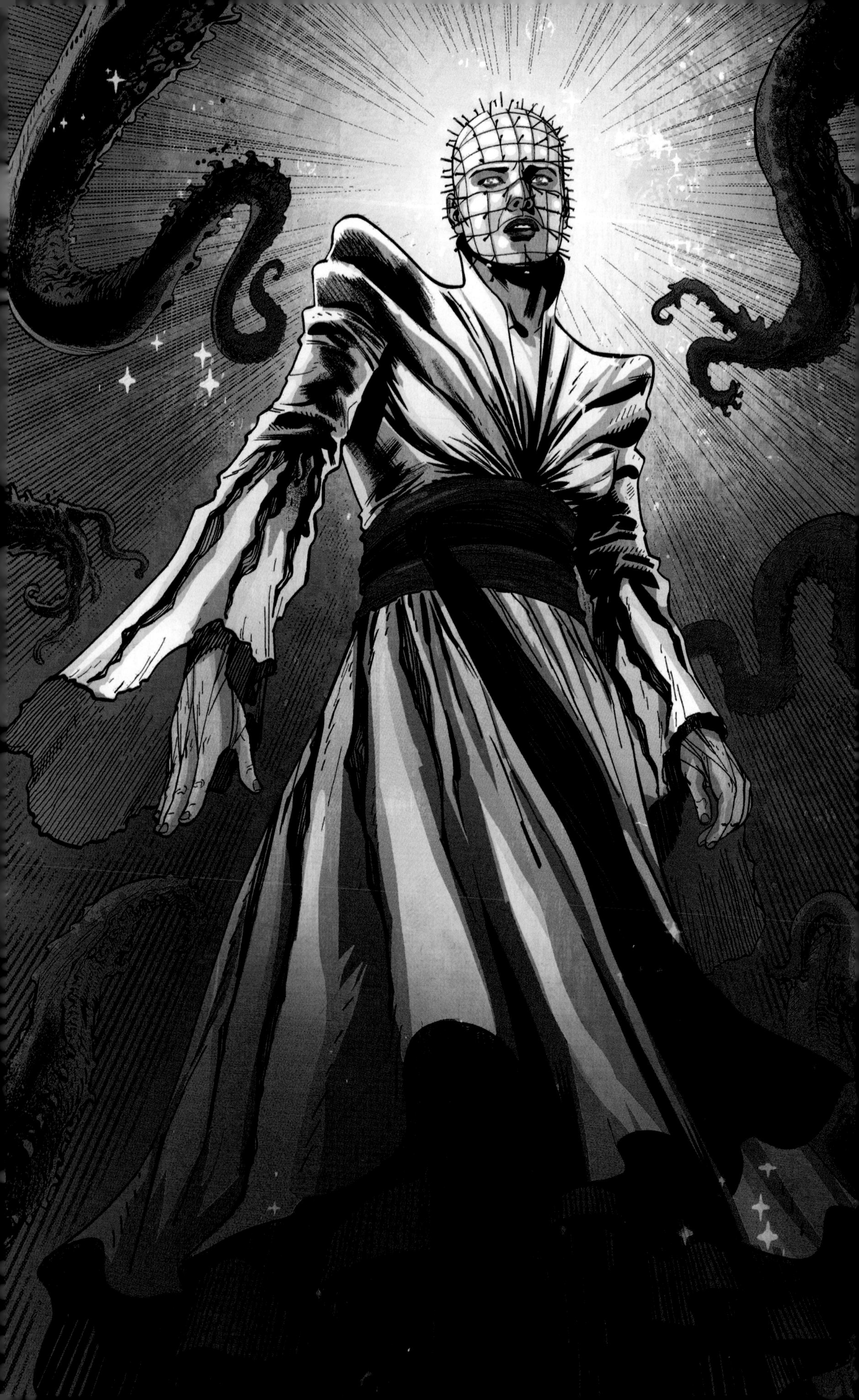

KIRSTY, THE PAINTER. THE CREATURE. THE MOTHER OF LIES.

IN THE BEGINNING, GOD CREATED... I THINK I'LL DO THE SAME.

WHAT IS THIS TRICK?

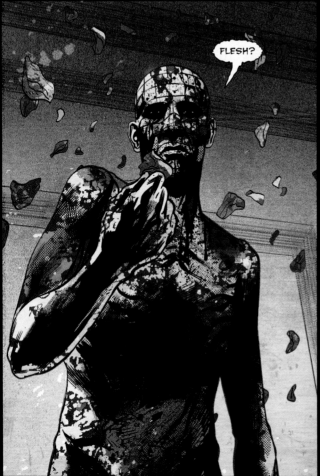

FLESH?

AKKKKK...

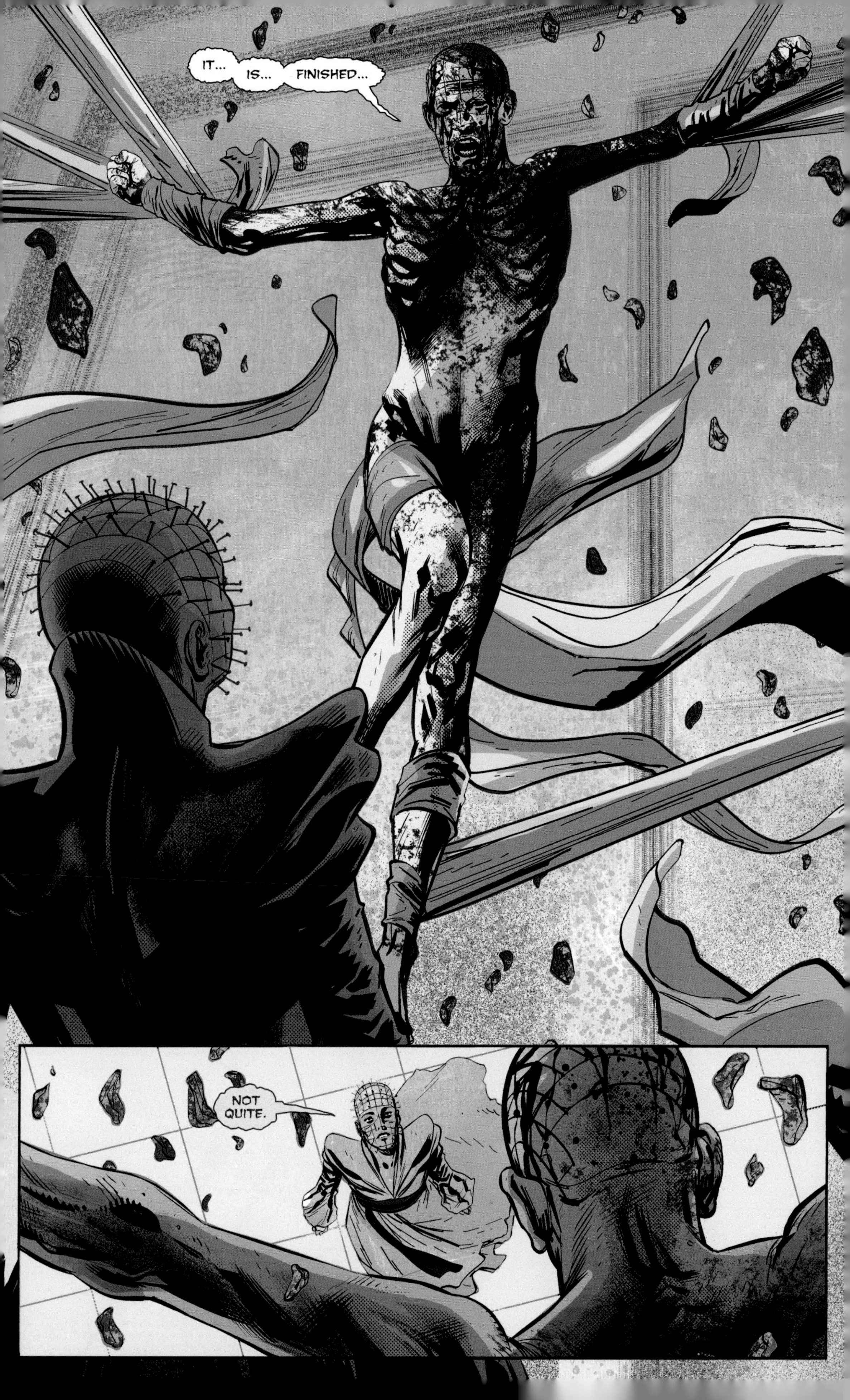
IT... IS... FINISHED...
NOT QUITE.

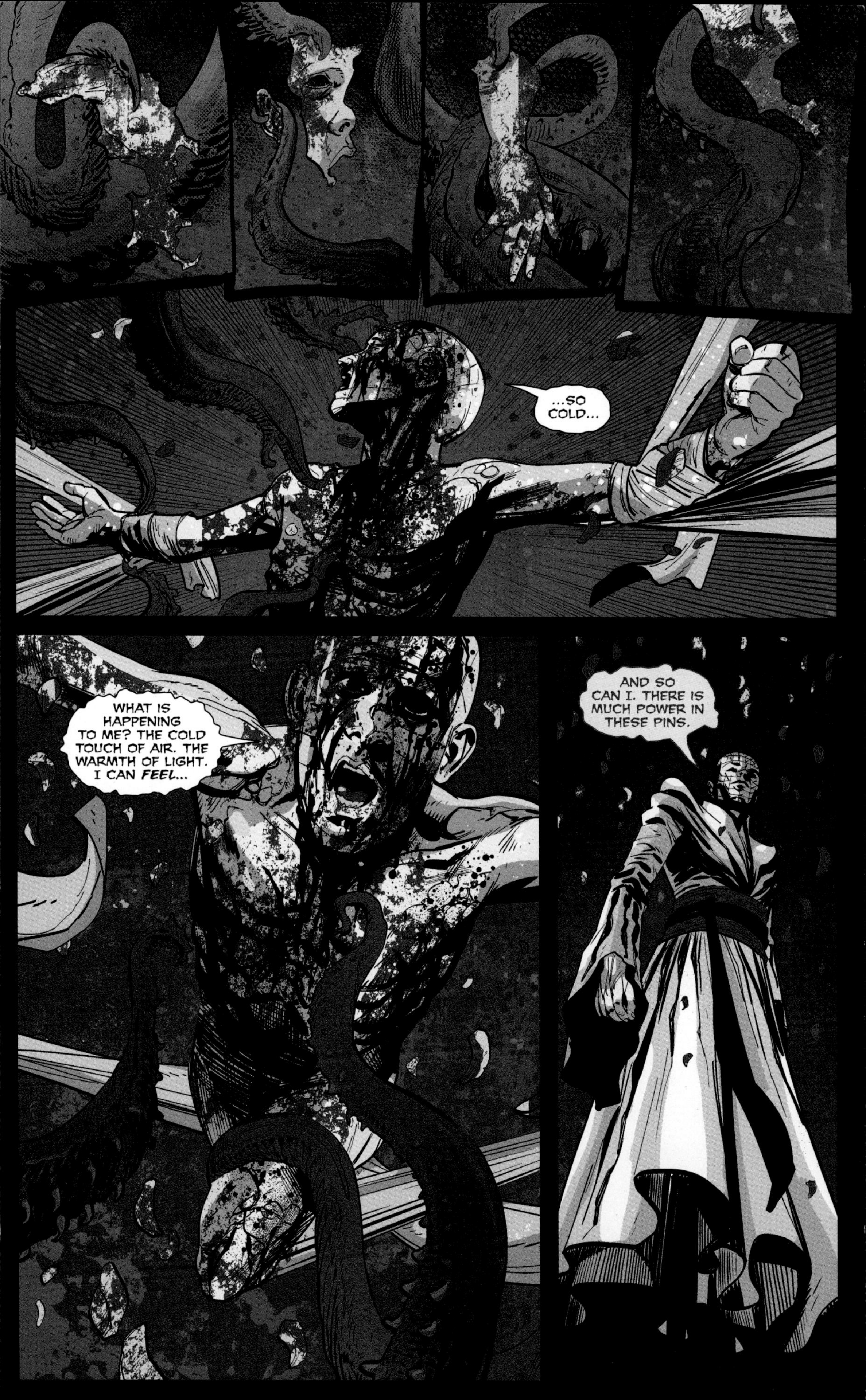
...SO COLD...
WHAT IS HAPPENING TO ME? THE COLD TOUCH OF AIR. THE WARMTH OF LIGHT. I CAN *FEEL*...
AND SO CAN I. THERE IS MUCH POWER IN THESE PINS.

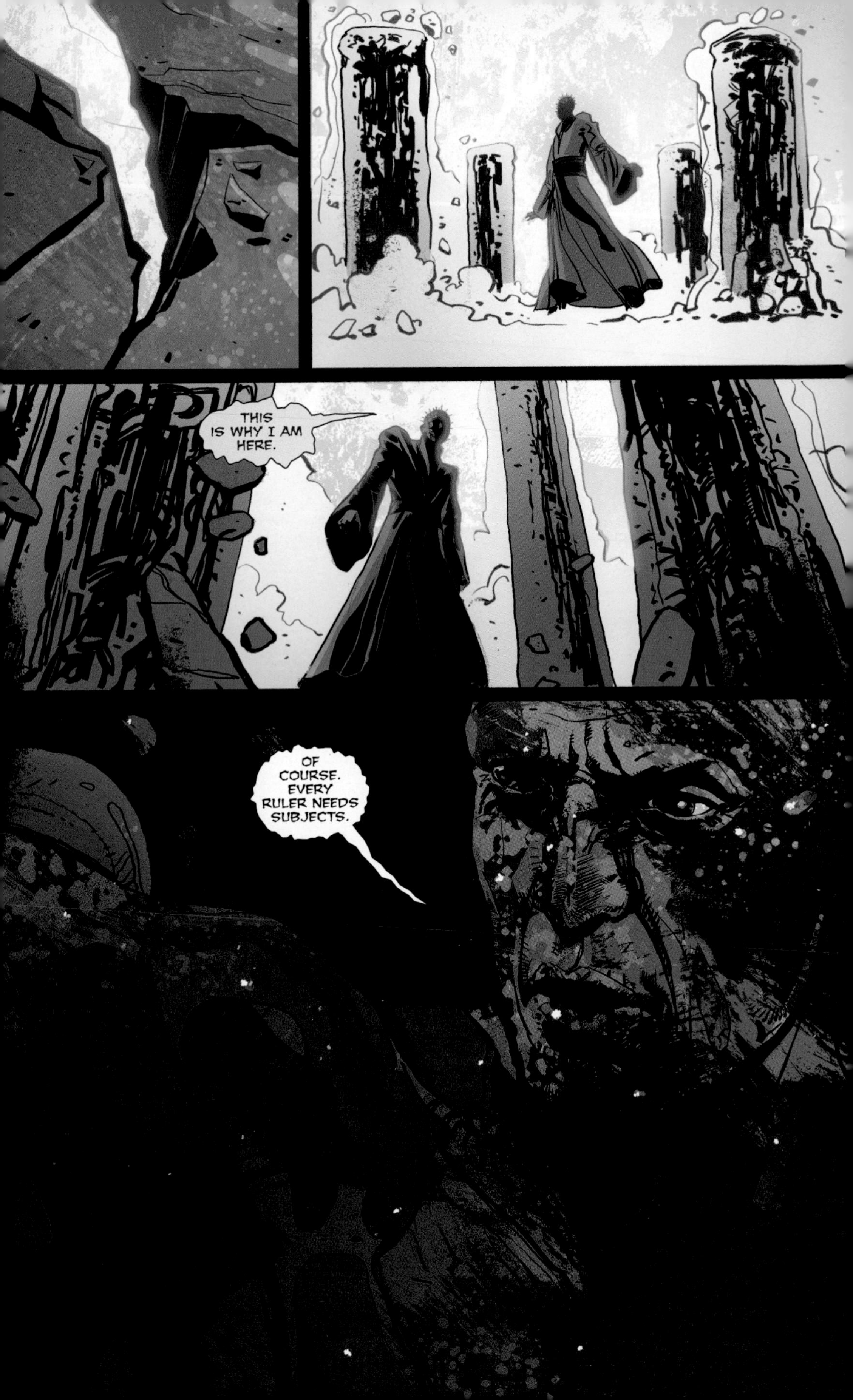
THIS IS WHY I AM HERE.
OF COURSE. EVERY RULER NEEDS SUBJECTS.

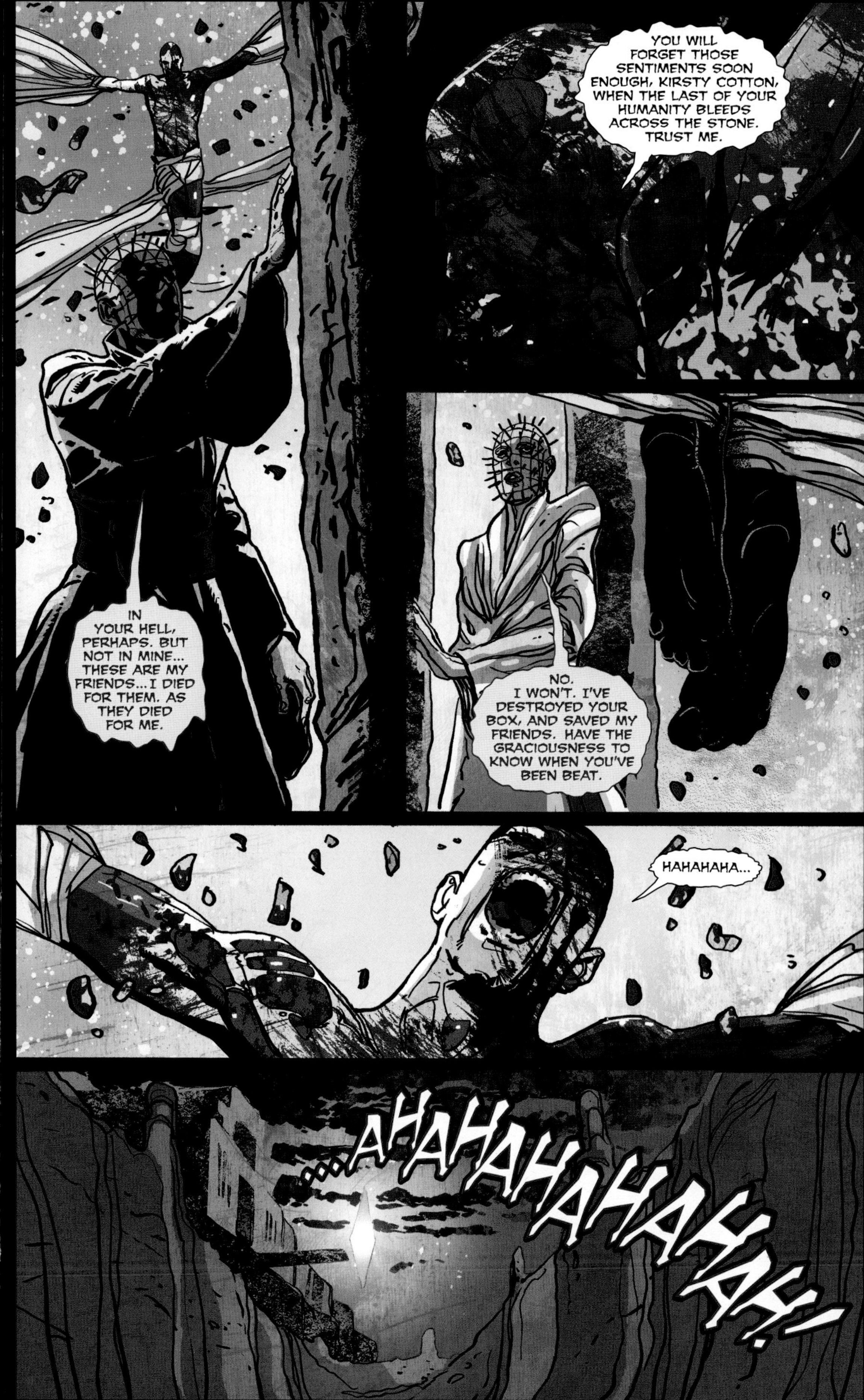
YOU WILL FORGET THOSE SENTIMENTS SOON ENOUGH, KIRSTY COTTON, WHEN THE LAST OF YOUR HUMANITY BLEEDS ACROSS THE STONE. TRUST ME.
IN YOUR HELL, PERHAPS. BUT NOT IN MINE... THESE ARE MY FRIENDS...I DIED FOR THEM. AS THEY DIED FOR ME.
NO. I WON'T. I'VE DESTROYED YOUR BOX, AND SAVED MY FRIENDS. HAVE THE GRACIOUSNESS TO KNOW WHEN YOU'VE BEEN BEAT.
HAHAHAHA...
...AHAHAHAHAHAHAH!!

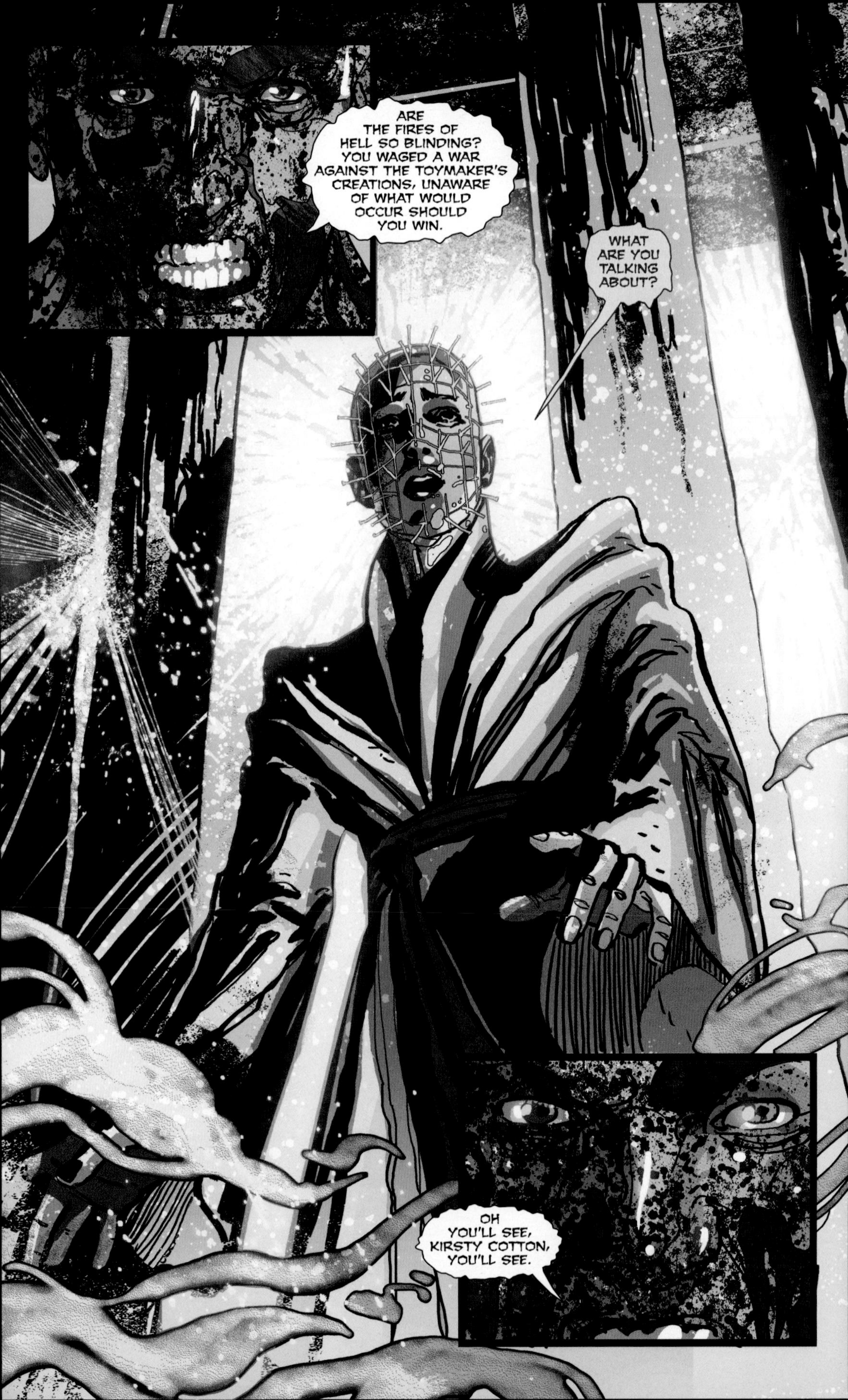
ARE THE FIRES OF HELL SO BLINDING? YOU WAGED A WAR AGAINST THE TOYMAKER'S CREATIONS, UNAWARE OF WHAT WOULD OCCUR SHOULD YOU WIN.
WHAT ARE YOU TALKING ABOUT?
OH YOU'LL SEE, KIRSTY COTTON, YOU'LL SEE.

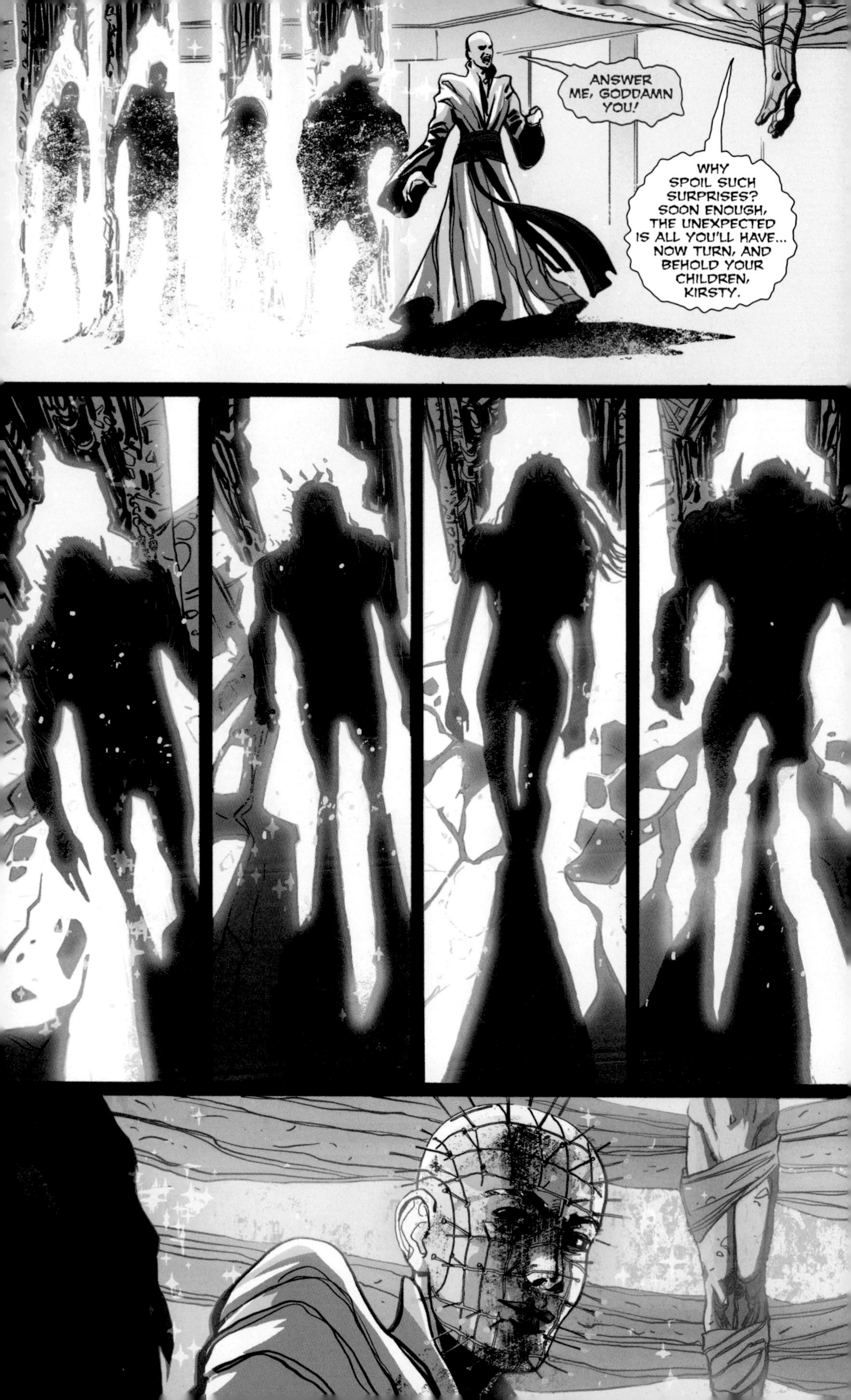
ANSWER ME, GODDAMN YOU!
WHY SPOIL SUCH SURPRISES? SOON ENOUGH, THE UNEXPECTED IS ALL YOU'LL HAVE... NOW TURN, AND BEHOLD YOUR CHILDREN, KIRSTY.

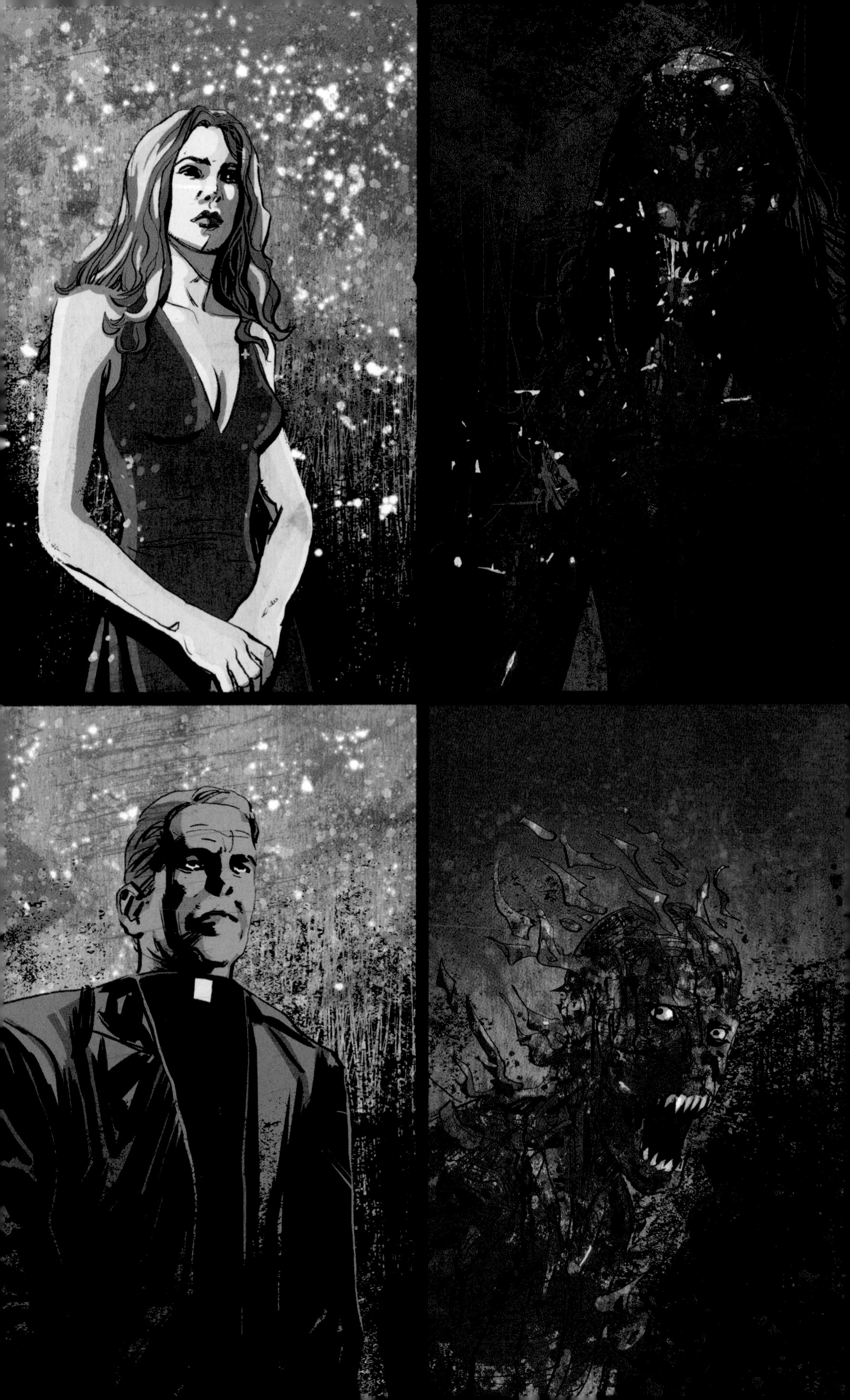

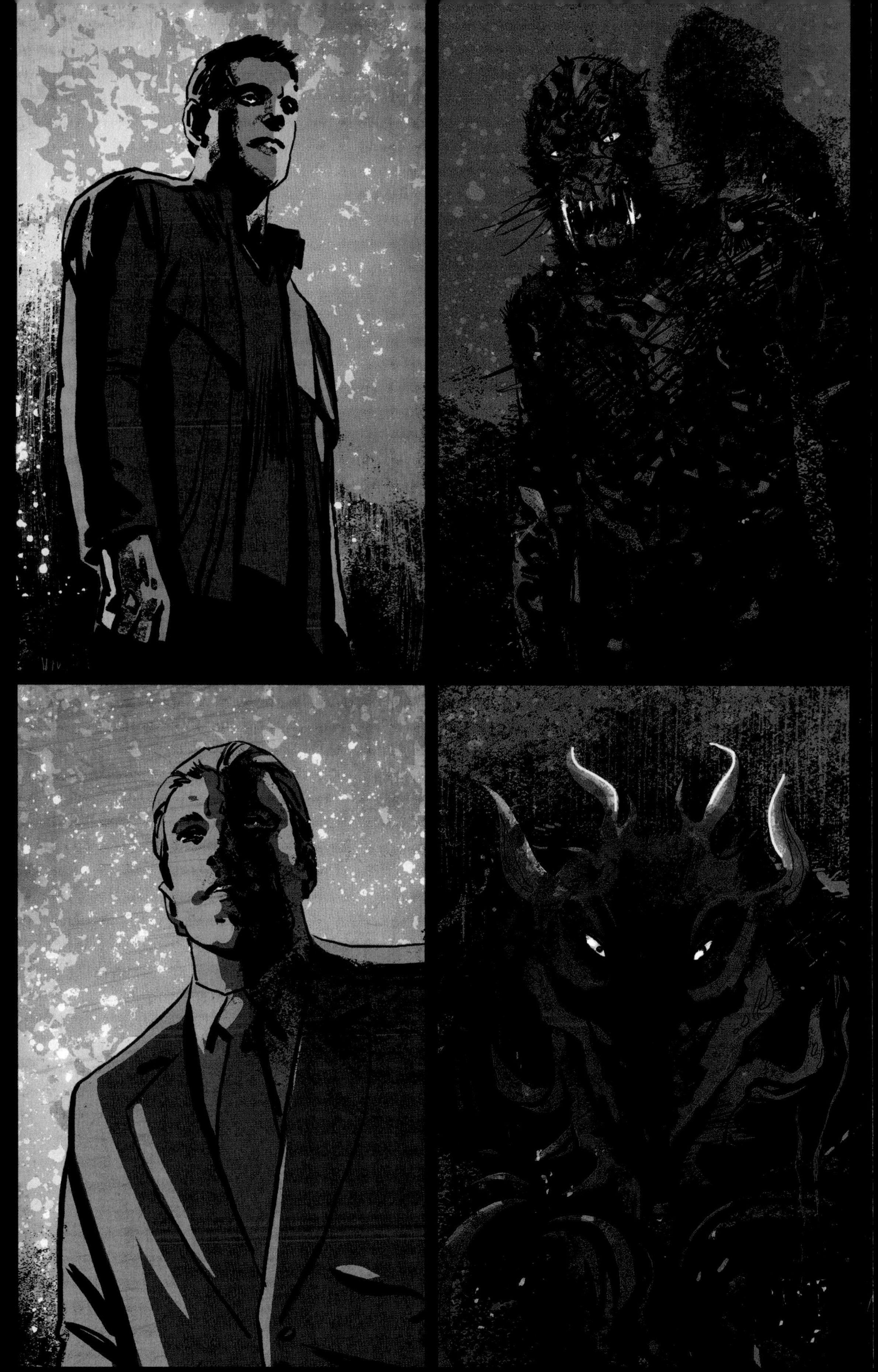

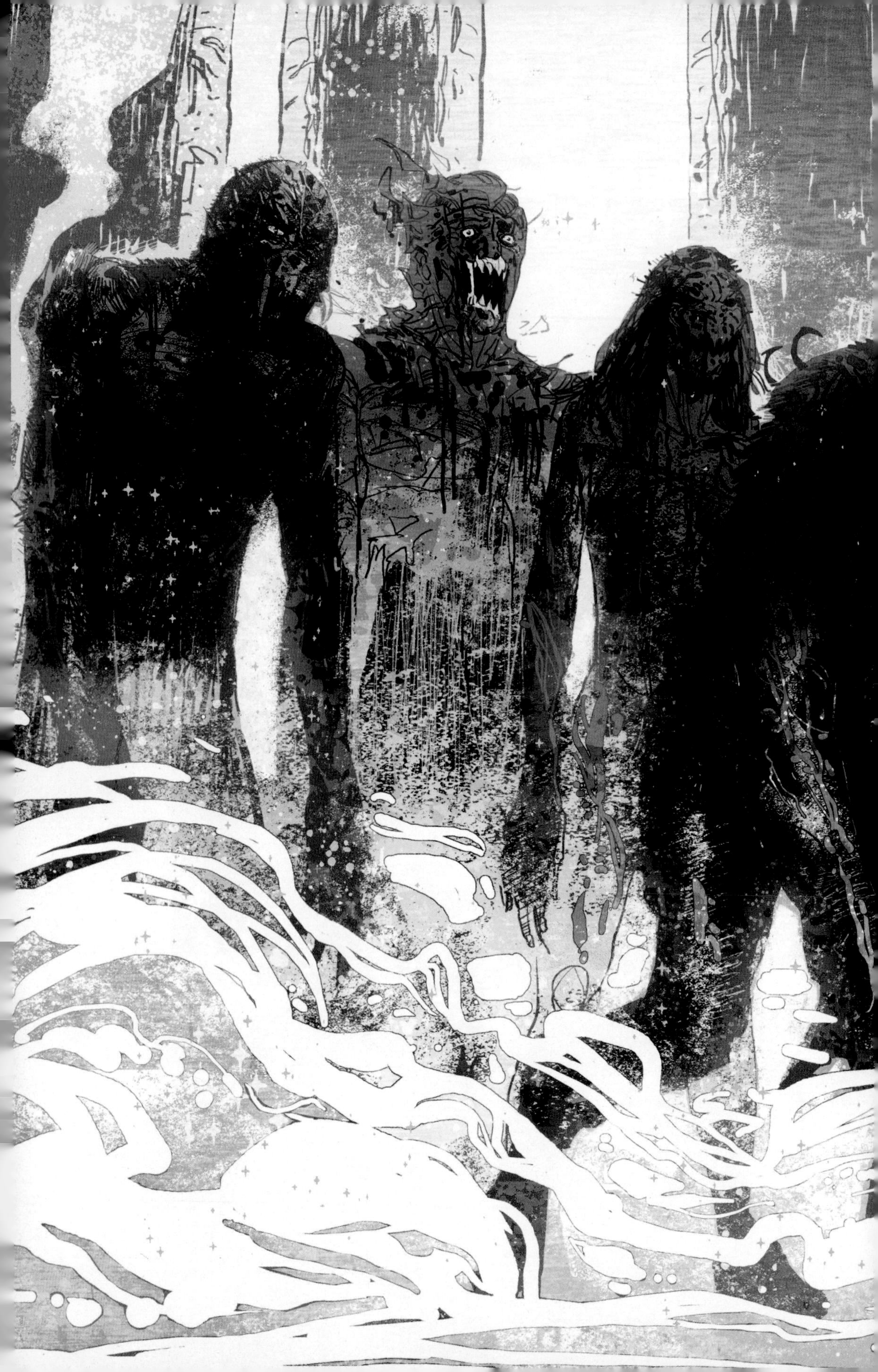

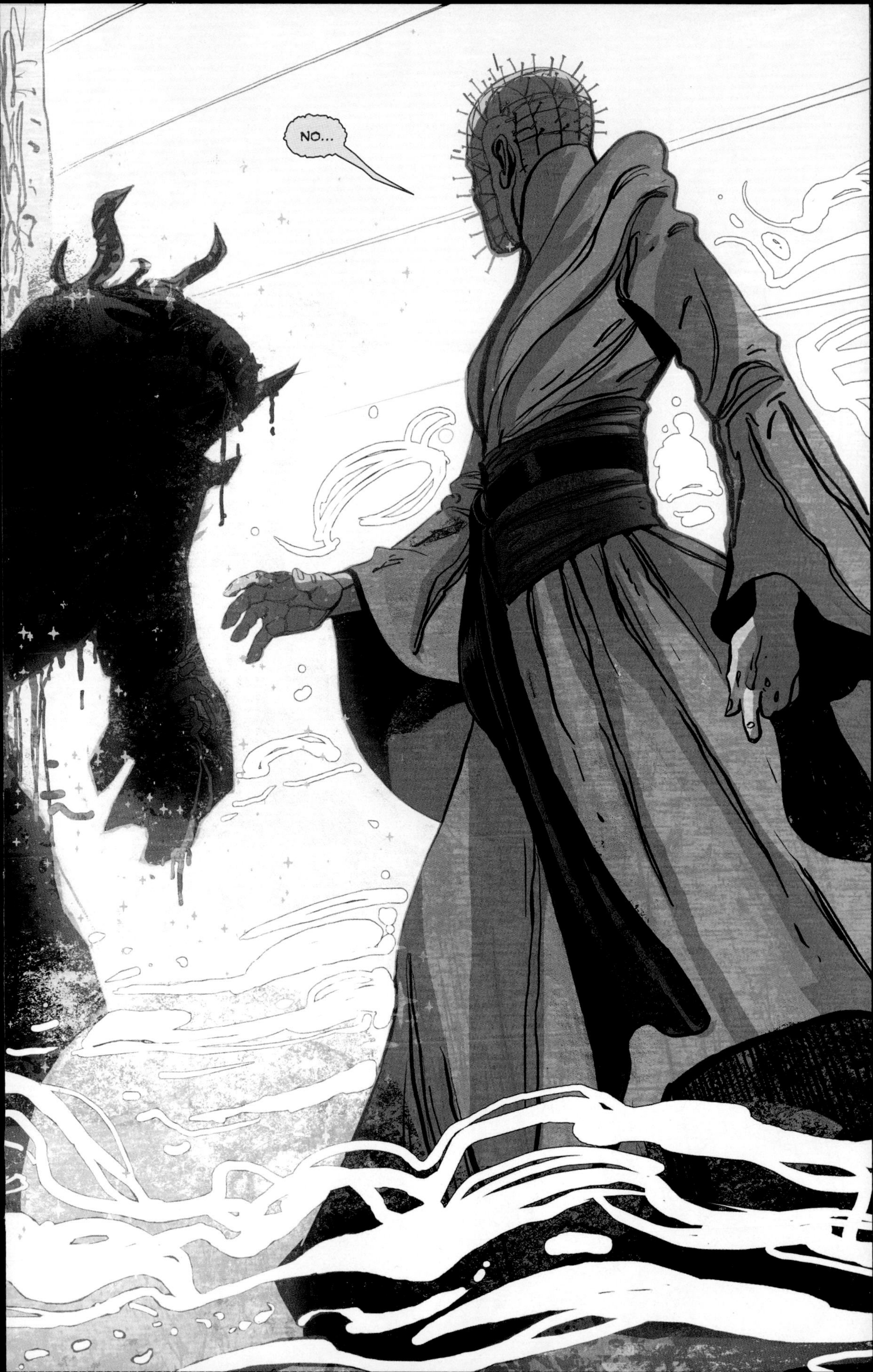
NO...

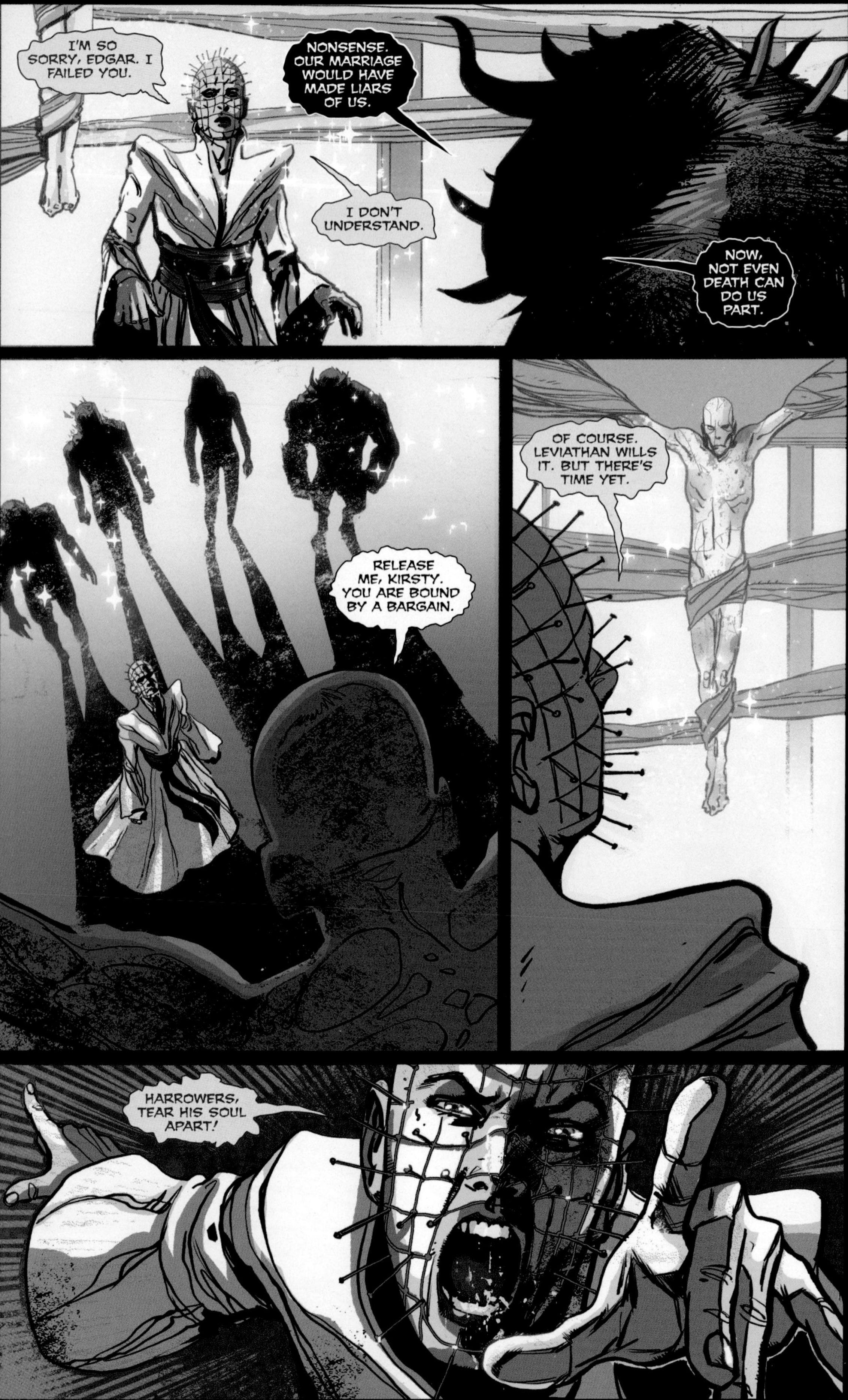
I'M SO SORRY, EDGAR. I FAILED YOU.
NONSENSE. OUR MARRIAGE WOULD HAVE MADE LIARS OF US.
I DON'T UNDERSTAND.
NOW, NOT EVEN DEATH CAN DO US PART.
RELEASE ME, KIRSTY. YOU ARE BOUND BY A BARGAIN.
OF COURSE. LEVIATHAN WILLS IT. BUT THERE'S TIME YET.
HARROWERS, TEAR HIS SOUL APART!

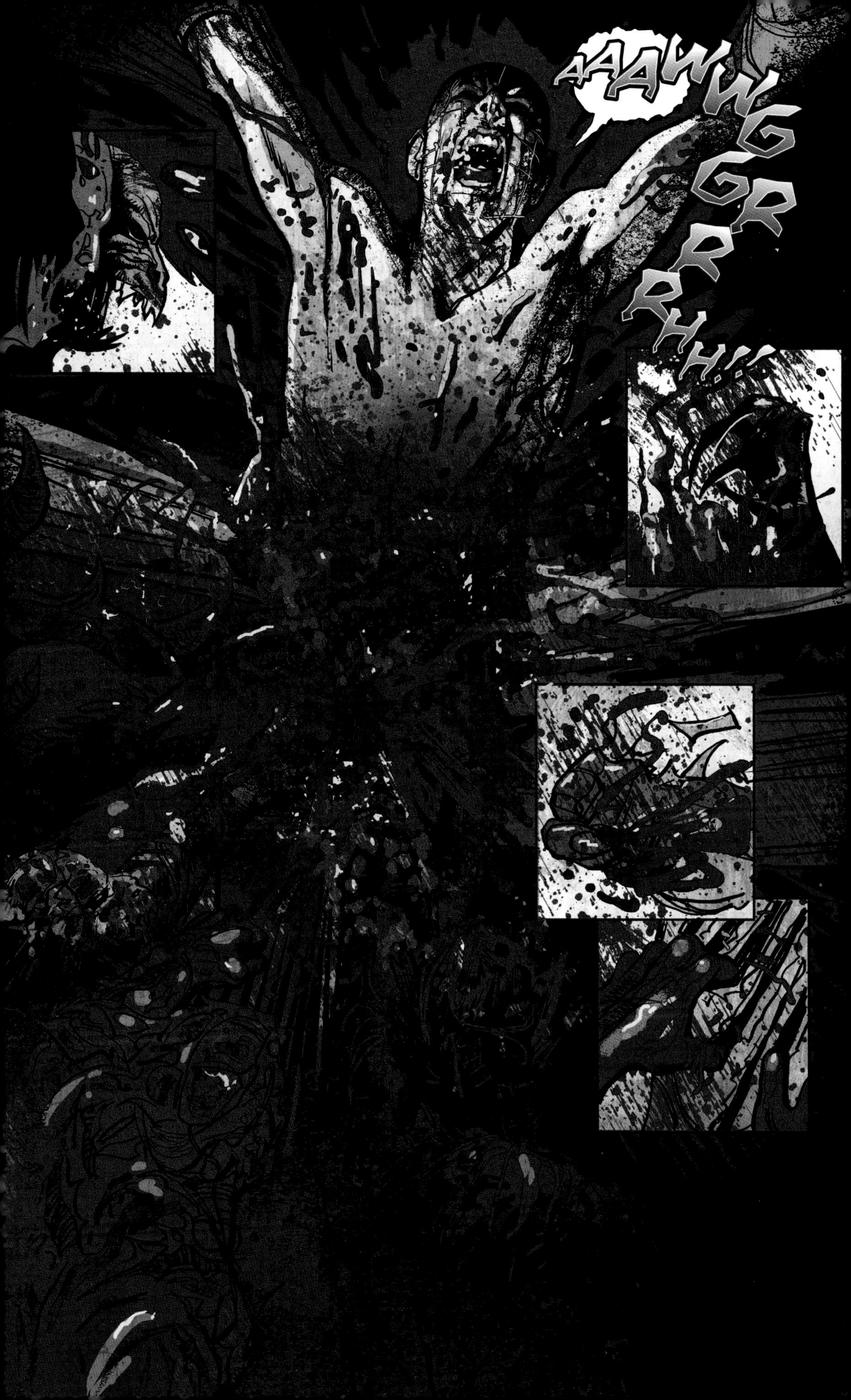
AAAWWGGRRRRHH!!

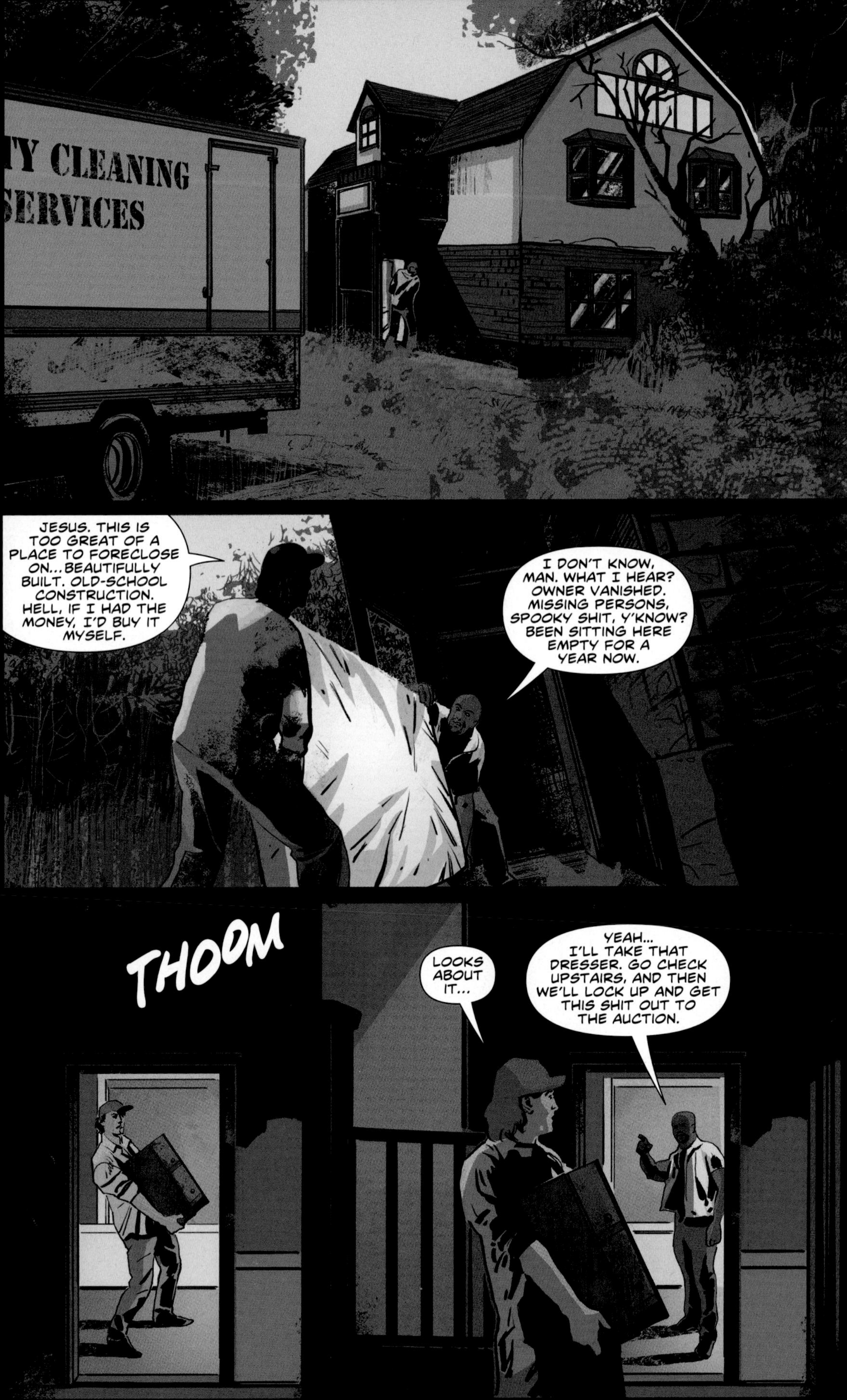

TY CLEANING
SERVICES
JESUS. THIS IS TOO GREAT OF A PLACE TO FORECLOSE ON...BEAUTIFULLY BUILT. OLD-SCHOOL CONSTRUCTION. HELL, IF I HAD THE MONEY, I'D BUY IT MYSELF.
I DON'T KNOW, MAN. WHAT I HEAR? OWNER VANISHED. MISSING PERSONS, SPOOKY SHIT, Y'KNOW? BEEN SITTING HERE EMPTY FOR A YEAR NOW.
THOOM
LOOKS ABOUT IT...
YEAH... I'LL TAKE THAT DRESSER. GO CHECK UPSTAIRS, AND THEN WE'LL LOCK UP AND GET THIS SHIT OUT TO THE AUCTION.

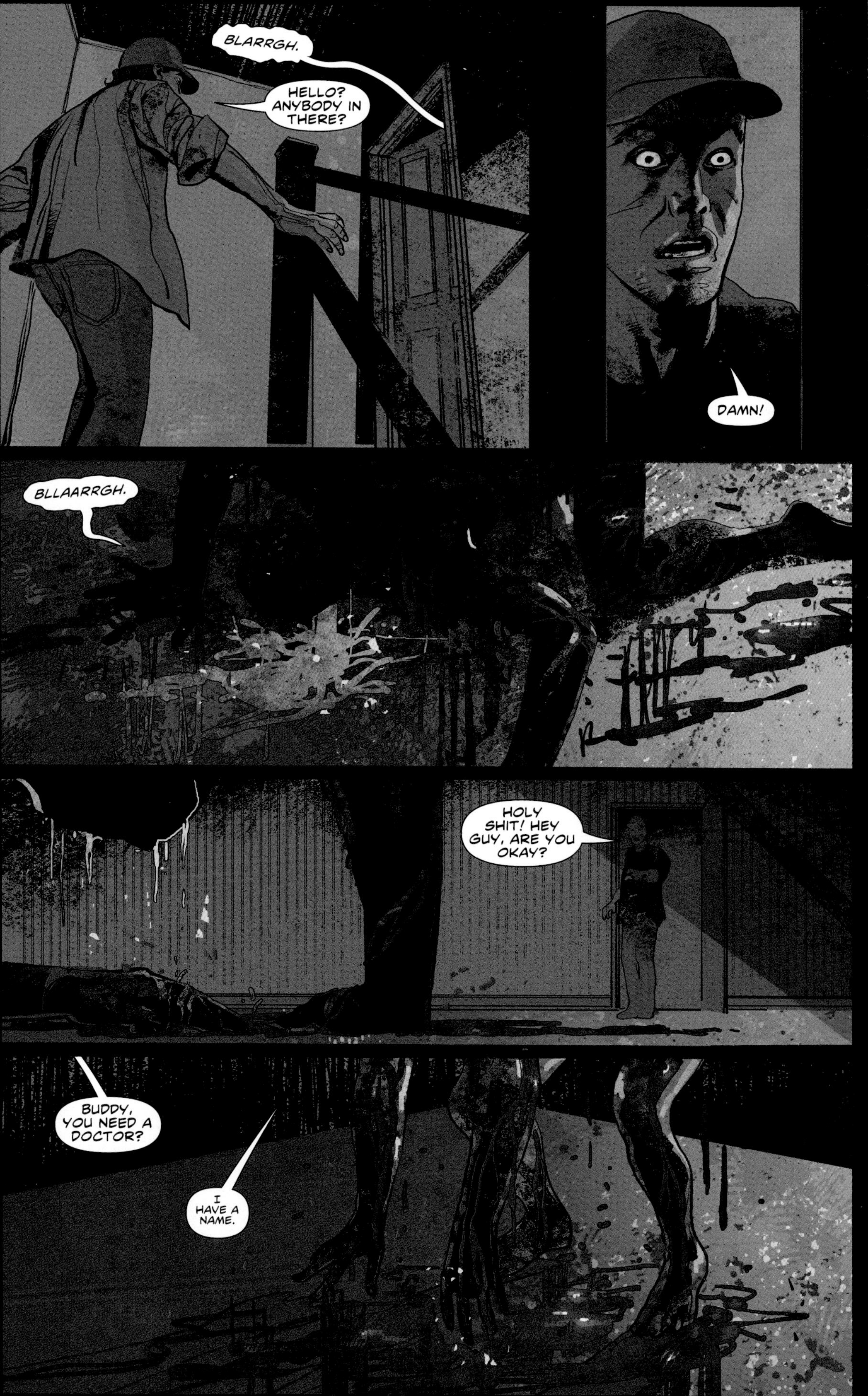
BLARRGH.
HELLO? ANYBODY IN THERE?
DAMN!
BLLAARRGH.
HOLY SHIT! HEY GUY, ARE YOU OKAY?
BUDDY, YOU NEED A DOCTOR?
I HAVE A NAME.

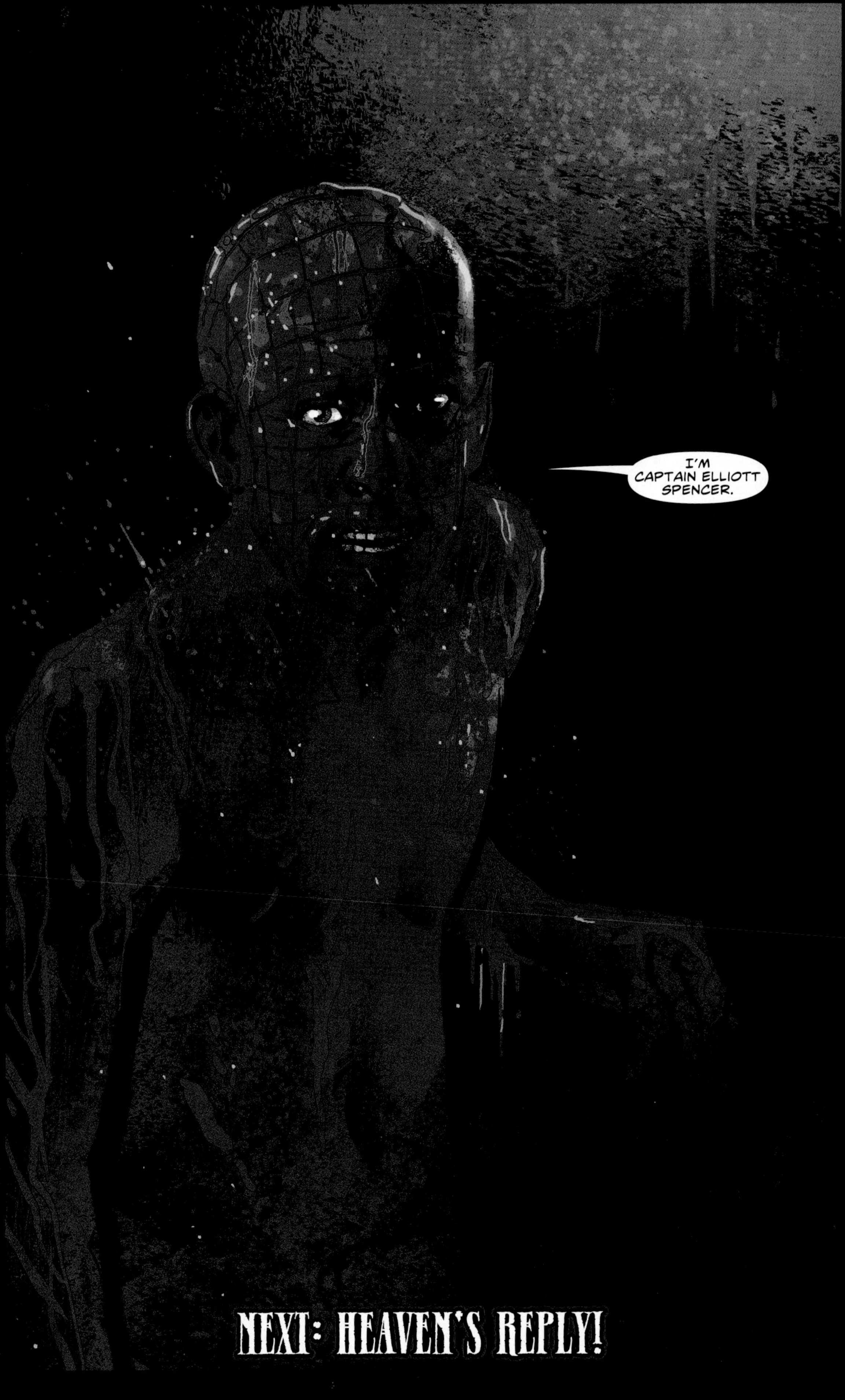
I'M CAPTAIN ELLIOTT SPENCER.

NEXT: HEAVEN'S REPLY!

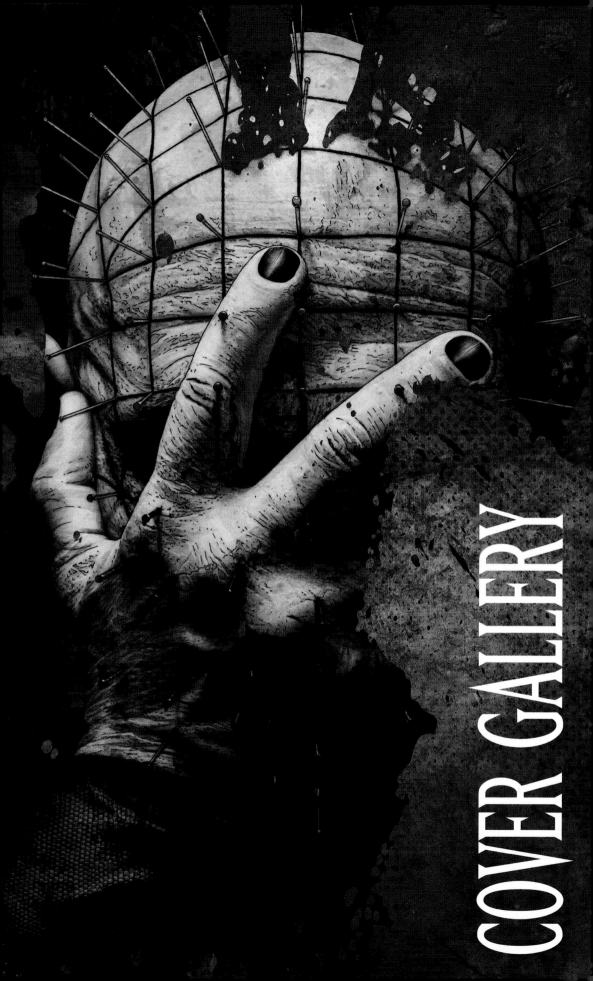

COVER GALLERY

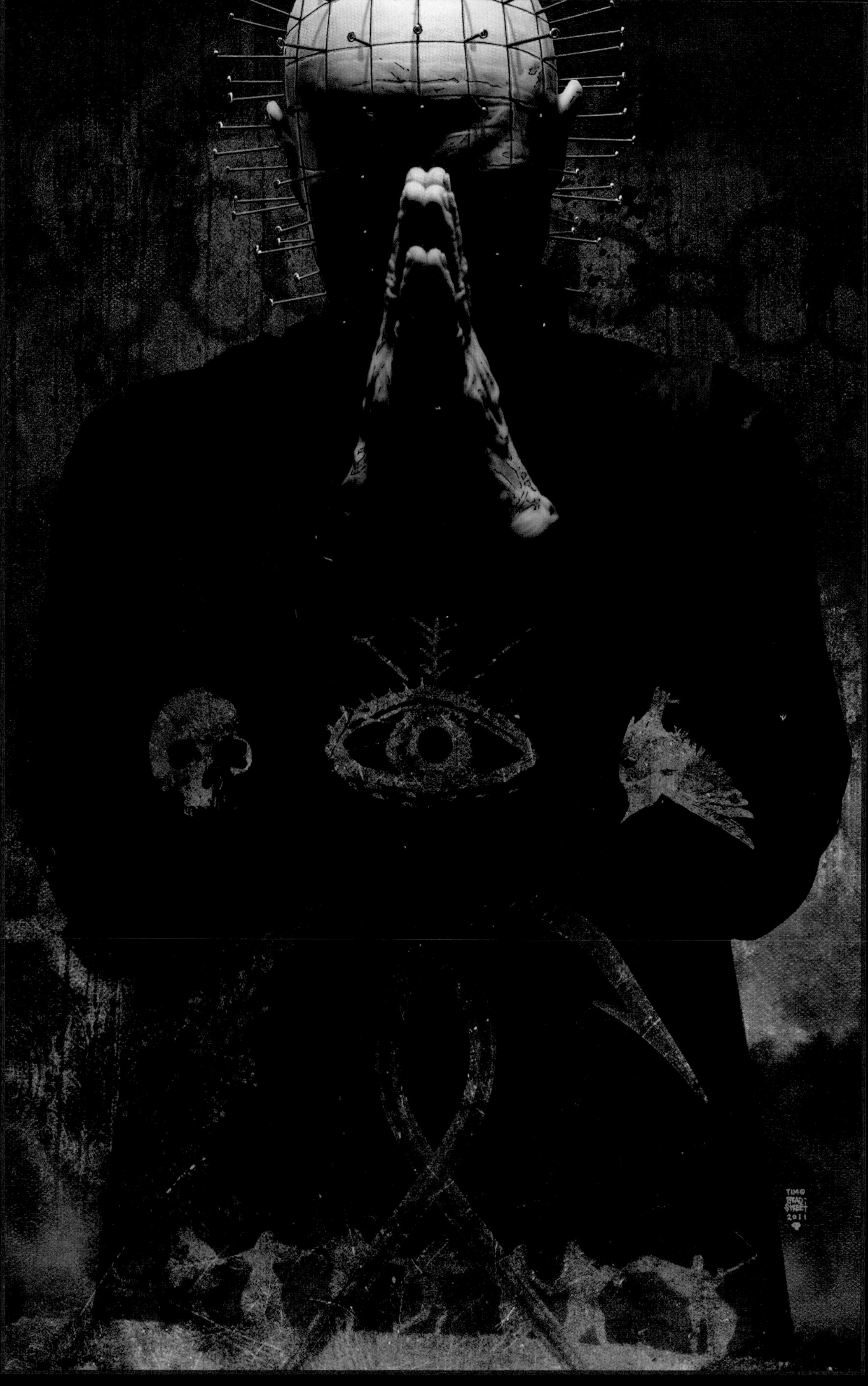
TIM© BRAD-STREET 2011

COVER 5A: TIM BRADSTREET

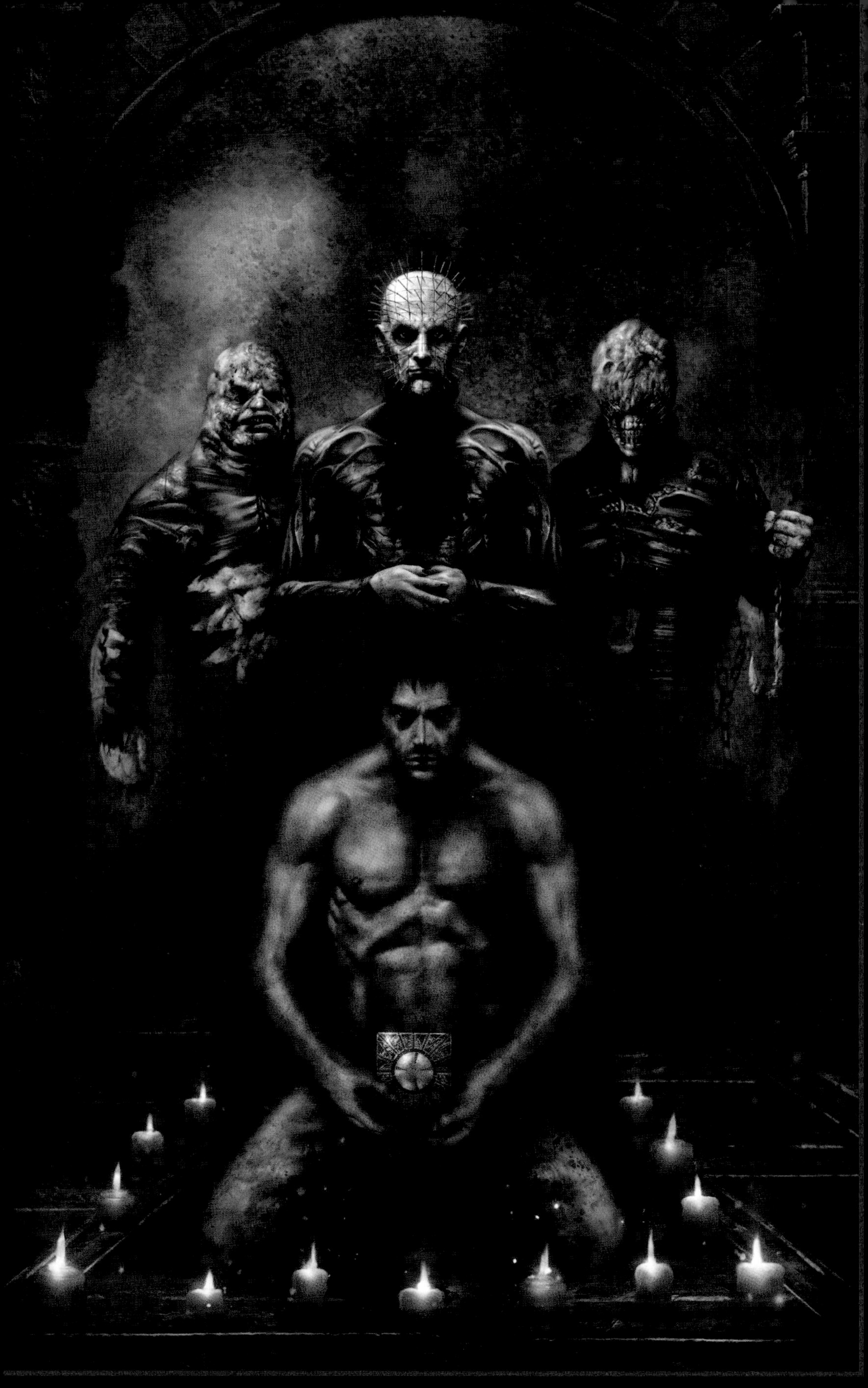

COVER 5B: NICK PERCIVAL

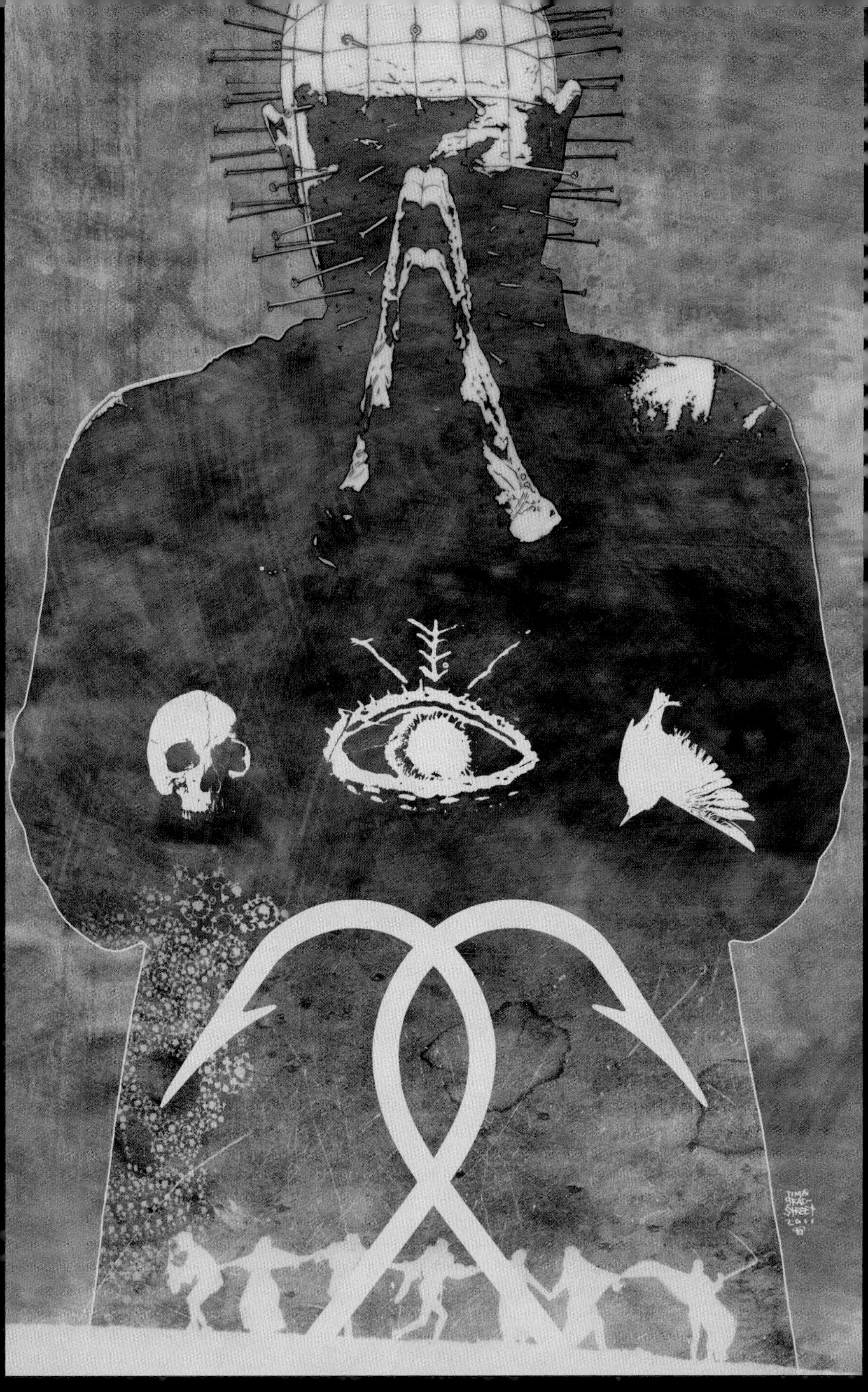
TIM BRAD-STREET 2011

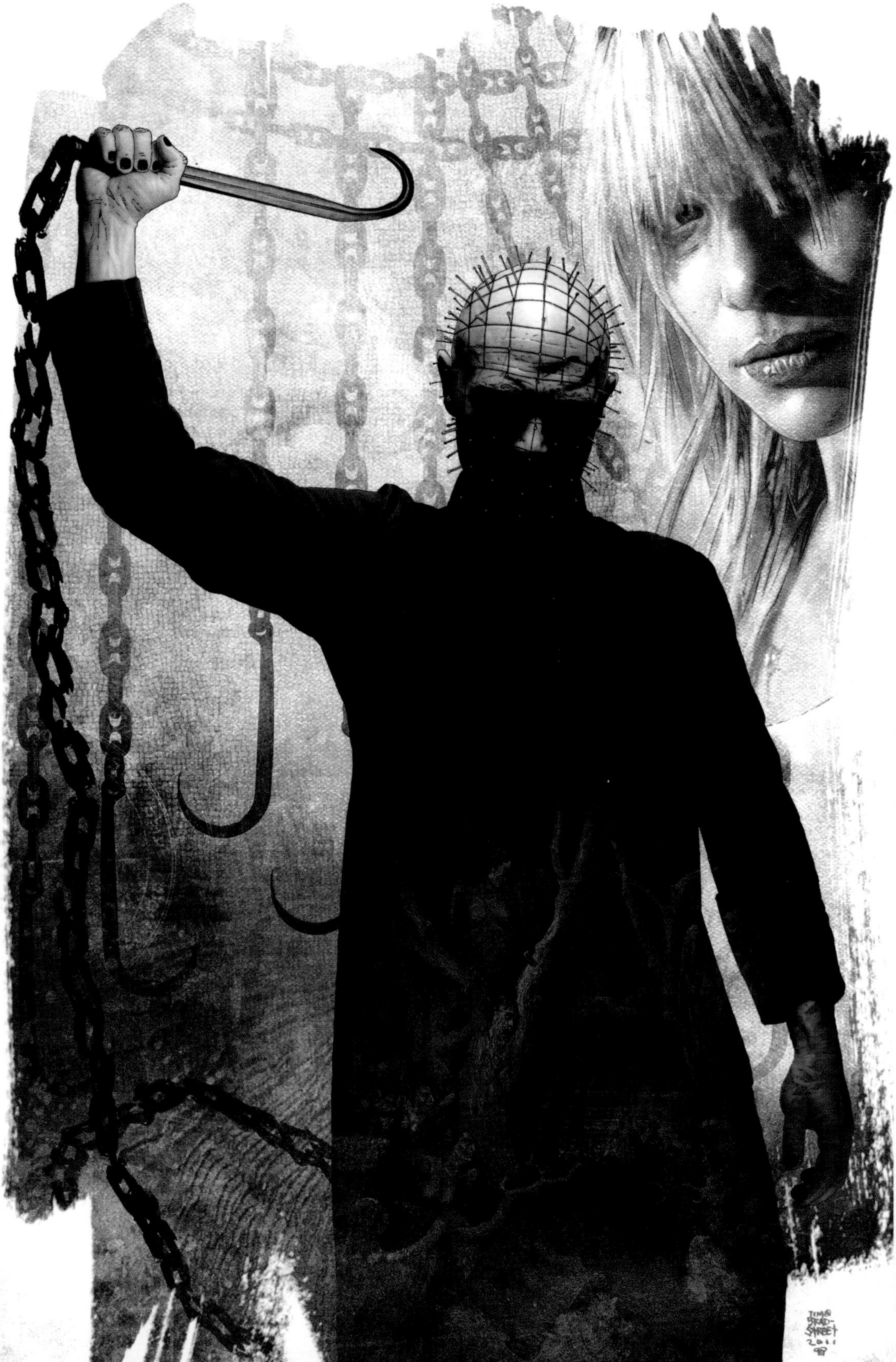

COVER 6A: TIM BRADSTREET

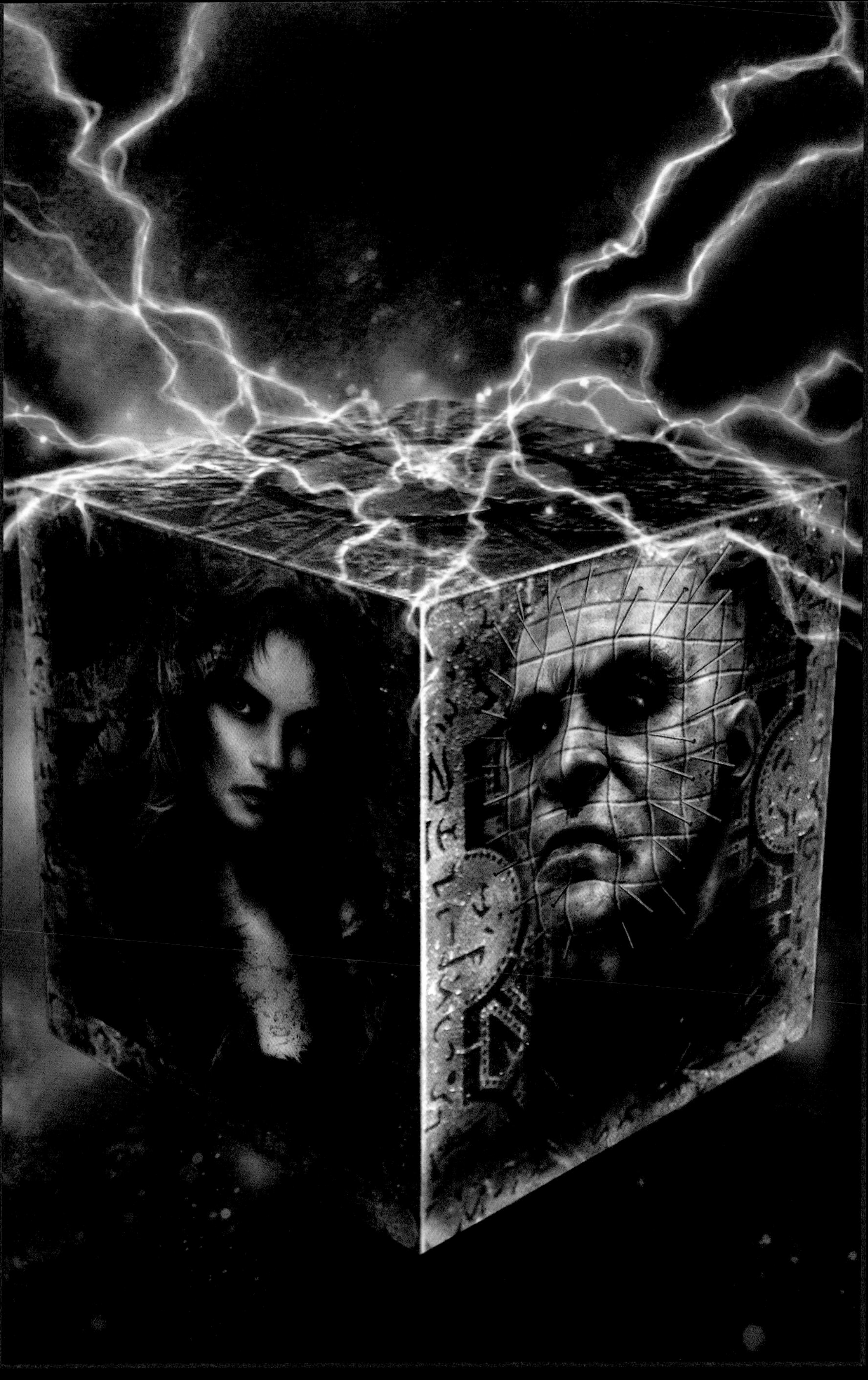

COVER 6B: NICK PERCIVAL

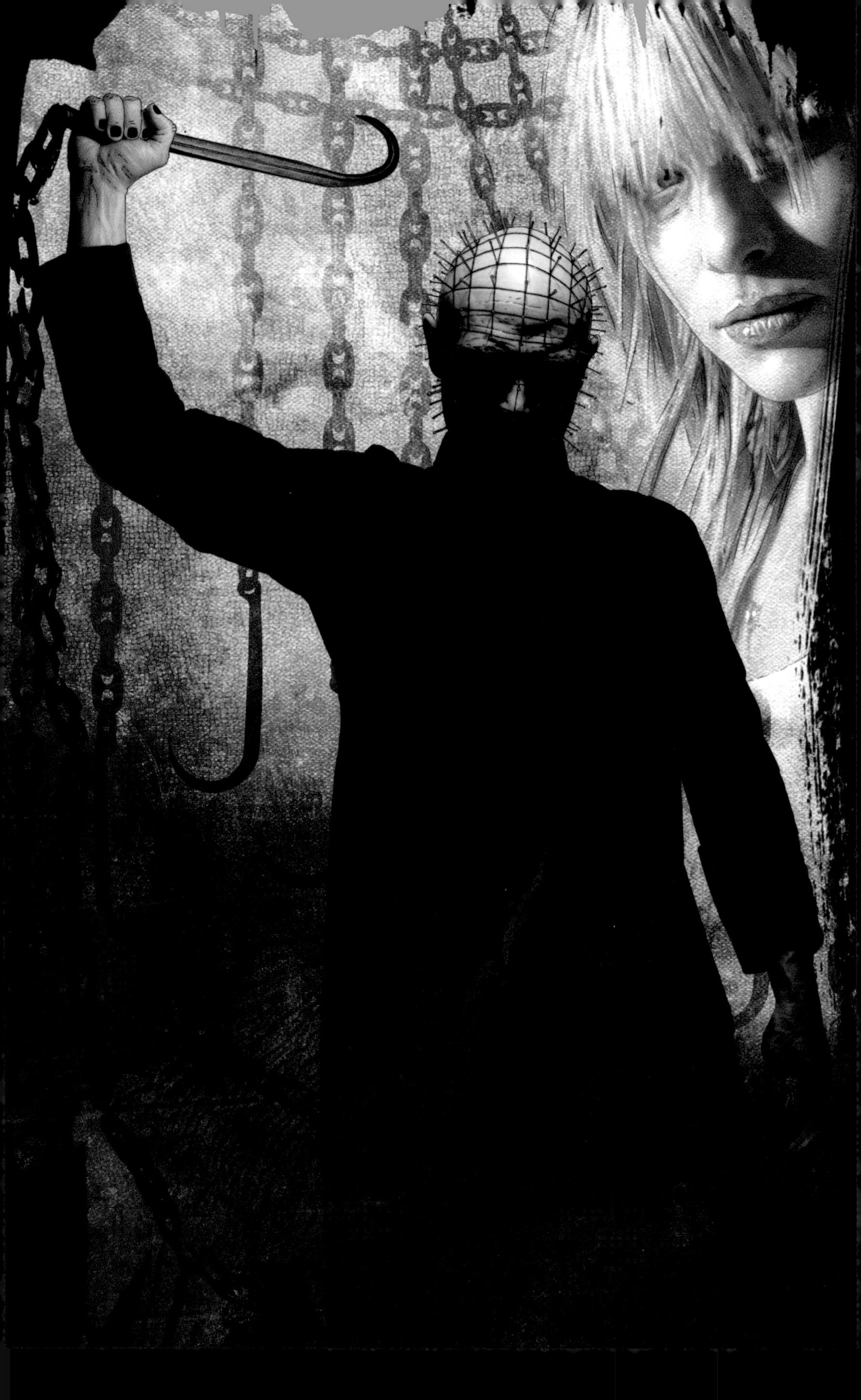

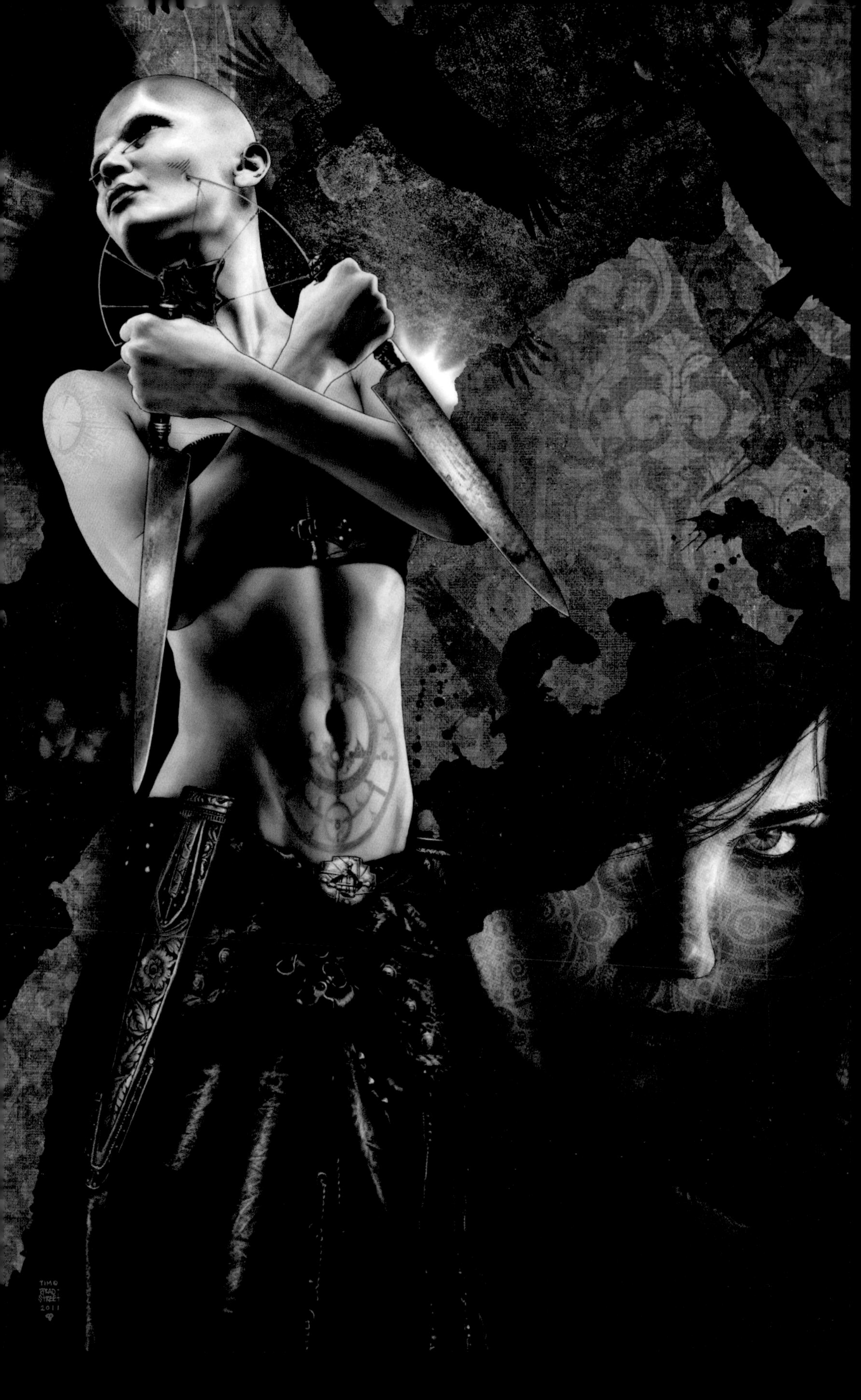
TIM BRAD-STREET 2011

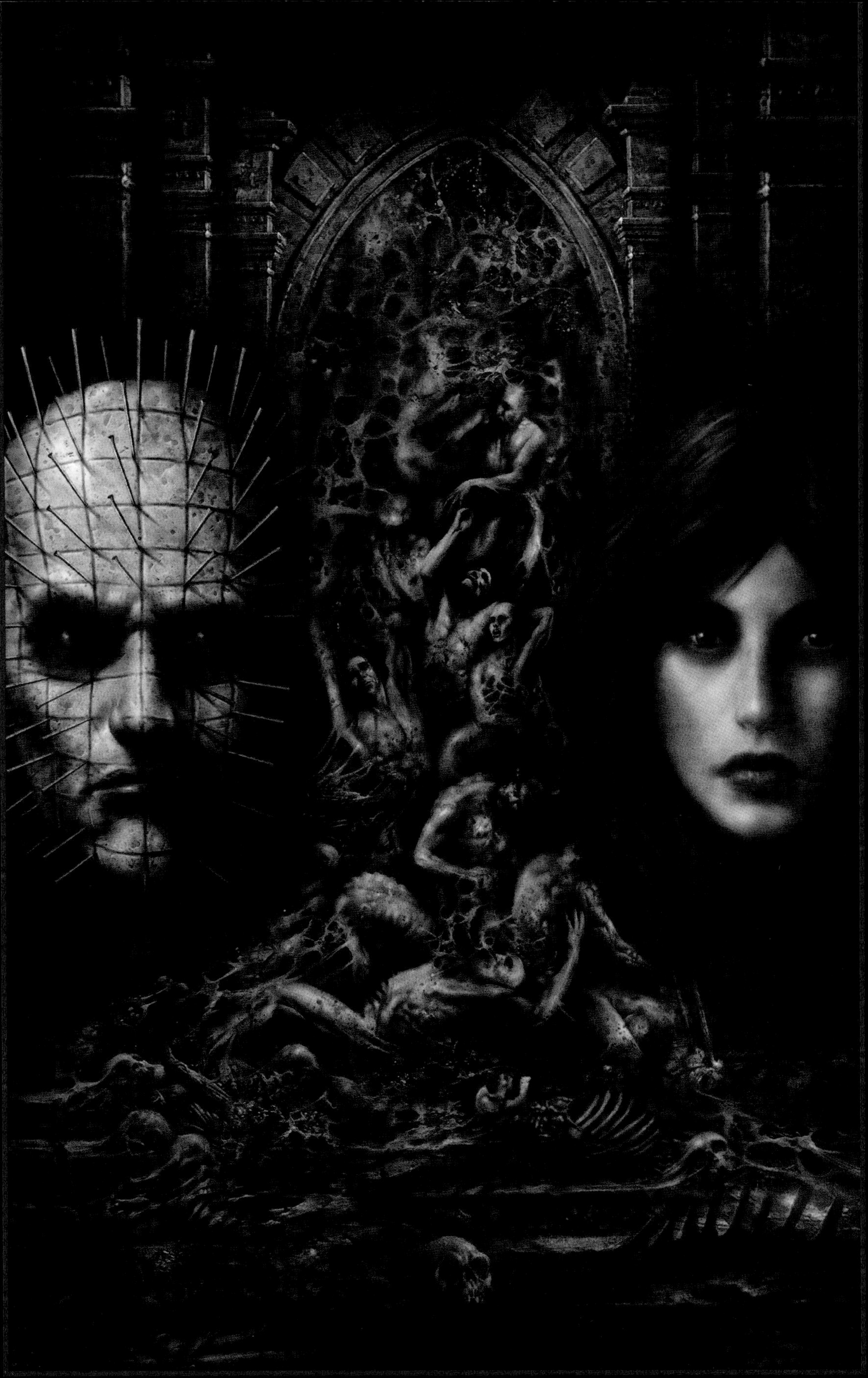

COVER 7B: NICK PERCIVAL

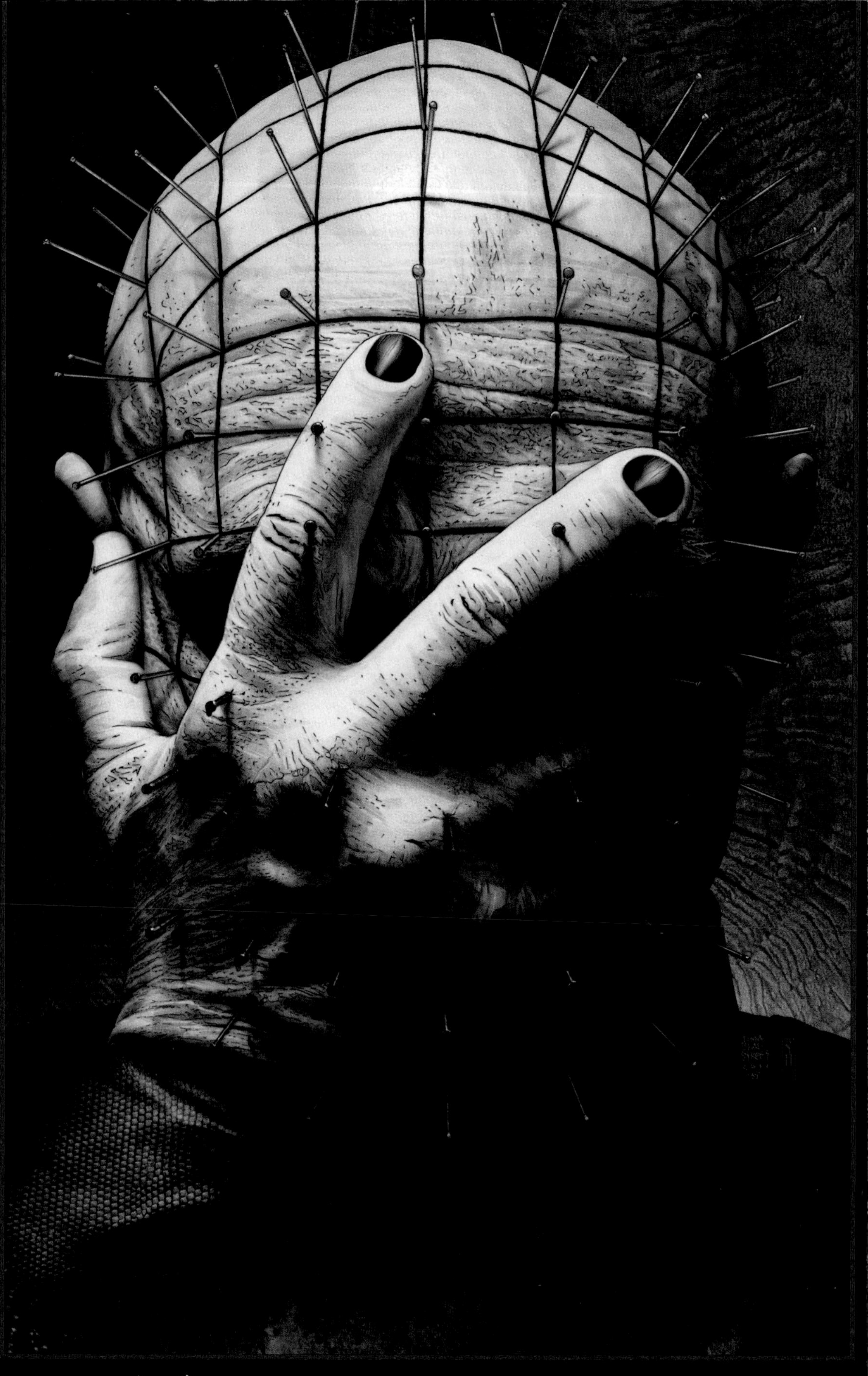

COVER 8A: TIM BRADSTREET

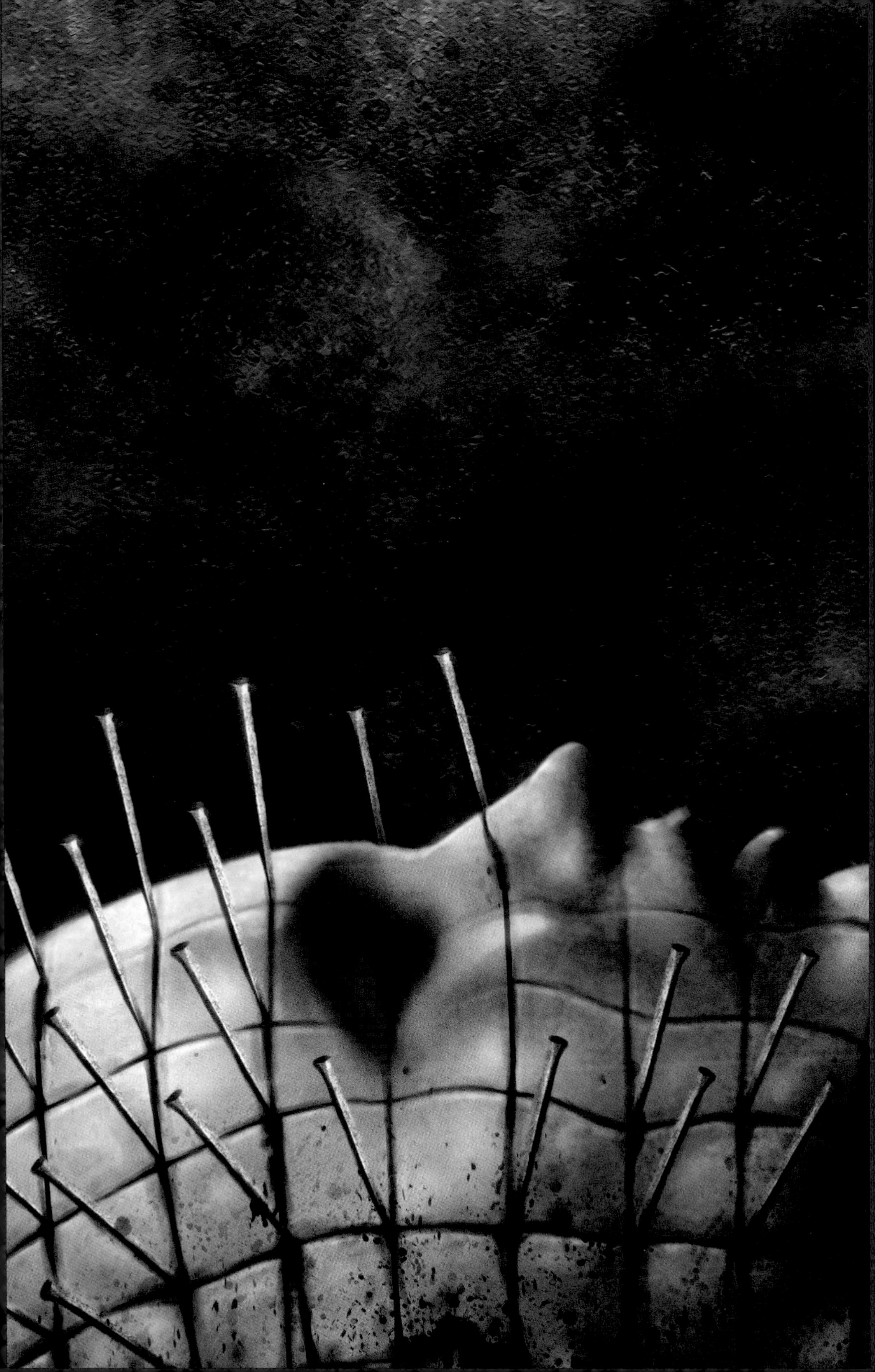

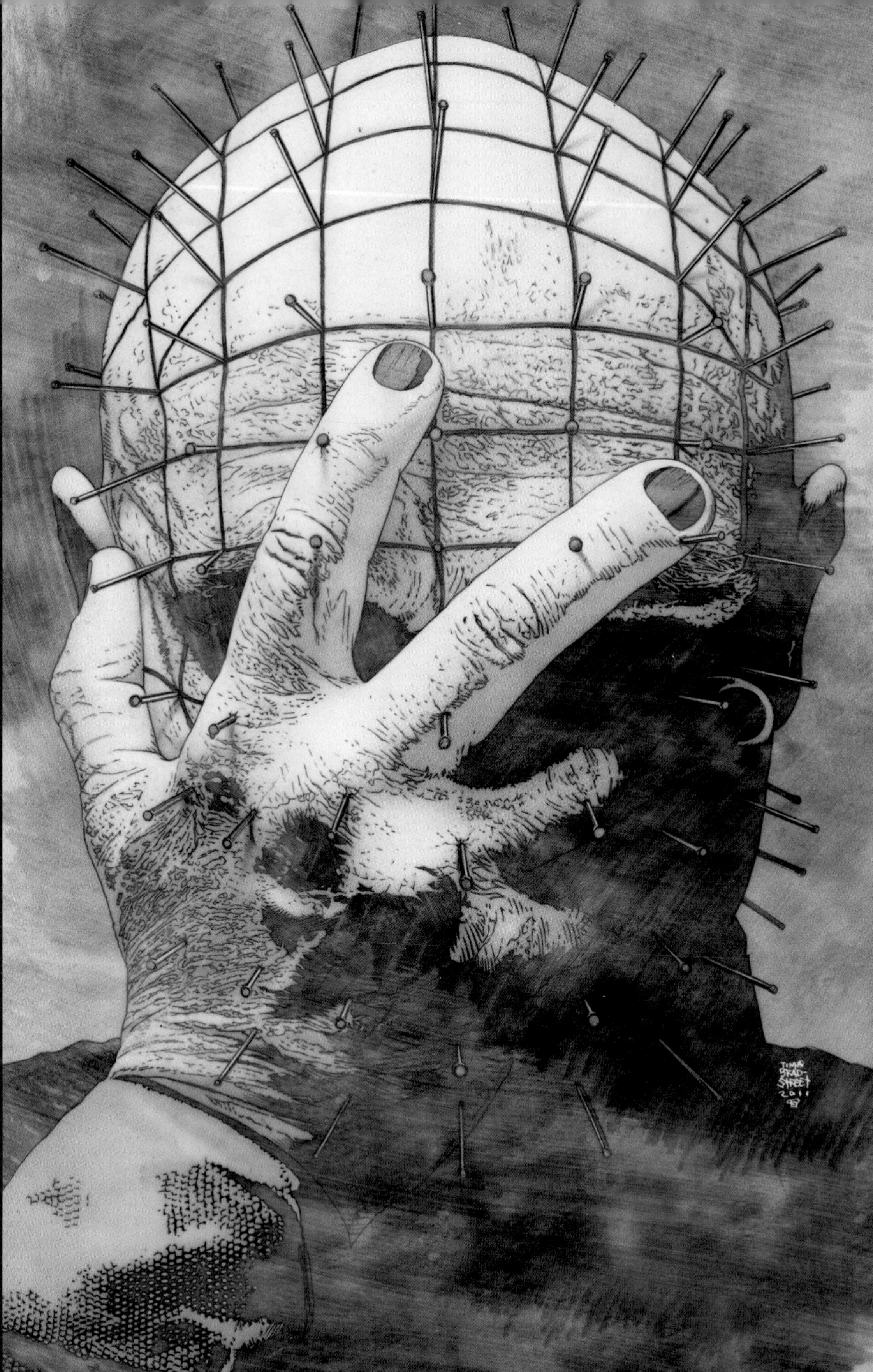